Women Political Leaders

Women Political Leaders

Breaking the Highest Glass Ceiling

Jane S. Jensen

WOMEN POLITICAL LEADERS
Copyright © Jane S. Jensen, 2008.

All rights reserved.

First published in 2008 by
PALGRAVE MACMILLAN®
in the United States—a division of St. Martin's Press LLC,
175 Fifth Avenue, New York, NY 10010.

Where this book is distributed in the UK, Europe and the rest of the world, this is by Palgrave Macmillan, a division of Macmillan Publishers Limited, registered in England, company number 785998, of Houndmills, Basingstoke, Hampshire RG21 6XS.

Palgrave Macmillan is the global academic imprint of the above companies and has companies and representatives throughout the world.

Palgrave® and Macmillan® are registered trademarks in the United States, the United Kingdom, Europe and other countries.

ISBN-13: 978–0–312–22338–0
ISBN-10: 0–312–22338–2

Library of Congress Cataloging-in-Publication Data

Jensen, Jane S.
  Women political leaders : breaking the highest glass ceiling / Jane S. Jensen.
    p. cm.
  Includes bibliographical references and index.
  ISBN 0–312–22338–2
  1. Women heads of state. 2. Women cabinet officers. 3. Women in politics. 4. Women heads of state—Biography. 5. Women cabinet officers—Biography. I. Title.

HQ1236.J46 2008
920.72—dc22   2008017171

A catalogue record of the book is available from the British Library.

Design by Newgen Imaging Systems (P) Ltd., Chennai, India.

First edition: December 2008

10 9 8 7 6 5 4 3 2 1

Printed in the United States of America.

*To my husband, Lloyd Jensen,
who has been my most
ardent critic and my
most enthusiastic supporter*

Contents

Preface		xi
One	**Introduction**	1
	Acquiring the Right to the Franchise	5
	Why So Few Women in Politics	6
	Where Women Hold Sway	10
	Those Who Became Leaders	12
Two	**Political Legacies**	15
	Widows	15
	Daughters	26
	Conclusions	35
Three	**Professional Politicians**	37
	Stopgap Appointment	37
	Challengers for Party Leadership	39
	Appointments to Aid Faltering Parties and Troubled Governments	45
	Leaders of Former Soviet Republics	52
	The Finnish Duo	54
	Leaders of Plural Executives	55
	Leaders of Micro States	56
	Elected Executive Presidents	59
	Conclusions	60
Four	**Temporaries, Tokens, and Ceremonial Leaders**	63
	Leaders Overseeing Elections	63
	Leaders Chosen to Deal with Civil Conflict	67
	Interim Leaders	69
	Tokens	72
	Ceremonial Leaders	73
	Conclusions	77
Five	**The Early Years**	79
	Parental Political Activities	79
	The Father/Daughter Relationship	85

	The Mother/Daughter Relationship	89
	Sibling Relationships	94
	Conclusions	95
Six	**Educational Experiences**	**97**
	Formal Education	98
	Extracurricular Activities	107
	Conclusions	109
Seven	**Balancing Family and Political Career**	**111**
	Ambivalence about Marriage and Family	117
	Husbands as Political Liabilities	120
	Divorce and Widowhood	125
	Conclusions	126
Eight	**Early Political Experience**	**127**
	Getting Started in Politics	128
	Climbing the Political Ladder	134
	Starting at the Top: Widows and Daughters	140
	A Push up the Ladder: The Role of Mentors	144
	Conclusions	146
Nine	**Running for Office**	**149**
	Physical Characteristics of Leaders	150
	Coping with the Rigors of a Campaign	152
	Meeting Her Family Responsibilities	155
	Is She Competent?	156
	Is She Tough?	159
	The Special Case of Widows and Daughters	162
	Running against a Woman	165
	Conclusions	170
Ten	**Forming Governments**	**173**
	Cabinet Selection	174
	Presidential Systems	178
	Dual Systems	179
	Plural Executive and Multiparty Systems	180
	Military Dominated States	182
	Selection by Widows and Daughters	182
	Selection by Temporary Leaders	186
	Portfolios Assumed by Leaders	187
	Conclusions	188

Eleven	**Political Decision Making and Management Styles**	**191**
	The Cabinet's Role in Decision Making	192
	Alternatives to Formal Cabinet Decision Making	195
	Personal Advisers and Outside Experts	197
	Management Style	202
	Conclusions	204
Twelve	**Political Leadership**	**207**
	Party Leadership	208
	Legislative Leadership	212
	Popular Leadership	214
	Responding to Leadership Challenges	216
	Conclusions	221

Epilogue		223
Appendix: Background of Women Leaders		229
Notes		235
Index		261

Preface

As a student of South Asian politics, I became interested in women political leaders as this region has surprisingly accounted for a number of women presidents and prime ministers. Sirimavo Bandaranaike of Ceylon (now Sri Lanka) became the first woman prime minister, followed by Indira Gandhi of India. Among those women who rose to the top in 2007 was Pratibha Patil who was elected president of India, a largely ceremonial post. In the interim, Benazir Bhutto served as prime minister of Pakistan and Chandrika Kumaratunga served as both prime minister and president of Sri Lanka. Two women, Khaleda Zia and Sheikh Hasina have dominated Bangladesh politics since 1991.

Since more than 60 women have now reached the top, we can begin to make more meaningful generalizations about those women who have broken the highest glass ceiling and compare them to their male counterparts. I was curious to know if anything set them apart from other women. How did their early years prepare them for political office? Did women have special problems in getting nominated for office and in running for office once nominated? What sorts of problems did they encounter in balancing family obligations and the demands of a career? Finally, how successful have they been in office and how have their decision making and management styles varied?

I wish to thank the staffs of the many libraries in the United States and abroad that made it easier for me to use their collections of books, periodicals, and newspapers. Especially useful for my purposes were the Library of Congress, the British Library, and the Library of the University of Pennsylvania. Some smaller specialized ones in London were found helpful. Also, I wish to thank my family, friends, and colleagues who encouraged me to stay with the project.

Chapter One

Introduction

Sirimavo Bandaranaike, a 44-year-old homemaker with relatively no political experience, in 1960 became prime minister of Ceylon (now Sri Lanka), a small island located off the tip of India. Sensitive to her special place in history as the first woman to head a government in modern times, Bandaranaike, who followed in the footsteps of her late husband, remarked at a reception in London several months after she took office: "I have often been asked what it is to be the first woman prime minister. I must confess that this has given me a feeling of anxiety and trepidation. For, I do feel that if I fail in my office I will be letting down womankind. That has made me work with still greater determination."[1]

Although the selection of Bandaranaike signaled the opening of new opportunities for women in politics, women rulers had reined in many countries before the advent of the democratic era, despite fairly universal misgivings about women as leaders.[2] From such disparate sources as the *Mahabharata*, sacred Hindu writings; the *Talmud*, a collection of Jewish law; the teachings of Confucius, an ancient Chinese philosopher; and the writings of John Knox, a sixteenth century Scottish religious reformer, there were warnings of the dangers of female rule. Since women were viewed as weak, inferior, unreliable, and even cruel, they were seen as unfit to exercise power. But given the reliance on hereditary succession as an effective means of choosing leaders, some women, despite widespread concerns, assumed power even though a preference for men was built into the rules governing leadership selection.

Like Bandaranaike, many of the women rulers of the predemocratic period came to office on the death of a husband. The widow usually served until a son was old enough to take over the reins of power, often remaining under the watchful eye of male advisers during her tenure. Typical of such a ruler was Anne of Austria who governed France as regent after the death of her husband in 1643 until her son, Louis XIV, came of age. Power during her reign was in effect ceded to Cardinal Mazarin, a shrewd politician, who subsequently became the first minister to the young king.

In contrast, Blanche of Castile, who, along with her betrothed, had been educated in the household of her future father-in-law, played an active role in governing France following her husband's death in 1226.[3] She successfully mobilized support for her rule against those who sought to unseat her and extended the authority of the French sovereign to more remote geographical regions. Gradually she turned over the responsibilities of leadership to her son, Louis IX.

Although the regent usually moved aside once the son assumed office, some regents such as Catherine de Medici of France, the daughter of a Florentine ruler, found it difficult to part with power.[4] After the accidental death of her husband, Henri II, in 1559 and the death the following year of her son, Francis II, Catherine ruled as regent for her second son, Charles IX. Unlike Blanche, who continued to serve merely as an adviser to her son, Catherine played an active role even after Charles, who was predisposed to do her bidding, came of age. In fact, Catherine remained a significant political actor in her adopted land until her death in 1589 although Henri III, who succeeded his brother, was more willing to resist his mother's intervention. Driven by concern to keep her family in power and the country intact, Catherine skillfully played off the warring Protestant and Catholic forces against one another. She plotted the murder of her opponents within both groups to ensure her political dominance.

Tz'u-hsi, a royal concubine who bore the only son of the emperor of China, Hsien Feng, also continued to dominate the political scene after each of her two stints as regent had officially come to an end. In effect, she ruled her country from 1860 until her death in 1908.[5] Following the passing of the emperor, Tz'u-hsi took over as regent[6] and remained the key actor in the political affairs of her country even after her son came of age. T'ung-chih did not take his duties seriously but instead pursued a reckless lifestyle, neglecting his formal education. After his death at the age of 19, Tz'u-hsi arranged for a four-year-old nephew, Hsuan T'ung, to be named heir to the throne, and she once again governed as regent. Though she stepped aside when Hsuan T'ung reached his majority, those who opposed the young ruler's moves to open China to foreign contacts set the stage for her return to power. With the support of the military, Tz'u-hsi assumed the political leadership of her country, taking over from her nephew and confining him to the palace.

A key factor favoring male leaders stemmed from the custom of rulers personally to command their armies during military engagements. Since women rulers were forced to rely on others to perform this critical task of leadership, they were at a disadvantage in exercising power although this practice also offered opportunities for women to rule. Since transportation and communication systems were quite slow, a king who journeyed far from home to lead his troops was not able to attend to the affairs of the realm. Mothers and wives were called upon to take over the task of governing, ruling as regents when a king was out of the country for an extended period. The grandmother of Blanche of Castile, Eleanor of Aquitaine, who was married first to a king of France and then to a king of England, ruled England from 1191 to 1198 while her son, Richard I, was fighting in the Holy Land. Concerned to protect his interests in the kingdom, Eleanor successfully held off his rivals for power.[7] Blanche herself had a second stint as ruler, taking over for her son when he joined the Crusades in 1247. During her husband's extended absences, Catherine de Medici improved her popular image when she assumed the role of regent, attending to such responsibilities as raising funds for the military operations that occupied the attention of Henri II.

Some women who governed as regent following the death of a husband did not step aside for a son but, instead, took over the reins of power as a full sovereign. Two such women were Empress Wu Chao, a seventh century ruler of China,[8] and Queen Didda of Kashmir, who was an important actor in the politics of the Indian subcontinent in the tenth century. Both assumed extraordinary power while their husbands were still alive, and, as regents, they played dominant roles in the affairs of state. Both have been described as ruthless as they were not reluctant to resort to murder, torture, and intrigue to achieve their objectives.

Finally, a few leaders who came to office after the death of a husband did not govern as regents but from the beginning assumed power in their own right. One such example is Catherine the Great, who ruled Russia from 1762 to 1796, following the ouster of her husband Peter III.[9] The daughter of a minor German prince, Catherine had been exposed to the world of political maneuver in the court of Frederick the Great and was attracted to power. She enthusiastically approached her marriage to the heir of the Russian throne despite Peter's crude and cruel manner, and she noted in her memoirs that she was sustained by the belief she would realize her ambition to become the Empress of Russia, ruling the empire in her own right. Following her marriage, which was not consummated for several years because of physical problems of the crown prince, Catherine made the most of her situation, busying herself with the study of the Russian language and religion while pursuing potential allies at court.

During his brief tenure as ruler, Peter, who greatly admired the Prussian leadership and used his country's resources in support of

German interests, proved to be quite unpopular. Taking advantage of the disaffection with Peter in the Russian military and the civil bureaucracies, Catherine built on the support she had fostered through the years among these groups by appealing to Russian nationalism. The concern that her husband would soon cast her aside to marry his mistress provided the impetus to move ahead with coup plans that were carried out by her lover, Gregory Orlov, and his brothers. During Peter's absence from the capital Catherine was declared empress, and the king was arrested. While incarcerated, he was murdered by his wife's supporters. Although there is no evidence that Catherine ordered the assassination of her husband, she had much to gain from his death.

Women were more likely to come to power as full sovereigns in situations in which a ruling family failed to produce a male heir. Because of the intense opposition to female leadership, there was special concern on the part of ruling families to produce a son to ensure the long-term viability of the family's status. In some cases, extraordinary measures were taken. Henry VIII, who ruled England from 1509 to 1547, for example, married several different women in an attempt to produce a male heir, but his only son Edward VI died following a short reign. A daughter, Mary Tudor, became queen, and she was followed by a second daughter, Elizabeth.

One of the misgivings about women as rulers grew out of concern as to the possible effects of their choice of a husband on a country's well-being. Delicate balances among countries as well as domestic political alliances might be affected by her choice of spouse. While a woman who inherited a throne was considered the lawful ruler, it was expected that she would marry and that her husband would take over many of the responsibilities associated with governing.

While Mary I of England married, her sister Elizabeth I chose to remain single throughout her 45-year reign that began in 1558.[10] Perhaps Elizabeth was made wary by the unhappy and politically damaging marriage of Mary to Philip II of Spain. Philip used the union with Mary to pursue his own agenda by involving England in his conflict with France. Elizabeth's refusal to take a husband and produce an heir created anxiety for her subjects, but her encouragement of potential suitors as a political tool to affect both domestic and foreign policy was a key to her successful rule. For example, by holding out prospects of an alliance with France through marriage to a son of Catherine de Medici, she was able to thwart the territorial ambitions of her brother-in-law.

Some women who inherited a throne ruled jointly with a husband. Isabella, Queen of Castile, and her husband Ferdinand of Aragon, who were responsible for the unification of Spain, agreed on the tasks each would perform. While both were involved in the making of basic decisions, Isabella focused on administrative matters. Ferdinand was the military strategist although during the fighting that resulted in the Moors' being pushed out of Spain, Isabella spent much time on the battlefield even when she was pregnant.[11]

Another woman who inherited a throne, Mary II, ruled England along with her husband, William of Orange, during the latter part of the eighteenth century. Mary took responsibility for managing the affairs of state while her husband was away, but when he was at home, she left the duties of governing to him. In her memoirs, she noted the appeal of this arrangement: "Being freed from care and business...I immediately gave my self to my own ease and carelessness...believing it very unnecessary for me to medle or trouble my head, when the King was here...."[12]

Since rulers were prone to expect that at some point they would produce a son, daughters often did not receive adequate training in the ways of politics. Elizabeth I was fortunate in that she acquired valuable lessons in the art of governing during the brief reigns of her brother and sister. On the other hand, Maria Theresa, who ruled the Hapsburg Empire from 1740 to 1780, had little preparation in governing a state.[13]

Charles V, Maria Theresa's father, was skeptical that a woman would be able to hold the loosely held empire together. When it appeared that it was unlikely he would have a son, he did promulgate an act making it possible for a female to succeed to the domain of the Hapsburgs. He also sought the support of the several components of the empire for a female leader although he held to the belief that if his daughter did assume the throne, her husband would exercise power.

Maria Theresa was married at the age of 19 to Francis Stephen of Lorraine. Though her relationship with her husband was a close one, on assuming the throne, she refused to let him make decisions. She took seriously her duty to preserve the empire by developing a strong military and creating a new alliance system to isolate neighboring Prussia.

Acquiring the Right to the Franchise

As popularly elected governments made their appearance during the eighteenth and nineteenth centuries and the franchise was extended to include most men, the fortunes of women in the political arena did not keep pace.[14] In 1849, the Danish constituent assembly declared that "it is everywhere accepted that neither incompetents, children, women nor criminals should vote." Before the beginning of the twentieth century, New Zealand was the only state to permit women to vote. Australia recognized the right of women to vote in 1902; Finland, in 1906; and Norway, in 1913; but most of the European states as well as the United States did not get around to extending the franchise to women until after the First World War. France held out until 1944; and Switzerland, until 1971. Protracted struggles, in some cases taking place over more than a century and occasionally leading to outbreaks of violence, preceded the extension of the franchise to women.[15]

For the most part, women in the developing countries were spared this particular clash as the new states, after acquiring self-rule, were inclined to give women the right to vote. The former colonies were concerned to show that they were progressive and able to handle the responsibilities of an independent state. An exception is found in the states of the Middle East, where women in Kuwait voted for the first time in 2006.

The fact that women were denied the right to vote as well as hold public office on the grounds that these were tasks that by nature belonged to men did not deter some women from participating in political activity. In addition to those who took part in the suffrage movement, other women worked on behalf of husbands or other male relatives. In Britain, for example, following the passage of reform legislation in 1883, women played an active role in developing support for political parties. As boosters of their husbands' careers, they mobilized the newly enfranchised voters and assisted with the conduct of campaigns by canvassing, organizing a variety of community activities, and addressing campaign literature. Since these middle-class women had time available as well as experience as volunteers in their communities, they were especially suited to influence potential party supporters.[16]

Why So Few Women in Politics

The political experience women acquired during the struggle to secure the vote as well as that acquired in assisting politically active male relatives did not translate into high-level positions in the political arena. It was many years later that the first woman became a national leader, and she was not a professional politician but the widow of a martyr. Although many women have risen to positions of power since Sirimavo Bandaranaike's selection as prime minister in 1960, in most countries the political arena continues to be dominated by men. Even with the inclusion of lower-level officials, women do not represent anything like their proportion of the population in political life.

Though there has been a gradual increase in the participation of women in politics throughout the world, the numbers are still relatively small. Data collected by the Interparliamentary Union put the number of women in the world's national legislatures in December 2007 at 17.2 percent, but this figure varied widely among the states.[17] For example, the percentage of women in the parliament of Finland was 47.3, while in the U.S. House of Representatives and Senate the number stood at 16.2 percent. In the British parliament, the figure was 19.7 percent and in the lower house of the German parliament, 31.6 percent. Regional averages for the Americas, Sub-Sahara Africa, and Asia were slightly higher than those of the United States, scoring 19.5, 17.0, and 16.5 percent, respectively. Arab and Pacific states each averaged slightly less than 10 percent women.

The number of women cabinet ministers in the world has almost doubled in less than a decade. In 1999 it stood at 8.7 percent whereas by July 2007 it had risen to 15.2 percent.[18] Women ministers have been concentrated in departments that deal with traditional concerns of women. Fifty-six percent of the women cabinet ministers headed departments focusing on health, education, welfare, and consumer affairs, while only 15 percent held posts dealing with the economy.[19]

Various explanations have been offered as to why so few women have entered the political arena as well as why so few of them have risen to leadership positions.[20] One of the most frequently mentioned is the incompatibility of the demands of public office and the responsibilities of women for the care of children and a home. Women have been socialized to attend to and nourish the family and have been discouraged from engaging in activities that might detract from the performance of these tasks. Those who have seen fit to take on other obligations have quite likely experienced feelings of guilt. Given the lengthy period in which children remain dependent, those women who entered politics may choose to do so later in life than their male counterparts, making it difficult for them to acquire the experience necessary to break the highest glass ceiling.

The fact that historically women have been discouraged from pursuing activities outside the home as well as entering certain professions and trades also worked to keep them from playing an active role in public life. Women who are isolated in the home and preoccupied with the care of children have little chance to develop an interest in broad political issues nor do they have an opportunity to make contacts that would support a run for office. To the extent that women have held jobs outside the home, these have not been the kinds of positions that provide the flexibility necessary to seek public office nor that provide the exposure to groups that are sources of financial and organizational support. Instead, those who have sought office have often relied on experiences as volunteers in community activities to create an electoral base and raise funds in preparation for seeking political office.

Women have been socialized to see politics as outside their area of concern, and since so few of them have played an active role in the political arena, they have neither grown up with expectations of becoming politicians nor do they dream about influencing public affairs. Women who have aspired to a political career have gone against the traditional view of their role, and they have been confronted with questions about their suitability for office because of their gender. The high-profile areas, such as finance and national security, have not been viewed as the "appropriate" concern of women, and women have risked social disapproval if they chose to pursue such interests.

Although there has been a paucity of female role models as well as an absence of a tradition of female political involvement, failure to launch a political career has, until more recently, reflected a realistic assessment of the prospects for success. Using one's time and resources in pursuit of such goals would merely have proved to be a futile exercise.

Another explanation places the responsibility on men in that they, so the argument goes, have conspired to keep women from positions of political power, and certainly women have historically been denied access to the educational steppingstones to political office. They have not taken part in activities that foster the development of skills necessary for political action. In political parties, more often than not, they have dealt with the menial tasks rather than those associated with policy making. Because of their gender, they have found it difficult to participate in informal sessions where contacts are developed and information important for pursuing a political career is gathered. For example, while serving in various ministries, Edith Cresson, who was appointed prime minister of France in 1991, was not invited to attend the regularly scheduled breakfast meetings held at the prime minister's office as were her colleagues. Although such treatment may not be evidence of a conspiracy, the very limited opportunities that have been available to women suggests that men tend to view people like themselves, that is, other males, as the ones appropriate to fill important political roles.

Women who do enter the political realm must win the approval of their predominantly male colleagues, and, apart from any prejudice that may exist, men may fear that voters will not support women candidates, making it difficult for women to secure nominations for seats in legislative bodies or raise funds for campaign purposes. In parliamentary systems women may be given those seats that are considered safe for the opposition, and in presidential systems they may not be encouraged to run in those races in which there is a good chance of electoral success. This is not to suggest that men also do not seek office in districts that are considered safe for the opposition. In fact, seeking office from such a district can provide valuable training as well as demonstrate one's commitment to a political party.

Once in office, women are dependent on the male-dominated power structure for their success and ability to retain their positions. Since women may be more likely to rely on an accommodative and collaborative style of decision making, they may find it uncomfortable to adjust to the confrontational approach characteristic of legislative bodies and the hierarchical organization favored by men. The European Parliament, where emphasis is placed on decision making by committees, boasts a fairly high proportion of women, currently numbering approximately one-third of the membership. Also, there is less competition for these positions since the European Parliament has little power, and the slots available to a member country may be used to reward party workers, many of whom are women.[21]

Another explanation for the paucity of women in politics is related to the belief that women do not exhibit essential leadership qualities. Instead, they have been described as emotional, sensitive, and dependent as well as lacking in drive. Men, on the other hand, are seen as ambitious, competitive, and decisive—characteristics believed necessary for effective leadership—but in women these traits may be viewed not only as absent but also as inappropriate.

Although these several explanations as to why there are so few women in politics are of interest from an historical point of view, some of them have lost a measure of their validity. During the period since the early 1970s women have gained greater acceptance in the political arena—a development in part attributable to the women's movement—while, at the same time, the number of women eligible for public office has increased. With more educational opportunities available to women, their numbers in the professions, especially law, have risen.

Despite changes in attitudes toward women in politics as well as the increased size of the pool of women eligible to serve, the representation of women in national politics has remained low. Though the fact that incumbents have an advantage in electoral contests over challengers has undoubtedly worked against the election of women, this explanation is not sufficient. The authors of a study conducted in the United States of several general elections in the 1980s and 1990s for state legislatures as well as for the Congress from 1972 to 1994 concluded that the reason there are so few female representatives is that women do not see fit to seek office.[22] By examining the records of more than 61,000 candidates, the researchers found that the success rate for women candidates was comparable to those of the men who sought public office.

While earlier, women may have been discouraged from pursuing a political career as they had relatively little chance of success, they may remain reluctant to enter the political fray. Potential supporters may resist assisting with campaigns, in view of the persistent and widespread belief, despite evidence to the contrary, that women have difficulty getting elected.[23] Women may also be deterred from seeking political office because of lingering doubts about their own ability to handle the job and, perhaps even more so, because of concern about whether they will be taken seriously and viewed as equals by their colleagues in the male-dominated political institutions.

Where Women Hold Sway

The Scandinavian states provide an exception to the relatively low figures found throughout much of the world for women's representation in public office. Iceland, Norway, and Finland have all had women prime ministers or presidents and for a brief period in 2003 in Finland both positions were held by women.

Scandinavian women occupied 41.8 percent of the parliamentary seats in 2007.[24] They also held 55.1 percent of the cabinet posts in Finland, more than 47.4 percent in Norway, and 40.9 percent in Sweden.[25] These have included some of the more important cabinet positions. In Sweden, for example, four women in a row served as foreign minister, beginning in 1991, and women have also served as justice minister. In neighboring Norway, both the finance and defense ministries were headed by women in 2005.

A number of elements, taken together, set these countries apart.[26] First, there are the historical experiences and the cultural traits. The

Scandinavian states have a strong tradition of egalitarianism and social justice, dating to the Viking Age. From the earliest times women enjoyed some civic rights although they were considered inferior to men, and these states were among the first to grant women the right to vote, well ahead of most other countries.

Many Scandinavian men earned their livelihood as sailors and were away from home for extended periods. Women filled in the gaps, assuming the responsibilities associated with governing and established a tradition of female involvement in the affairs of the community.[27] With the emphasis placed on the development of social welfare programs since the end of the nineteenth century, the traditional expertise of women in caring for the home assumed importance in the political arena.

Other elements that affect the numbers of women serving in public office include the institutional arrangements for the selection of political leaders. There is general agreement that a system of proportional representation, the method used by the Scandinavian states to select their leaders, encourages or at least does not discourage the election of women.[28] Proportional representation, as opposed to the single-member district used in Britain and the United States, tends to place less importance on the characteristics of the individual candidate, as the voters cast their ballots for a party slate rather than a single candidate. The reasoning goes that voters are more likely to cast their ballot for a woman if she is included on a list of candidates. Party leaders are more willing to place a woman on a list, especially if the party is likely to win several seats in a multimember district,[29] than they are to select her as the sole candidate seeking office from a single-member district.[30]

Women's organizations, which have been especially strong in the Scandinavian states, played a crucial role in securing increased numbers of women in public office. In Norway, for example, the feminist organizations that were created in the 1960s and 1970s were able to form a coalition with the established women's organizations attached to political parties to push for greater numbers of women in political office.[31] These groups also provided needed encouragement and support for prospective female candidates.

Finally, during the 1980s there was a movement in some of the Scandinavian states to adopt a quota system to encourage an increase in the number of women seeking parliamentary office. While legislation failed of passage, individual parties put into effect a rule that required at least 40 percent of candidates be women. With the inclusion of more women on candidate lists, other parties were pressed to make similar moves to hold on to the support of an important constituency.[32]

Those Who Became Leaders

Apart from considerations of democracy and social justice as well as the most efficient use of human resources, female participation in politics, particularly at the highest levels is seen as important since it provides representation for another point of view. As Kim Campbell, who became prime minister of Canada in 1993, remarked when she was appointed to head the justice ministry some three years earlier, "the importance of having strong representation of women in government is because women experience the world differently from men."[33] In decrying the paucity of women in the power structure of her country, Kazimiera Prunskiene, who served for a brief period as prime minister of Lithuania, said: "Society loses much by not giving the woman a chance to realize her own approach to life, based on construction, tenderness, care and compromise."[34] Although not suggesting that women are essentially different, Gro Brundtland, who in 1981 became the first woman to serve as prime minister of Norway, noted that women's "traditions, culture and background, the nurturing of children and thinking ahead are what they have been already into for generations. It makes them see things differently."[35] Jenny Shipley of New Zealand, who led a coup of sorts within her party in 1997 to become prime minister, noted the importance of both genders to policy making when she said: "Women and men together make the best decisions." She went on to point to the special role women are able to play when she noted that "the skills and knowledge [being a mother] brings are very important in understanding the hopes and aspirations of your people."[36]

Despite the advantages of having more women in the decision making process, the fact remains that very few women have been able to reach the top. In an effort to better understand why so few women have reached the political pinnacle as well as what it takes to do so, the experiences of the 64 women who were able to accomplish that feat as of the end of 2007 will be examined. The specific routes that they followed to achieve this goal are detailed in the next three chapters. Some acquired their positions as legacies of national political leaders, while others worked their way up the political ladder, serving in a variety of positions. Finally, some were temporary or interim appointees, tokens, or ceremonial leaders.

In subsequent chapters, the focus will be on the role the families of these women played in setting their daughters off on a course that eventually led to a career in politics. Parents are important in helping a child develop a sense of self-esteem necessary to pursue public office as well as serving as role models. In examining the family background, the extent of involvement in politics or community affairs of the families in which these women grew up will be explored. The schools these women attended, the graduate and professional schools in which they were enrolled, and the various school activities in which they participated will be noted.

The hurdles confronted by women leaders, such as balancing a demanding career with the responsibilities of caring for a family, will next be examined. Since most of the women who have risen to the top were married and had children, they were confronted with the problems that affect most women who have both a family and a career, such as making provision for adequate child care and dealing with feelings of guilt about not spending enough time with their families.

The following two chapters will explore the challenging paths the various women took to reach the top. These often included political positions at the local or provincial levels. Even after reaching the national parliament they were often assigned ministry positions dealing with women or family issues. The difficulties of running for the highest office as a woman are then discussed.

The remaining three chapters will be devoted to a consideration of the performance of these women in office. Focus will be on their skills in forming and managing governments as well as on their general decision making and leadership qualities.

Chapter Two

Political Legacies

After women acquired the right to vote and seek public office, the first to enter the political arena were not those who had played key roles in the struggles as they had become disillusioned because of the modest gains made by women.[1] Instead, widows and daughters of prominent politicians were the first to take advantage of the newly acquired rights. For example, one-third of the women who entered the U.S. Congress between 1916 and 1963 were widows of politicians.[2] Of the 26 women to win a parliamentary election in Ireland before 1981, 13 were widows of male members of parliament or male members of the independence struggle, 4 were daughters, 3 were sisters, and 1 was a granddaughter.[3] In Sri Lanka, of the 17 women elected to the parliament between 1947 and 1977, more than one-half were elected as a replacement for a husband or father.[4]

Likewise, among the first women to rise to the top in the political arena were widows and daughters of prominent political leaders. These women were usually prodded by the close associates of their male relative, who in several cases had died a martyr's death, to assume the role he occupied in the hope that their jobs or the prospects of their political party might be salvaged.

Widows

Sirimavo Bandaranaike (1960–1964; 1970–1977; 1994–2000)

As the first woman to head a government since the dawn of the democratic era, Sirimavo Bandaranaike began the journey to the top following the assassination of her husband, who was at the time serving as prime minister. Sensing her voter appeal as well as their own political vulnerability, the leaders of the Sri Lanka Freedom Party (SLFP) urged Bandaranaike to become the head of her husband's party, but she refused. Three months before his death she had told a woman's group that "knowing fully well the responsibilities that devolve on a Prime Minister, and how difficult it is for a human being to cater to all the requirements of a nation and satisfy them, I will not accept the post of Premier even if it is offered to me."[5] She reluctantly agreed to work for the SLFP during the election campaign that was held in March 1960.

Despite Bandaranaike's efforts on behalf of her party, the SLFP did not win enough seats to form a government, but Bandaranaike was persuaded to assume the presidency of the party before a second election held a few months later. It was made clear that she would be the prime minister if the party prevailed at the polls. Remaining uncertain about the pursuit of power, she refused to seek a seat in the parliament. Instead, she was appointed to the upper chamber of the parliament, leaving the more powerful lower house virtually leaderless.

During the second campaign, Bandaranaike spoke of her husband's accomplishments and stressed that she was giving up the comforts of her home to ensure that his work would be continued. On many occasions she was led to tears as she spoke of his death and the sacrifices she and her three children had made. In the election held in July, her party won a majority of the seats in the parliament, and she was sworn in as prime minister. Perhaps to reassure the voters as well as bolster her decision to enter the political fray, Bandaranaike expressed confidence about her ability to handle the job when she said in a speech following the election: "I know what politics is and its ups and downs. I have strength and courage to face what comes when I am assigned to do a job. What is wrong for me to follow in the steps of my late husband in trying to serve the people?"[6]

After one term in office and a bitter election campaign, Bandaranaike's SLFP was defeated in the 1965 electoral contest. Her party was returned to power in 1970, and she once again became prime minister, serving until 1977 when the SLFP's bid for reelection failed. With more than 20 percent of the workforce unemployed and essential goods in short supply, the United National Party (UNP), which projected an image of honesty and purity, overwhelmingly defeated the SLFP although Bandaranaike and her son were able to hold on to their seats.

On the recommendation of a commission appointed to look into allegations of corruption and abuse of power in her government, Bandaranaike was stripped of her civic rights in 1980 and was barred from holding public office for seven years although she was granted a pardon some five years later. Accusing the government of political assassination, she took her case to the people, traveling throughout the country addressing various meetings and attacking the government over the high cost of living and corrupt practices. Playing the role of the martyr, she taunted her opponents by asking, "Why is the president afraid of a woman like me?"[7]

In the meantime, provision for a strong president was put in place by the UNP-led government. Bandaranaike, who continued to head her party, attempted a comeback in the 1988 presidential contest in a campaign held in the midst of widespread communal violence. Though in some circles Bandaranaike was believed to be the favorite in view of the deteriorating security situation and a faltering economy, she received only 44.9 percent of the vote while her opponent, the UNP's Ranasinghe Premadasa, polled 50.4 percent. Making no attempt to hide her disappointment, she was slow to begin her party's campaign for the parliamentary elections to be held some two months later. The left-oriented alliance that she led was in disarray, and violence stalked the campaign. Bandaranaike herself suffered a slight injury when smoke grenades and homemade bombs were thrown at the platform during one of her appearances. Although she managed to win her own seat, the SLFP won only 67 seats out of 225. But Bandaranaike's political career was not to end on this note. Her younger daughter, Chandrika Kumaratunga, was elected president in November 1994, and she appointed her ailing mother as prime minister. Bandaranaike resigned just months before the general election in 2000, saying that by stepping down she would allow her daughter to appoint someone who would be able to campaign actively. The veteran politician died two months later.

Khaleda Zia (1991–1996; 2001–2006)

Some 30 years after Bandaranaike became the first woman to serve as prime minister, Khaleda Zia, whose husband, Bangladesh President Ziaur Rahman, had been assassinated in 1981 by a group of army officers, became the prime minister in the newly adopted parliamentary system. In contrast to the apprehension expressed by Bandaranaike, Zia noted that "there is nothing special about being a woman in power."[8] Not only had a number of women governed states during the years that intervened, but Zia herself had acquired some political experience—first as a mediator of disputes within her party and then as leader of the Bangladesh Nationalist Party (BNP).

Up to the time of her husband's death, Zia, like Bandaranaike, had played the part of the dutiful wife, but shortly after the assassination there was discussion, especially among the disgruntled left-wing elements within the BNP, to the effect that she become the party's nominee for president in the upcoming election. The fact that the opposition Awami League (AL) had just elected Sheikh Hasina Wajed, the daughter of the founder and first leader of Bangladesh, Sheikh Mujibur Rahman, as its president made the prospect particularly appealing. Though Zia toyed with the notion of taking over the leadership of the BNP, she decided, under pressure from supporters of the incumbent president, Abdus Sattar, to forego the challenge at this time.

In 1982, a coup led by the army chief of staff, Lieutenant General H. M. Ershad, whom Zia suspected played a role in the murder of her husband, ousted the Sattar government. With many of the BNP supporters placed under arrest, renewed pressure was put on Zia to take over the leadership of the wounded party, and the following year she agreed to do so. In explaining why she had changed her mind, she stressed her connection to her husband, saying that his "ideal was to establish a just and oppression-free society on the basis of Bangladesh nationalism...As the wife of that great leader, it is my object to fulfil that idealism."[9]

To legitimize his rule, Ershad attempted to hold an election, but the leaders of the two principal opposition parties laid down conditions to be met before they would agree to take part. They called for an end to martial law and the release of political prisoners, insisting that the only way a free and fair election could be held was if the president resigned and a caretaker government took over.

Ershad on several occasions set a date for an election, offering concessions to his opponents, but each time they rejected his offer. Demonstrations and rallies followed, with Zia herself often leading her party's protests. Ershad responded by canceling the scheduled election and arresting the opposition leaders.

Although the two party leaders shared opposition to the Ershad government, they did not personally get along with one another. Sheikh Hasina believed that Zia's husband had protected those responsible for the assassination of her father from prosecution, and Zia suspected that the AL may also have been involved in the assassination of her husband. It was only under pressure from student-led demonstrators and after Ershad announced his intention to contest the election scheduled for 1990 that the two women leaders put aside their differences and came together to oust the government. Strikes and rallies were organized. With the country virtually paralyzed, Ershad resigned and was subsequently placed under house arrest.

The campaign that followed was a hectic one with the two women promising to pursue the policies of their politically prominent male relatives. The BNP captured the most seats in the parliament although the party did not secure a majority. With the support of Jamaat-I-Islam, the party of the mullahs, Zia was able to form a government despite the belief of some of the religious leaders that it was not appropriate for a woman to rule an Islamic state. In 1996, her bid for a second term was rejected by the voters, but in 2001 she regained office for a five-year term following another bitter election campaign.

Janet Jagan (1997–1999)

Janet Jagan, who was elected president of Guyana in 1997, drew a distinction between herself and the other widows who rose to the top when she said: "From the start, Cheddi [her late husband] and I went in together and started everything together. I have always been my own person."[10]

Following their marriage in 1943, the Jagans moved to Guyana, formerly British Guiana, a small country located on the northeast coast of South America and populated by people from India and Africa. The Chicago-born Jagan, who had studied nursing, and her Northwestern-trained husband set up a dental clinic, but they soon took to politics. They founded the leftist People's Progressive Party in 1950 and pushed for independence from Britain. They were imprisoned for several months in 1953 out of concern about their Marxist leanings. While Cheddi occupied a number of positions through the years, including that of president from 1992 until his death in 1997, Janet served as a member of the parliament for many years and held several different cabinet posts. After the death of her husband she was appointed interim prime minister.

Jagan was encouraged by supporters in her party to seek the presidency, but, despite her considerable experience, she expressed reluctance to take on the responsibilities of the highest office. She said that she "tussled with the party for months, trying to encourage them to leave me out." But she gave into the pressure to run, indicating that she was aware of the "magic" of the Jagan name.[11] Like Bandaranaike, Jagan waged the campaign by focusing on the accomplishments of her husband, stressing her intention to carry on with his work.

Despite the attempts of her opponents to stress her age and Jewish ethnicity, referring to her as "a Caucasian Old Lady," 77-year-old Jagan was successful in her bid for office. She won more than 50 percent of the vote in a 3-person race. Her victory was tarnished by the fact that the opposition leader did not recognize her government, alleging that there were election irregularities. She remained in office for less than two years, resigning for health reasons in August 1999.

Isabel Peron (1974–1976) and Mireya Moscoso (1999–2004)

Two widows, 43-year-old Isabel Peron, who as vice president at the time of her husband's death in 1974 became president of Argentina, and 52-year-old Mireya Moscoso, who was elected president of Panama in 1999, lived for some time in exile with their politically prominent husbands. Peron, who was 35 years younger than her husband, met him in Panama where he was living after he was ousted as president of Argentina in 1955. Having trained as a dancer, Isabel was working in a cabaret, but she chose to give up her show business career, such as it was, to become General Juan Peron's secretary and companion. Following the couple's move to Spain and under pressure from friends, they were married some six years later.

Throughout his years in exile, General Peron maintained contact with his followers in Argentina and sought to influence events in his country. In 1973, he returned to seek the presidency and chose his wife to be his running mate. There is disagreement as to whether the General wanted his wife on the ticket.[12] Some believe that she was chosen because she would neither upstage him nor offer resistance to his agenda. Others suggest that he would have preferred someone else, but there was no agreement among his supporters as to a suitable vice presidential candidate. To avoid alienating any of the factions within the Peronist movement, the General settled on his wife.

Although many of Peron's followers opposed the idea of a woman, particularly one who only had the equivalent of a sixth grade education, they were able to take comfort in the belief that even if the General died in office, his wife would not likely come to power. The military would simply not permit it.[13] Attempting to reassure his supporters, General Peron said that he had trained her for the position although this assertion is rejected by his biographer who argued that she had been confined to the carrying out of household tasks.[14] Isabel repeated the claim, saying "we talked about politics the day we first met and afterwards he trained me to be his political representative."[15]

Others believe that General Peron was persuaded to include her by Isabel herself and his private secretary, Jose Lopez Rega, a retired police corporal and astrologer, who saw in her his path to increased influence. Isabel had met Lopez when he attended her during a trip she made to Argentina in 1966, and he accompanied her when she returned to Spain, eventually becoming a key adviser to the General. According to a member of the opposition Radical Party, General Peron acknowledged the role his wife played when he observed: "At this late stage in my life, I simply could not resist the pressure from within my own bedroom."[16]

By securing a place on the ticket with her husband, Isabel accomplished what Eva Peron, the General's second wife, had been unable to do. Eva, an effective speaker, was instrumental in mobilizing the support of labor and the poor for her husband, but her attempt to become vice president failed. Though she succeeded in getting Peron to include her on the ticket in 1951, under pressure from the military, she was persuaded to withdraw.

Isabel used the election campaign to bolster her standing with her husband's supporters. Traveling throughout the country speaking to many groups, she patterned her personal appearance as well as her views after those of the popular Eva, hoping to stir the voters by evoking memories of the charismatic figure.

After she assumed the presidency, Isabel promised to pursue the same path as her late husband in national as well as international affairs, but she was unable to unite the disparate forces among the Peron supporters and stem the political violence. Her regime was toppled by the military in March 1976. She was charged with corruption and fraud and was placed under house arrest. In 1981, she was released and permitted to go into exile in Spain, but she remained nominal head of the Peronist party, Justicialist, until 1985.

Unlike General Peron, Mireya Moscoso's late husband, Arnulto Arias, did nothing to encourage his wife, who was 45 years younger than he, to seek office. Instead, he warned her not to enter politics. Arias was elected president of Panama three times but each time he was removed by his opponents. Following the military coup that swept him from office for a final time in 1968, he moved to Miami where he lived until his death. It was there that he married Mireya who had worked as a secretary at a government agency and as a sales manager at a coffee company owned by Arias. Because of her close connection to the ousted leader, she also had fled Panama after the military coup.

Following Arias' death and the removal of strongman Manual Noriega by the United State in 1989, Moscoso returned to Panama to carry on with her husband's work, taking up the leadership of the

Arnulfista Party. Her first bid for office in 1994 failed, but five years later she entered the race for president once again. She was able to overcome a poor showing in the polls and lead her party to victory. Moscoso seemed unable to deal with the faltering economy as well as widespread corruption, and support for her plummeted. Limited by the constitution to one five-year term, she was unable to seek reelection in 2004.

Corazon Aquino (1986–1992) and Violeta Chamorro (1990–1996)

Two other widows, 53-year-old Corazon Aquino, who became president of the Philippines in February 1986, and 60-year-old Violeta Chamorro, who was elected president of Nicaragua in February 1990, did not succeed a husband as head of state but, instead, took up the banner of a politically active, martyred husband. Benigno Aquino was a former provincial governor and a member of the Senate. He, along with others who opposed the Ferdinand Marcos regime, was jailed in 1972 and was later accused of murder, illegal possession of firearms, and subversion, but in 1980 he was permitted to leave the country to seek medical treatment in the United States. Marcos, concerned about Benigno's popularity, perhaps saw this as an acceptable way of removing the potential threat represented by this rival. On his return to the Philippines some three years later, Benigno was assassinated at the Manila airport as he left the plane. Many, including his wife, believed that President Marcos had ordered the assassination though the military officers accused of planning the murder were acquitted.

Opposition to Marcos's rule intensified. The regime, viewed as oppressive and corrupt, was also saddled with a worsening economy as unemployment was on the rise and the world price of locally important products such as sugar and coconut oil had collapsed. Demonstrations and rallies that attracted large, diverse crowds were organized. Though Corazon Aquino was not a good speaker, she became a familiar figure in the "parliament of the streets." Addressing her audience in a monotone, she described her husband's imprisonment, often leaving those who came to hear her in tears. She sprinkled her message with quotations from Benigno and urged action against the Marcos regime.

Under pressure from the United States to institute reforms, President Marcos spoke of calling an election, and Aquino was mentioned as a possible candidate. Having painted herself as a victim of Marcos, she had become the symbol of opposition to the regime and appeared to be the one candidate around whom the disparate forces could unify.

Like other widows who came to power after the death of their husbands, Aquino was hesitant about seeking office and fearful of assuming the responsibilities of governing. Perhaps as a way of slowing the movement of events, she made her decision to run contingent upon the calling of a snap election by Marcos and the collection of a million signatures in support of her candidacy. Finding little difficulty in gathering the signatures, her supporters put increased pressure on her to make a commitment after Marcos unexpectedly called for an election to be held in February 1986. She responded to the challenge, announcing her intention to seek office two days after the acquittal of the military leaders accused of assassinating her husband. In an interview she said, "...it came to the point I just said oh gosh, I just have to do this otherwise I will really blame myself for not having tried...it would really bother me if things turned out for the worst and I would always ask myself, could I have made a difference."[17] In addition to soliciting the advice of her family as well as politicians and priests, Aquino, who was a religious person, prayed before making her decision. She told a friend that accepting the will of God and the will of the people was "the cross I have to bear. It's a heavy cross and I can't drop it."[18]

Her candidacy immediately ran into a snag. Doy Laurel, a close associate of her husband, who had been traveling around the country for several years building a political organization, resented the fact that Aquino had taken so long before deciding to seek office. In the interest of unity and with some pressure from the Archbishop of Manila, Jaime Cardinal Sin, Laurel eventually agreed to run for vice president, creating a ticket that combined his organization and her popularity.

Aquino, who relied on members of her family for advice, traveled throughout the country during the two-month campaign, attracting large, enthusiastic crowds. She focused on the now-familiar story of her husband's imprisonment and assassination. In response to questions about her lack of experience, she replied that for 20 years "we've had one of the most brilliant Filipinos, and look what we've got—despair."[19]

Following the voting, the government contended that Marcos had won his reelection bid by 1.5 million votes, and Aquino was invited to join an advisory body to formulate policy. Rejecting this overture, she declared herself the winner, arguing that the election process was marked by fraud. An observer group as well as some independent counting agents supported her claims. She called for strikes and an economic boycott of government-controlled companies. She also lent her support to a rebellion against the regime launched by military reform leaders who had been plotting a coup. Aquino urged her supporters to take to the streets in a "people's power" protest to prevent action by the troops loyal to Marcos against the reform forces that had recognized her victory. Under pressure from the United States Marcos left the country, and Aquino was sworn in as president.

In an interview a few months after she took office, Aquino made clear that she would not seek a second term, saying that she "was needed just for the transition, when people had to find somebody they could believe in... But I am sure that six years from now, there will be many qualified people, and I will have earned a well-deserved rest."[20] Holding to her initial appraisal of the situation and remaining wary of political activity, she retired at the end of her term in 1992.

Violeta Chamorro's husband Pedro, the owner of the newspaper, *La Prensa*, had never held office, but he was a persistent critic of the Somoza regime. Pedro Chamorro was seen as a likely alternative to dictatorial rule, and his attempts at political organization led to repeated arrests.

One morning in early January 1978, as Chamorro was driving to his office in Managua, his car was forced off the road, and he was shot through the windshield. Despite the arrest and conviction of several men, theories as to who instigated Chamorro's murder abound, with many asserting that the assassination was planned by the Somoza forces. Others speculate that those interested in the removal of the Somoza regime saw the elimination of Chamorro as the most likely way to ensure that the opponents of strongman rule would be spurred on to take action to end the dictatorship.[21]

Following the assassination of Pedro Chamorro, the opponents of the Somoza regime began to mobilize, gathering support among those who had gone along with dictatorial rule. Perhaps out of concern for their own long-term safety, these newcomers to opposition politics among the middle and upper classes questioned the continued usefulness of the Somoza regime to the country.[22] An armed rebellion led by the relatively small, rural-based Sandinista National Liberation Front (FSLN) followed, and the dictator, who was under pressure from the United States to resign, left office 18 months after the assassination.

Inheriting the responsibilities of governing, the FSLN formed a five-person junta to exercise executive power. Violeta Chamorro, who had lent her personal as well as financial support to the rebellion, was asked to join the ruling council. Though she was reluctant, she felt that she could not refuse. As she said, "they told me that they needed me, they needed the name of my husband, and the name of *La Prensa*. It wouldn't have been patriotic to refuse."[23]

Chamorro's tenure in the junta was short-lived, for after nine months she left her post, pleading health problems. Though she had suffered a broken foot, she later acknowledged that she "didn't tell the truth," saying that she "gave that reason because I did not want people who had hope and faith in me to desert democracy."[24] She had misgivings about the direction in which the new government headed by Daniel was moving. She noted that "it was going to be democratic, it was going to be pluralistic, but it turned out to be just the opposite. It is a Marxist, Communist Government that has betrayed the Nicaraguan people."[25]

During the months that followed, Nicaragua became a battle ground of the cold war. The United States opposed the rule of the left-oriented Sandinista regime and imposed a trade embargo, withdrew aid programs, and provided military assistance to forces fighting the government. The Nicaraguan economy shrank by more than one-half in the next decade, and the country was thrust into a civil conflict.

In an attempt to check the threat to the stability of the region, Central American rulers under the leadership of Costa Rican President Oscar Arias sought a solution. After extensive negotiations, an agreement was reached that called, among other things, for the holding of an election in early 1990.

After the date for the election was set, 14 small parties, including conservative and liberal parties, banded together to form the National Opposition Union (UNO). When it came time to select a candidate to contest the presidential election, the UNO turned to Chamorro. In addition to her position as the widow of the martyred opposition leader, her role as publisher of *La Prensa* had kept her in the limelight.

Her lack of political experience was viewed as an asset, especially in such a bitterly divided country in which members of families, even the members of the Chamorro family, found themselves on opposite sides. As one of her economic advisers put it, since the country was so fragmented, the fact that she did not represent a particular point of view made her the popular choice.[26] Another reason her candidacy was considered viable was the fact that she was acceptable to the United States, and it was expected, accurately so it turned out, that the UNO would receive financial support from its neighbor to the north if Chamorro were the nominee.

Like the other widows who followed in the footsteps of their husbands, Chamorro reminded her audiences during the campaign of her husband's work. As a deeply religious woman, she indicated that she had consulted with God as well as her dead husband before she accepted the nomination. Seeing the task ahead of her as a duty, she said, in terms similar to those used by Aquino, "I am not a politician, but I believe this is my destiny. I have to do this for Pedro and my country."[27] When asked whether she felt prepared to assume the presidency, she confidently told an interviewer: "Of course I am. I have enormous faith in God. He will illuminate me and show me how to do what my conscience dictates."[28]

To the surprise of many pundits and contrary to the poll projections, Chamorro won the presidency, taking approximately 55 percent of the vote. Her electoral alliance won 51 of 92 seats in the National Assembly. The Nicaraguan people were looking for a way to end the war, and the fact that the United States had made it clear that the war would not end so long as the Sandinistas were in power may have encouraged some to vote for the UNO candidates. Perhaps equally surprising to many was the fact that Chamorro was able to complete her six-year term, a feat she was not able to repeat since the constitution prohibited her from seeking a second term.

Daughters

Indira Gandhi (1966–1977; 1980–1984)

In addition to widows, daughters of politically prominent men were urged to enter the political arena in the expectation that they would be able to garner support for their political parties. But, in some instances, daughters proved to be a disappointment to their backers as they were more likely than the widows to have an independent agenda. They represented a different generation and were concerned to create an identity separate from that of their parents.

The first of the daughters to rise to the top was Indira Gandhi whose father was the popular Jawaharlal Nehru, India's first prime minister. Although there had been some discussion of her succeeding her father, and a poll conducted in 1964 by the Indian Institute of Public Opinion on the question of Nehru's successor ranked her third in terms of preference, she did not appear interested in the position at that time. In a letter to Dorothy Norman, an American writer friend, she wrote just a few days before her father's death in May 1964: "I must settle outside India at least for a year or so...The desire to be out of India and the malice, jealousies and envy, with which one is surrounded, are now overwhelming."[29]

By the time of Nehru's death much support had gathered around Lal Bahadur Shastri. Despite Gandhi's expression of "a desire to be out of India," she chose to join the new government, accepting the post of minister for information and broadcasting. She may have felt that to eschew office at that time would cut her off from future political activity as she would have no official position from which to cultivate a power base. In a letter written to her aunt in December 1965, she said: "I did not want to come either to Parliament or to be in Government. However, there were certain compelling reasons at the time for my acceptance of this portfolio. Now there are so many crises...that every time seems to be the wrong time for getting out...."[30]

When Shastri died unexpectedly within months of taking office, Gandhi's candidacy was actively pushed by the Congress Party president, Kumaraswamy Kamaraj, who was concerned to find someone who could be more easily influenced than Shastri and who could defeat Morarji Desai, the chief contender whose views and manner were considered rigid and dogmatic. It was believed that Gandhi as a woman could be manipulated, particularly in view of her unimpressive performance as a member of the cabinet as well as her tendency to rely on the advice of others. Although women had held high-level office in India and had played an active role in the long and tumultuous struggle for independence, it was not expected that a woman would be able to exert dynamic leadership.

Other considerations that made her a strong candidate were her lack of a regional attachment in a country plagued by conflicts among numerous religious, linguistic, and cultural groups as well as her popularity with Muslims. She also had extensive campaign experience, and an election was scheduled to be held within a few months. She appeared to have considerable popular appeal, and it was believed that she could win the support of women who were voting in increasing numbers. The many international contacts she had developed while serving as hostess for her father could prove invaluable for India, particularly in its search for aid.

When the chief ministers of the Indian states, eager to play a larger role in policy making, announced that they would support her, the Syndicate, a powerful group of Congress Party bosses, joined the bandwagon though many of them disliked her personally because of the role she played as gatekeeper for Nehru.

Gandhi was not so reluctant to assume power as the widows were. Following her election, she remarked to a friend and later wrote to her elder son Rajiv that she had thought of the lines of a poem by Robert Frost entitled "How Hard It Is to Keep from Being King, When It's in You and in the Situation." At the same time, she did not wish to appear to be seeking the office. Renunciation or detachment, an important ingredient in liberation from the cycle of rebirths, is central to Hindu thought. The office must seek her she reminded those who gathered at her home following Shastri's death. Even after announcing her candidacy, she continued to keep a low profile and did not appear to be campaigning actively. She said that she had agreed to be a candidate when asked by Kamaraj out of a sense of duty, and the canvassing was left to her supporters.

Despite the efforts of the party leadership to orchestrate her selection, Desai insisted on entering the race, and an election for the post of party leader was held. Gandhi polled 355 votes while Desai won 169. Still not wishing to appear overly eager, on assuming office, she remarked to reporters that she felt "neither excited nor nervous," for being prime minister was "just another job I have to do."[31]

Gandhi served as prime minister from 1966 until her defeat in 1977 following a period of emergency rule set in motion in 1975 by the prime minister to ensure her continuation in office. In contrast to Bandaranaike and her politically active son, Gandhi and her younger son, Sanjay, did not win their seats in the 1977 election. Gandhi again led her party to victory in the 1980 election. She spent the intervening years responding to the numerous legal actions brought against her by her opponents, and she traveled throughout the country, building up her support. Her second term of office beginning in 1980 was cut short when she was assassinated by her Sikh bodyguards in 1984.

Benazir Bhutto (1988–1990; 1993–1996)

Unlike Gandhi, Benazir Bhutto, who became prime minister of Pakistan in 1988, actively campaigned for the position that had been held by her father, Zulfikar Ali Bhutto. She had indicated to friends that she did not want to go into politics,[32] and in her autobiography she wrote that she had "no intention of becoming a politician, having seen firsthand the pressures and strains of life in politics."[33] But after her father's execution, she became intent on avenging his death.

In the 1977 election Zulfikar Ali Bhutto's party won a majority of the seats, but he was deposed by a military coup and arrested on charges of corruption and conspiracy to murder. Following a controversial trial, he was executed in 1979. Benazir, who had returned just days before the coup from several years of study in the United States and England, was forced to set aside the plans she had made for a career as a diplomat.

In her autobiography, Bhutto wrote that when her father was first imprisoned, he warned her of the difficulties that lay ahead, indicating that if she decided to leave the country, he would understand.[34] With her siblings away at school, she decided to remain at home to help her parents. She visited her father in prison when she was permitted to do so and participated in the preparations for his defense. Her political career began modestly during this period as she made appearances on her father's behalf, giving speeches to energize his supporters and settling intraparty disputes. She was arrested on several occasions as were many of the workers in the Pakistan People's Party (PPP), for the authorities were concerned about the effect the daughter of a popular politician might have on a restless electorate.

After the execution of her father, Benazir continued to work on behalf of the PPP, spending time in prison because of her political activities. The years under arrest took a toll on her health and, among other things, she developed a chronic ear infection. Near the end of 1983, she was given permission to leave the country to seek medical treatment in London. She told an interviewer that she reluctantly made the decision to go abroad, because she felt that her incarceration was "a matter of psychological encouragement to all our party workers heroically facing the odds against martial law."[35]

Bhutto took advantage of her stay in Europe to drum up support for her campaign to oust the military ruler, Mohammad Zia ul-Haq. She traveled extensively and met with foreign leaders while maintaining contact with the party workers in Pakistan, and she developed relationships with the members of the old guard who were living in exile. In 1986, following the lifting of martial law by Zia ul-Haq, Bhutto returned to Pakistan, attracting enormous crowds to her rallies designed to whip up support for early elections. After yet another arrest, Bhutto's campaign to oust the regime lost momentum, but she had gathered sufficient popular support that the old guard of the PPP began to take her seriously and accepted her as leader of the party.

Just months before he was killed in a plane crash, Zia ul-Haq, under increasing pressure even from those within his circle of supporters, announced that an election would be held in 1988. Although he doubted that Muslim Pakistan would vote for a woman, he scheduled the election for November so that Bhutto would not be able to meet her campaign commitments. She was pregnant at the time and though she never revealed the projected delivery date, it was believed that the baby was due in November. Actually her son was born in September.

Bhutto, despite a kidney infection, was able to conduct a vigorous campaign and lead the PPP to victory, but since the party did not secure a majority of seats, she was not immediately sworn in as prime minister. The military expressed reservations about her leadership, but she was able to overcome these concerns by agreeing not to cut the military budget and pledging to keep on certain key officials. Though Muslim leaders argued that Islam did not permit a woman to serve as head of government or state, Bhutto was asked to form a government.

Less than two years later, this government was dismissed by the president on grounds that it was guilty of corruption, nepotism, and abuse of power. Many of her supporters as well as her husband were arrested, and charges were brought against her in special tribunals set up for the purpose of hearing these cases. In the election that followed her ouster, Bhutto's party was soundly defeated, winning only 45 seats compared to 105 for her principal opponents.

As the leader of the opposition, Bhutto pressed for new elections, arguing that those held after her dismissal had been rigged although independent observers rejected this claim. To end the stalemate that had plagued the country for several months, the army stepped in and secured the resignation of the president and prime minister, paving the way for a caretaker government to oversee another election. Bhutto's party won a plurality of the votes in the election held in October 1993, and, with the support of independent and minority members, she was able to form another government.

In November 1996 Bhutto's government was dismissed for a second time on grounds of corruption and financial mismanagement. In the election that followed, her party was defeated, and she again assumed the position as leader of the opposition. To escape arrest and prosecution, Bhutto went into exile in 1999 but remained the chair of her party. She sought to return to run for office in the 2002 election, but her nomination papers were rejected by the military government.

Following eight years in exile, Bhutto returned to Pakistan in the fall of 2007 to lead her party in an upcoming parliamentary election. Her plans for a third chance at governing were never put into play as she was assassinated at a campaign rally in Rawalpindi in December.

Chandrika Kumaratunga (1994–2005)

Chandrika Kumaratunga, the younger daughter of S.W.R.D. and Sirimavo Bandaranaike, became prime minister and then president of Sri Lanka in 1994 at the age of 49. It was expected that her brother, Anura, would follow in the footsteps of his parents when Sirimavo Bandaranaike stepped down, but he fell out of favor with his mother who suspended him from the party for a brief period in 1993 and let it be known that she was tilting toward Chandrika to succeed her. Bandaranaike was torn between her "level-headed son...and her firebrand daughter, who was much less predictable but whose passion for the poor came closer to her own feelings."[36] In the meantime, Anura joined the UNP with the promise of a cabinet post, making it unnecessary for Bandaranaike to choose between the two.

Kumaratunga and her husband, a popular film actor turned politician who was assassinated in 1988, had founded a political party some four years before his death when it became apparent that they would not be able to move the SLFP to the left. After the assassination, Chandrika spent the next three years in London out of concern for her safety and that of her two children. Her political career began in earnest when she returned to Sri Lanka in 1991 and rejoined the SLFP fold. Taking advantage of the voters' frustration with the many years of conflict, Kumaratunga called for new peace initiatives and promised unconditional negotiations with the Tamils, a minority community seeking independence. She expanded the base of support for her party, putting together an alliance made up of the SLFP and several leftist parties.

The People's Alliance performed well in local elections that were held during the early months of 1994. In fact, the coalition had done so well that the president of Sri Lanka decided to call for the general election a few months early in hopes of catching the opposition unprepared. At the time the SLFP was bogged down in a conflict over who would be the leader of the party, Kumaratunga or her mother.

As the campaign proceeded, the leadership decision was made in the daughter's favor, and her alliance won 105 seats, just a few short of the number needed to form a government. When it appeared that the UNP was not likely to be able to put together a governing coalition, Kumaratunga was asked to form a government. With the support of some Tamil groups and the Muslim Congress, she succeeded in ending 17 years of rule by the UNP.

After serving as prime minister for approximately two months, Kumaratunga entered the race for president, the more powerful of the two offices. She won by an overwhelming margin, defeating Srima Dissanayake, the widow of her initial opponent who was assassinated during the campaign. Pledging to amend the constitution and return to a traditional parliamentary system in which the prime minister is the more important figure, she proceeded to appoint her mother as prime minister. Speculation at the time held that with her mother in the position, it would be easy for Kumaratunga to become prime minister again once she had succeeded in restoring power to that office.

Unable to get a new constitution in place, Kumaratunga successfully sought reelection as president in December 1999, one year ahead of schedule. During the last days of the campaign an assassination attempt against her resulted in the loss of sight in one eye, assuring Kumaratunga's return to office. Her party did not win enough seats in the 2001 parliamentary election to form a government, but she staged a comeback in the 2004 parliamentary election. Since Kumaratunga was limited to two terms, she was not a contender in the 2005 presidential contest, retiring after 11 years in the office.

Sheikh Hasina Wajed (1996–2001)

After years of conflict, alternating with brief periods of cooperation, between the two principal political leaders in Bangladesh, 48-year-old Sheikh Hasina defeated her rival, Khaleda Zia, in the 1996 election. Hasina, the daughter of Sheikh Mujibur Rahman, the founder of his country, had lived in exile in India since her father's assassination in 1975. She made her debut on the political stage in 1981 when she was selected to head the Awami League. It was believed that she would be able to repair a severely divided party and encourage her father's supporters.

Hasina sought to oust her chief rival within months of Zia's election victory in 1991. Protests and strikes dotted the political landscape, and in 1994 Hasina led her party in a boycott of the parliament. Among other things, Zia's government was accused of corruption, voter fraud, and incompetence. When Zia would not agree to the appointment of a caretaker government to supervise the election to be held in early 1996, Hasina refused to participate. It was only after Zia gave in to the demands of her opponent that an election in which all the parties took part could be held.

The AL failed to win enough seats to govern without support from other quarters, forcing Hasina to form an alliance with Ershad's wife, who was primarily interested in getting her husband out of prison. In her quest for political office, Hasina was the beneficiary of the Zia government's failure to maintain public order, but she likewise disappointed the voters and was turned out in 2001.

Gloria Macapagal Arroyo (2001–) and Megawati Sukarnoputri (2001–2004)

Two other Asian women who rose to the top—Gloria Macapagal Arroyo who became president of the Philippines in January 2001 and Megawati Sukarnoputri who took over as president of Indonesia approximately six months later—were the daughters of former political leaders. Arroyo was the daughter of Diosdado Macapagal who was president of the Philippines (1961–1965) while Megawati was the eldest daughter of Achmed Sukarno who was the founding president of Indonesia (1949–1967). Both of these women served as vice president and ascended to the presidency following the forced resignation of presidents who left office under a cloud. Unlike the other daughters who followed fathers into a leadership position, these women entered politics many years after their fathers held public office, but they were quick to remind the voters of their relationship to the popular politicians.

Though she declared her intention to seek the presidency in 1998, Arroyo, who received no party endorsements, began her journey to the top when the newly elected president, Joseph Estrada, a former film star, came under heavy criticism. Among other things, he allegedly took bribes from illegal gambling syndicates and kickbacks from various business deals. The vice president resigned her cabinet post in October 2000 and began putting together an alternative governing coalition made up of a mixed bag of interests such as business groups, left-wing activists, and university students. She urged President Estrada to step down, declaring that the shadow administration she had put together was preparing an agenda.[37] Despite the discontent with Estrada, Arroyo's push to set up a shadow government was widely criticized as she was seen as overly eager to assume power.

The crisis intensified in January 2001 when the Philippine Senate by a vote of 11 to 10 refused to allow the presentation of evidence of corruption against Estrada, effectively shutting down impeachment proceedings that had been authorized by the House. Mass demonstrations, supported by both the church and the military, were organized. Several members of the cabinet resigned, but Estrada refused to leave office. In the midst of the turmoil, the Philippine Supreme Court declared Arroyo to be president. Deserted by the army and with protesters marching to demand his resignation, Estrada was forced out of office.

The 53-year-old former economics professor, a devout Catholic who said that she rose to the top only because God had ordained it,[38] said she did not like politics but was drawn to it out of a sense of duty instilled by her father.[39] Arroyo served the remainder of the term but was ambivalent about facing the electorate in 2004. Her popularity ratings had fallen precipitously after taking office and she was not able to overcome the animosity of Estrada's followers. But by October 2003, her poll numbers were on the rise and she bowed to pressure from her supporters to seek election for a full term, taking approximately 40 percent of the vote in a crowded field.

Megawati Sukarnoputri's rise to the top began in 1993 when she became leader of the Indonesian Democratic Party (PDIP), one of two minority parties allowed by the government. Basically a quiet person, Megawati used this position to conduct a low-key campaign against the corrupt and dictatorial regime of President Suharto who had forced her father from the presidency some 30 years earlier. Megawati did not directly attack her adversaries out of concern for the safety of her supporters,[40] and in a culture that values silence and reticence, her "go slow" approach served to enhance her popularity. Megawati's dismissal in 1996 by a government-backed faction in the PDIP, and an attack by Suharto's troops on the party's headquarters gave her martyr-like status. Using the support she had put together, she formed a rival party, the Indonesia Party of Struggle.

With widespread rioting and a faltering economy tarnishing his image, Suharto resigned to be succeeded by B.J. Habibe who announced that an election would be held. The strength of Megawati's party was demonstrated as it won 34 percent of the popular vote and 30 percent of the parliamentary seats in the election held in 1999. Her closest rival among the 48 parties competing for power received only 22 percent of the vote.

With such an impressive showing, it was assumed by many, including Megawati, that she would be selected as president by the 700-member People's Consultative Assembly. To win the election, considerable deal making and promises of power sharing were required, but Megawati was uncomfortable with political maneuvering. She felt that she was entitled to the office because of her family connections and believed that all that was necessary was to ask for the support from the "pro-reform, pro-democracy, and anti-status quo" political parties.[41] Though the party of her ally, Abdurrahman

Wahid, an influential cleric, held only 11 percent of the seats in the legislative body, he was able to make the deals necessary to capture the top position, and he took advantage of the Muslim parties' opposition to a woman president. In a separate vote, Megawati won out in the election for vice president.

Wahid's tenure was short-lived. Disgust with his erratic behavior ultimately left him with little support. In February 2001, he was censured by the parliament over alleged corruption and incompetence. In desperation to stave off impeachment, Wahid offered to share power with the popular Megawati, but later reneged on these promises. In the end, Wahid could not resist the pressure as the army ignored his orders to suspend the National Assembly hours before it was to meet in July 2001. The Assembly voted 591 to 0, with 100 pro-Wahid deputies boycotting the session, to dismiss and replace him with the 54-year-old Megawati. Her detractors were reassured by the belief that she would be easily influenced and that she was not likely to remain in office for long. The latter prediction proved accurate as Megawati served only one three-year term, failing to be reelected in 2004.

Conclusions

A characteristic shared by the widows and to a lesser extent the daughters who have risen to the top is a lack of political experience. Few had held any elective office. Their opponents were quick to point to this weakness, but the women responded by noting a compensating factor—extensive exposure to politics. Bandaranaike put it this way shortly after becoming prime minister: "People forget I had twenty years of political education from my husband. I am not as inexperienced as they make me out."[42] During the 1985–1986 presidential campaign, Aquino pointed out that her husband had instructed her in the ways of politics: "I learned a lot from Ninoy. Ninoy taught me well."[43] Bhutto said that her father taught her about politics when she visited him in prison.

Although the inexperience of these women was a disadvantage in that they did not have the opportunity to hone their leadership skills over time, it also accounted for much of their appeal in that they had few political enemies. Because of their ties to martyrs or popular politicians, they enjoyed considerable trust and support among the electorate. They had no record of political corruption that could be used against them, and though it proved, for the most part, to be a miscalculation, it was believed by some who pushed their candidacies that they could easily be manipulated. The widows in particular expressed reluctance about assuming office, a response not unexpected given their inexperience. Once in office, their doubts seemed to pass, and most of them remained active in the political arena for many years. The widows and daughters stressed that they had come to politics out of a sense of duty. At least initially many of them did not have an agenda of their own but instead pointed to the political goals of their male relatives. By focusing on the programs of these relatives, they were able to reassure the voters and perhaps even allay some of their own doubts about their capabilities.

Another characteristic common to these women is that they hailed from developing countries. As new entities these countries had not yet acquired well established paths for the selection of their leaders. Given the importance of the family as the repository of continuity and stability in these rapidly changing societies, close relatives become a ready source of new leaders.[44]

The dominance of Asian women among those who reached the top and were related to prominent male politicians is puzzling since women in this part of the world do not enjoy the status of their counterparts in developed states.[45] When asked about participation of women in politics, Indira Gandhi indicated that the role played by women in the struggle for Indian independence accounted for their acceptance in the political arena. Women were encouraged to take part in the resistance movement as many of the men were in prison and unable to conduct the daily activities associated with the movement. The activities of the women were deemed acceptable despite the fact that they were defying the traditional female role. They were viewed as merely filling in for husbands or fathers.[46]

The fact that a number of Asian women have risen to the top political post has perhaps made it easier for others in the region to assume leadership positions. Since the voters have had experience with women in these roles, they may be more willing to accept women as leaders. Women of the region may, also, be less reluctant to assume such positions since they have many role models after whom they may pattern their careers. When asked whether she enjoyed doing things other girls did not do as a possible explanation for why she entered politics, Benazir Bhutto replied that "to me, these weren't things girls 'didn't do.' I saw Indira Gandhi in India and Mrs. Bandaranaike in Sri Lanka and Mrs. Fatima Jenna[47] in Pakistan."[48]

Chapter Three

Professional Politicians

Since women had little experience in campaigning for public office or in governing, beyond that acquired while assisting a husband or father, it was perhaps inevitable that among the first of their gender to rise to the top were those who were related to a male politician. With the unfolding of more opportunities for women in politics, some began to build careers in the fashion of many male politicians, serving a long apprenticeship in a variety of posts.

Stopgap Appointment

Golda Meir (1969–1974)

The first female professional politician to head a government was Golda Meir who emerged from retirement to become the prime minister of Israel in 1969, following the sudden death of Levi Eshkol. While she had a long and distinguished political career, serving in a variety of cabinet posts, including that of foreign minister, Meir was viewed at the time of her selection as a stopgap prime minister. Moshe Dayan and Yigal Allon, who represented different wings of the newly united Labor Alignment, were the principal contenders to succeed Eshkol. To avert a struggle over the succession, which might have led to a split in the party just before the election scheduled to be held later that year, Pinhas Sapir, secretary-general of the party, orchestrated Meir's selection as prime minister.

Her age and perhaps her gender as well made her the ideal stopgap leader. Since she was 70 years old, it was assumed that she had no long-term political ambitions. In fact, Meir had indicated only days before Eshkol's death that she did not intend to seek a seat in the Knesset in the forthcoming parliamentary election. As one of the last members of the founding generation, she had been a force within the party for many years, and, unlike her rivals, she was acceptable to all the factions. She was also popular with Jews around the world, having traveled extensively, speaking to various groups on behalf of her adopted land.

This is not to say that Meir did not have her detractors, particularly in view of her sometimes intractable manner. One writer suggested that "the choice was not quite unanimous, and there were objections from several sides that the voting procedure was not satisfactory in the party's Central Committee. The decision had been made, as so often before, by the Party's top leadership."[1]

Dayan's supporters were particularly reluctant to back Meir as they considered her too flexible on foreign policy matters. Her candidacy was also opposed by some religious leaders on the grounds that the religious law prohibits a woman's heading a Jewish government. Others rationalized their support for her, indicating that they were not voting for her as such but rather for the government of which she happened to be the leader, and that the president of Israel was the head of state.

Meir at first resisted the idea of becoming prime minister, particularly in view of her recurring health problems. She suffered from migraine headaches; she had experienced a minor stroke; and cancer of the lymphatic system had been diagnosed in 1963 although few were aware of this serious medical problem at the time she was asked to head the government.

When she accepted the position as prime minister, she said she had undertaken all her political posts with "awe and trepidation and endless doubts," and this one was no exception.[2] Her own misgivings were shared by many throughout Israel. One of her aides said that "the majority of Israelis saw her as a bitter politician... sick, old. They wanted national dynamic leadership and all they got was a grandmother."[3]

Soon after Meir assumed her new responsibilities, her own doubts as well as those of the voters about her ability to lead the nation began to fade. Her popularity ratings soared, reaching 80 percent approval within weeks of her becoming prime minister, and her health improved as well. Her personal strength and prestige restored a sense of confidence in the government.

While it had been expected that Meir would remain in office only until after the election, she early on expressed her intention to continue as prime minister following the campaign despite the fact that she had remarked to a visitor: "This is an awful job. It's not the work. God knows, before I came to this office I was not given an opportunity to be spoiled by leisure. I only dreamt about it. But the responsibility. It's an awful strain. I imagine it would be at any time, but at this time . . . ."[4]

The results of the October 1969 election proved disappointing as Meir was unable to translate her support into a parliamentary majority for her party. In fact, the Labor Alignment won even fewer seats than it held before the election, but Meir was called on to form a government since her party won more seats than any of its rivals. Additional seats were lost in the 1973 election as there was growing criticism of the government's handling of the Yom Kippur War and rancorous soul searching within the party itself, but Meir was again asked to put together a governing coalition. In April 1974, within weeks of this government's difficult birth and almost five years after she had been chosen as a stopgap candidate, she offered her resignation. Not only was she influenced by her dwindling support but she was also concerned that her health would not measure up to the tasks that lay ahead.

Challengers for Party Leadership

Margaret Thatcher (1979–1990)

Several women rose to the top after successfully challenging for the leadership of their respective parties. In some systems, the party leader assumes the top governmental position if the party holds a majority of the members of the parliament or the leader of the opposition if the party is in the minority. Margaret Thatcher spent four years as leader of the opposition before becoming prime minister following her party's victory in the 1979 British election.

Thatcher's quest for the prime ministership had its beginnings in 1974, following two consecutive Conservative Party general election defeats. Frustrated with the party's performance as well as that of its aloof leader, Edward Heath, Conservative backbenchers pushed for the election of a new leader. Reluctantly, Heath agreed to establish a committee to review the system of selection as there was no party machinery for replacing a leader who wished to remain in office. Ironically, the procedure adopted, which required that a ballot for the leadership be scheduled each session and that a candidate win a majority of all Conservative Party backbenchers and 15 percent more votes than the nearest rival, was used by Thatcher's opponents to oust her in 1990.

Following the withdrawal from the leadership contest of her long-time friend and political ally on the right, Keith Joseph, and with no one else coming forward, Thatcher decided to take the risky step of challenging Heath. Initially, her candidacy was not taken seriously, especially by the prime minister. Though Thatcher had served in the government and shadow cabinet with him for many years, she was neither close to Heath, nor had she been a member of his inner circle of advisers. He did not particularly like her but admired her abilities and believed that she was useful to the party.

Thatcher did not have the kind of experience considered necessary for a British prime minister as she had never held a major cabinet post. Her middle-class background represented a sharp contrast to that of the typical Conservative Party prime minister who hailed from the aristocracy. She had not interacted extensively among the backbenchers, nor was she particularly popular with party workers. The adverse publicity she had received during her stint as minister of education in the 1970s had not enhanced her reputation among the party members. Then there was the question as to whether the party and the country would accept a woman as leader. In June 1974, in reply to a question concerning the prospects of a woman as leader of the Conservative Party, Thatcher told a reporter that "it will be years before a woman either leads the Party or becomes Prime Minister. I don't see it happening in my time."[5]

To promote her candidacy, Thatcher's advisers encouraged those who wanted someone other than Heath to vote for her to ensure a second ballot. The prospect was held out that potential candidates, who remained loyal to Heath but who were preferred by party members, would come forward after the first ballot. To boost her support among the backbenchers, Airey Neave, a key strategist, arranged a series of meetings for her with members of parliament, especially those who had not yet committed themselves to a candidate. To court the press, she held luncheon meetings with members of the media.

As opposition spokesperson on Treasury and Economic Affairs, Thatcher had a platform from which to show off her skills in debate just before the leadership election. In mid-December 1974 her attack, punctuated with detailed arguments, against the Finance Bill implementing the Labor government's budget proposals was greeted with a cheer from the Tory MPs. In January she gave an impressive performance in opposing the government's proposed capital transfer tax to be imposed on gifts and bequests. Her aggressive debating style was a marked contrast to that of the pensive Heath and won her the support of a party suffering from recent electoral debacles.

Although some of her backing appeared to be slipping just before the party election, the result of the poll held on February 4 was Thatcher, 130; Heath, 119; and Hugh Fraser, a Scottish aristocrat who made no serious attempt to solicit support, 16. Following the resignation of Heath and the withdrawal of Fraser, four other candidates entered the race, but attempts by the former Heath loyalists to overcome her lead proved too late.

Since Thatcher had relatively little cabinet experience, the four-year period as leader of the opposition provided her the opportunity to learn her way around as well as make plans for a future Conservative government, but she soon became frustrated. Noting her penchant for action, she remarked that "[o]pposition can only question and exhort. Government can talk and act. I like to get on with things."[6]

Though the economy had begun to falter in the 1970s, by early 1979 Britain was faced with a worsening situation. Unions, the Labor government's principal supporters, were unwilling to go along with the policy of pay restraint as a means of controlling inflation. Strikes led to the closing of many services such as hospitals, schools, and transportation facilities. Public anger was intense. The Labor government found itself increasingly under attack, and it fell on a vote of no-confidence in March.

After years of planning and preparation, the five-week election campaign that followed was deftly managed by Thatcher and her advisers, and the Conservative Party secured a 44-seat majority over all other parties combined. Thatcher led her party to victory again in 1983. In 1987, she became the first British prime minister in 160 years to win a third consecutive term, but she was forced out some three years later when she lost the support of her cabinet members.

Tansu Ciller (1993–1996)

During her lengthy stay in office Thatcher was criticized for not helping other women interested in pursuing a political career, but after she retired, she came to the aid of a Turkish politician, Tansu Ciller. Thatcher, whose protégé shared many of the views of the veteran politician on the economy, traveled to Turkey at the invitation of Ciller just before the contest for the leadership of the True Path Party, the senior party in Turkey's governing coalition, and Thatcher stayed in Ciller's home. One British newspaper went so far as to suggest that in light of Thatcher's popularity in the Islamic world, she had been instrumental in making Ciller's subsequent victory possible.[7]

Ciller was a latecomer to the political arena as her career in politics did not begin until 1990 when she was invited by the leader of the opposition, Suleyman Demirel, to join the rural-based True Path

Party. Seeking to bolster his support within the business community and among the urban elite as well as with women, Demirel believed that as an educated young woman with extensive contacts among business leaders, Ciller would enhance the image of the party. In fact, during the 1991 parliamentary election campaign, pictures of her were used to project an image of a modern party ready to bring about change.[8]

Within less than two years after the election, the president of Turkey died, and Demirel assumed that office, leaving the position as leader of the True Path Party vacant. Ciller resigned as minister of state for the economy and entered the contest for the leadership—a high risk move as defeat would likely have spelled the end of her political career. Like Thatcher, she conducted a vigorous campaign, playing to the different segments within her party. For the benefit of the rural and religious interests she pointed to the importance of Islam, taking care to wear a scarf when entering a mosque, while for the urban business interests she stressed the significance of the country's connections to the West.

Though she did not have the support of Demirel and other party leaders, who found her emphasis on change and reform disquieting and her uncompromising manner difficult, the 47-year-old Ciller, a former economics professor, won the race for party leader and became prime minister in 1993. Surprising even some of her supporters given her political inexperience, she received 11 votes shy of a majority on the first ballot. Her two opponents withdrew from the contest, and she won on the second ballot.

Two years later, the governing coalition Ciller inherited collapsed as a result of the austerity measures pursued by her government to deal with an ailing economy. A major strike was called to protest the government's refusal to increase the wages of workers in state enterprises to compensate for triple-digit inflation, and the Social Democratic Party withdrew from the governing coalition. Because of Ciller's inability to assemble a satisfactory alternative government, she was forced to call an election. Though Ciller conducted a spirited campaign in 1993, she was not able to rise to the top again.

Jenny Shipley (1997–1999) and Helen Clark (1999–)

Two other women challenged rivals for the top position—Jenny Shipley and Helen Clark, both of New Zealand. The 45-year-old

Shipley, a former teacher, made her way to the top in 1997 by staging a coup of sorts. Amid growing dissatisfaction with the scandal-ridden and relatively ineffective governing coalition that had been formed the previous year, Shipley, who had served in the parliament for approximately 10 years and had held several cabinet posts, made plans to force out the incumbent prime minister. While Jim Bolger was out of the country attending a Commonwealth conference in Scotland, she circulated a letter for the signatures of the members of parliament, expressing support for a challenge. With the approval rating for the coalition at only 10 percent, she was able to get the signatures of 30 of the National Party's 44 MPs. When Bolger returned, Shipley confronted him, pointing out that he had little support in the party. Not wishing to face a vote of confidence that would likely have gone against him, he resigned and Shipley took over as party leader and prime minister.

As deputy leader of the Labor Party Helen Clark, a 49-year-old former college lecturer, who was first elected to parliament in 1981, successfully challenged the leader of her party for the top spot after the Labor Party lost the 1993 election. Her personal standing in the polls remained low, but Clark was able to hold her party together and lead it to a respectable showing in the 1996 election though she was unable to put together a governing coalition.

The 1999 election, a comparatively mild affair, pitted Shipley against Clark. While the two women did not differ extensively on social issues, with both taking a fairly liberal stance, Shipley favored policies that would ensure a market driven economy. Clark, on the other hand, pushed for a greater role for government with increased taxes to finance social programs. Though her party did not win enough seats to govern, Clark quickly put together a coalition with the backing of the left-leaning Alliance Party.

Shipley assumed the role of opposition leader, but her length of service in that role was cut short. The events that led to her departure in October 2001 bore some resemblance to those that allowed her to assume power in 1997. Although there had been rumors of an impending coup for some weeks, given the growing dissatisfaction with Shipley's performance as leader of the opposition, it was while she was on a trip abroad that her opponents began to mobilize. The seriousness of the situation was conveyed to her, but she did little to address the doubts about her leadership. Instead, on her return she urged her detractors to challenge her or give up the campaign to unseat her. When it became apparent that support for her was shifting, Shipley, like her predecessor, chose to resign.

In July 2002 Clark, whose government enjoyed favorable approval ratings, called a snap election four months early in response to the defection of some in the governing coalition. Although the proportional representation system used in New Zealand made it difficult to win an absolute majority, the prime minister did not seek to align with any of the minor parties. After winning a second term with 52 seats in a 120-seat parliament, she relied on ad hoc majorities that varied from issue to issue. This strategy paid off as she won a record third term in office in 2005.

Angela Merkel (2005–)

The 51-year-old physicist, Angela Merkel, who became the chancellor (prime minister) of Germany in 2005, took the first step up the political ladder when she turned against her mentor, Chancellor Helmut Kohl. The former chancellor, who referred to his protégé as "the girl," had become involved in a campaign finance scandal. Merkel responded to his troubles by writing a scathing article about him.

In 2000, Merkel took over leadership of the Christian Democratic Union (CDU), enabling her to play off her rivals against one another and leaving her in a position to assume the post of chancellor should her party win the next election. The 2005 German election was called a year earlier than was required by law as the incumbent chancellor, Gerhard Schroeder, of the governing Social Democratic Union (SDU) did not believe he would be able to hold his coalition together to move along his program for the faltering economy.

The election was won by the CDU and its centrist partner, the Christian Social Union (CSU), by a narrow but insufficient margin despite the fact that the CDU/CSU held a double digit percentage lead in the polls at the beginning of the campaign. Following failed efforts by both of the two major parties to put together a government, the decision was made to form a "grand coalition" to be headed by the CDU leader. Though Merkel had to make concessions to the SDU in terms of cabinet posts as well as policy priorities, she was able to salvage the chancellorship for herself.

Portia Simpson-Miller (2006–2007)

Following the 2006 decision of Percival Patterson to step down after 14 years as the prime minister of Jamaica and president of the ruling

People's Party (PNP), Portia Simpson-Miller sought to succeed him in those positions. In obtaining the party presidency Simpson-Miller, who had only a correspondence degree from a small college in Florida, beat out two candidates with doctorates and a physician. This party position enabled her to serve as prime minister until the next election that was held in September 2007 and which her party lost by a narrow margin.

Assuming the office of prime minister at the age of 60, Simpson-Miller had considerable political experience having served as vice president of the PNP since 1978 as well as making an unsuccessful run for the presidency of her party in 1993. A member of parliament since 1982, she also occupied a number of minor cabinet positions dealing with such issues as labor, social security, sports, and tourism.

Some expressed concern about her intellectual ability, perhaps in part because of her highly educated party rivals, but her strength lay in her sensitivity to the needs of the people, having come from a working-class background.[9] She fanned the flames of controversy when she spoke at the Rehoboth Apostolic Church insisting it was God who appointed her as prime minister and that "in light of this, Christians have a responsibility to support her."[10]

Appointments to Aid Faltering Parties and Troubled Governments

Just as widows and daughters of prominent politicians have been urged to seek office to salvage the electoral prospects of their political parties, some professional politicians have risen to the top in the belief that they would be able to restore support for faltering parties or aid troubled governments. Edith Cresson, who was chosen to be prime minister of France to improve her party's electoral prospects, was known to comment that "men turn to women when the situation is impossible."[11] At the 1998 summit of the Council of Women World Leaders, Hanna Suchocka said that she was of the opinion that men agreed to women's becoming prime minister only in very difficult times, and Kazimiera Prunskiene, noting that she came to office during a trying period for Lithuania, agreed with Suchocka.[12] Resorting to a bit of levity, Gro Brundtland, who became prime minister of Norway in 1981 during a period in which the nation faced severe economic difficulties, remarked in an interview that she and her women ministers were brought in "to do the dishes after the party."[13]

Although the appeal of those related to prominent male politicians lay in their name recognition, the professional politicians represented new faces that, it was hoped, would stimulate beleaguered parties or revitalize governments. Since women have been viewed as the "ultimate outsiders," popular women politicians offered prospects for victory to parties in distress or new life to governments in disarray as these women carried little of the baggage associated with those in power. The fact that the voters tend to see women as more honest only added to the appeal of these professional politicians and further shielded them from the negative consequences of their parties' or governments' misdeeds.

Gro Brundtland (1981; 1986–1989; 1990–1996)

Fearing defeat in the upcoming election, the leaders of the Norwegian Labor Party pressed for the resignation of the incumbent prime minister and in February 1981 chose Gro Brundtland, the popular 41-year-old deputy chair of the party, to fill out the remaining eight months of the term. Despite reservations about the effect her strong commitment to safeguarding the environment might have on the country's lucrative offshore oil drilling operations, the outpouring of support for Brundtland from the local party constituencies persuaded the leaders to place the fate of the party in the hands of this young, energetic woman. Though she conducted a spirited campaign, the Labor Party lost seats.

Unlike Ciller, Brundtland was able to overcome this loss and rise to the top again. While the Conservative-led-three-party coalition held on to the advantage after the 1985 election and once again formed a government, the coalition proved to be fragile. The Conservatives pushed for an increase in the gasoline tax to compensate for a drop in world oil prices, but a small right-wing party, holding the balance of power, refused to support the measure; and the government was defeated on a vote of confidence. Since the Norwegian parliament serves for a fixed four-year term, an election is not scheduled when a government loses a confidence vote, but rather another party leader is asked to put together a government. As the principal opposition leader in the parliament, Brundtland became prime minister again in May 1986. Although both of the major parties lost seats in the 1989 election, the Conservative Party was able to resurrect the three-party coalition.

The events that followed appeared to be a replay of those of the previous term. From the beginning, the governing coalition was plagued with serious policy differences, and the government resigned following the refusal of one of the coalition partners to support closer ties to the European Union. Brundtland staged another comeback, becoming prime minister in 1990.

In the 1993 election, Brundtland's party made modest gains, and she continued to serve as prime minister until 1996 when she resigned amid speculation that she was interested in becoming secretary-general of the United Nations. Brundtland ultimately accepted the position as head of the World Health Organization for a five-year term, beginning in 1998.

Kim Campbell (1993)

Another professional politician who was moved to the position of leader in the belief that she would enhance her party's chances in an upcoming election was Kim Campbell, a 45-year-old former litigator and college instructor from Vancouver who became prime minister of Canada in 1993. Campbell had caught the attention of Prime Minister Brian Mulroney in 1988 during her first race for a parliamentary seat. Labeling the opponents of free trade "wimpish and cowardly,"[14] she made a key element of her campaign strategy a strong defense of the North American Free Trade Agreement, a project in which Mulroney had invested considerable political capital. Under pressure to include more women in his government as well as to shore up his support in the western part of the country, about a year later Mulroney appointed this newcomer as minister of state for Indian affairs and northern development, and placed her on a number of cabinet committees. As a quick learner and one who early on showed she was a team player, Campbell made the most of these opportunities, and in 1990 she was chosen to head the justice ministry.

By February 1993, Mulroney's approval rating was at an all-time low, leading the prime minister to announce his intention to step down. Just weeks earlier, in readying his government for the general election, Mulroney reshuffled the cabinet, moving Campbell to the defense ministry. In addition to providing her contact with military veterans; as well as other powerful interests, the post afforded the opportunity to be identified in the minds of the voters with strength—a plus for a female politician in that apprehension remains about whether women are tough enough for national leadership, particularly in so far as security issues are concerned.

During the months that followed this appointment, Campbell had to walk a fine line, for while asserting her independence, she also had to show loyalty to Mulroney, especially since with her move to defense came a seat in the powerful inner circle. Attempting to make light of the situation and put down speculation as to her future in the party, she remarked: "Who needs a leadership race? I'll just stage a military coup," adding, "Don't mess with me. I have tanks."[15]

Following Mulroney's decision to retire from office, Campbell gained a commanding lead, and, except for Environment Minister Jean Charest, who was in his mid-30s, her rivals in the cabinet decided not to enter the contest. As the campaign progressed, the gap between the two principal contenders narrowed, for Campbell's outspoken manner created problems with the voters. Among her more controversial comments was her referral to those who were not roused by the debt and budget deficit as "enemies of Canadians." While noting that apathy "infuriated" her, she told an interviewer: "People who boast about how they've never been involved in a political party. Who do they think is working to keep this society intact so they can have the luxury of sitting back and being such condescending SOBs? To hell with them."[16]

In the same interview, she referred to the fact that she was confirmed in the Anglican Church while attending a Catholic school and observed that she supposed this step provided "a way of warding off the evil demons of the papacy."[17] Her opponents suggested that such statements were evidence of instability. Campbell responded by noting that she had always been outspoken and that she did not want to feel that she had to censor herself.

Despite the fact that the polls showed she would lose in an election, she was chosen at the party convention in June 1993 to head her party. Her superior organization, some of which was inherited from Mulroney, worked to her advantage while the youthfulness of her opponent discouraged some from rallying to his banner.

Mulroney's resignation, coming before the end of his term, allowed Campbell to run in the October election as the incumbent prime minister. Despite the edge this gave her party, the results of the election proved devastating. The Progressive Conservatives won only two seats in the parliament, and Campbell failed to carry her own constituency. An early lead had been squandered with a less than suitable performance, and, in the end, the dissatisfaction with the Mulroney government proved too great to overcome.

Edith Cresson (1991–1992)

Another professional politician whose selection was designed to improve the electoral prospects of a faltering party was Edith Cresson. She was appointed by President Francois Mitterrand in 1991 to head the French government as preparations were underway for parliamentary elections to be held in 1993. There was speculation that Mitterrand was concerned to have someone as prime minister who would do his bidding, and Cresson who had worked closely with him since his unsuccessful bid for the presidency in 1965 could be expected to follow her mentor's lead.

In the French system, which is a dual one or a hybrid of a parliamentary and a presidential form of government, the president has considerable latitude in selecting a prime minister, particularly if the dominant party in the assembly and that of the president are the same. The 57-year-old Cresson, a longtime protégé of Mitterrand, was chosen to replace the moderate Michel Rocard. It was believed that she would be able to energize the struggling Socialist Party, beset with a staggering economy and a campaign financing scandal. It was also expected that as a woman she would be able to garner support among women who made up a majority of French voters.

Cresson had a reputation for meeting challenges, but, like Campbell, she was outspoken, brash, and quick to express her views; and in the spotlight of high office, she became caught up in controversies that impeded her effectiveness as a political leader. Some may be put off by a male who is aggressive and uses crude language, but as the experience of both Campbell and Cresson suggest, for a woman who is expected to be nurturing and tolerant, such behavior may be especially harmful to her prospects for higher office.

Among Cresson's more damaging comments were those made about the Japanese whom she described as "ants," saying "they sit up all night thinking of ways to screw the Americans and the Europeans. They are our common enemy."[18] From her days as trade minister, she had been a critic of Japanese trading practices. Just months before being appointed prime minister, she left her post in the European affairs ministry, accusing Rocard of not providing adequate assistance to French industry.

After she became prime minister, Cresson continued to attack the way the Japanese conducted business. Describing the system as "hermetically sealed," she offered little room for maneuver in dealing with the Asian state when in a television interview she said: "Japan is another universe, which wants to conquer. That's the way they are."[19]

While such comments were harmful to Japanese-French relations, other ill-considered statements—for example, those suggesting that illegal immigrants should be returned to their homes in plane loads—cost her support within her own party.

During the months that followed her appointment, Cresson's popularity declined dramatically. One poll that initially found her approval rating to be approximately 43 percent registered a drop to 18 percent within two months.[20] Instead of an asset she had become a liability to her party. Following local elections held in 1992 in which the Socialists suffered a serious defeat, she was urged by Mitterrand, despite her protestations, to resign.

Hanna Suchocka (1992–1993)

An ideal candidate to assist a troubled government is a woman with relatively little political experience and, therefore, with few political enemies and/or one who has skills that are appropriate to the situation. Among the former are the temporaries whose paths to office will be sketched in the next chapter. Among the latter are professional politicians such as Hanna Suchocka of Poland, a former law instructor, who had a reputation for responding to problems in a low-key manner. The 46-year-old Suchocka became prime minister in 1992, at a time when many disputes divided the Polish state, including disagreements over the structure of the government itself.

Following the collapse of communist rule in 1989, Poland, with 29 parties represented in the parliament, had a number of short-lived governments, the longest surviving only a few months. When the fourth such government was not able to put together a governing coalition, the leaders turned to Suchocka who had served in the legislative body for several years but never in a leadership position. When she was nominated, President Lech Walesa did not even know who she was. She told an interviewer: "Walesa said, 'Hanna? Hanna Suchocka? Who's that? Oh, yes, I know her.' He thought it was Hanna Skowronska [another politician]. He told me, 'It was a real surprise for me when you came.'"[21]

It was hoped that as one who was seen as a conscientious worker and a conciliator, Suchocka would be able to fashion a government. She enjoyed the trust of moderates in the parliament as well as the newly organized Catholic parties, for she was conservative on social issues, supporting a strict ban on abortion. One insider said that after her name was suggested, legislators were "shocked" and "surprised" that a woman should head the government, but none could come up with a reason to oppose her.[22]

A shy, private person, Suchocka did not share the enthusiasm of her colleagues for her candidacy. When informed of the decision while traveling in England, she said: "I am not able. I am not prepared for such a job. What you are talking about is not within my competence. The answer is no."[23]

Suchocka eventually gave in to those who urged her to come forward, and she did not disappoint her supporters as she quickly managed to unite seven disparate parties to form a majority government. Shortly after she left office, she suggested that her success in forming the coalition might have been because as a woman she was able to calm the feuding parties. She added: "Women are usually looking for peaceful solutions."[24]

As a strict adherent of market reform, the Suchocka government fell victim later that year to a no-confidence vote called by Solidarity, a party on which the governing coalition was dependent for its survival. While President Walesa, who initially expressed reservations about a woman leading a nation, described Suchocka as the "best premier we have had,"[25] other Solidarity leaders were disturbed that the government refused to grant pay raises to striking hospital workers and teachers on the grounds that such increases would boost the budget deficit. She lost on the no-confidence motion by just one vote when a former minister of justice whom she had removed from the cabinet a week earlier arrived too late to cast his ballot.

In the election that followed the dissolution of the parliament, Suchocka's Democratic Union received only approximately 10 percent of the vote, but she was able to hold on to her seat. Although she enjoyed a 60 to 70 percent public approval rating, her policies were viewed as too harsh in a country that had come to rely on social welfare programs.

Beatriz Merino (2003)

As part of an effort to save the government of President Alejandro Toledo following the resignation of his entire cabinet in June 2003, Beatriz Merino, the head of the Peruvian tax collection agency and a veteran politician, was appointed prime minister. After asking several men to take over as prime minister and being rejected by all of them, the president was finally able to persuade the last person on his list, 54-year-old Merino, into taking the position. In accepting the prime ministership, Merino asserted that she would "co-govern" with Toledo. She took issue with the idea of a man dominating her even if he were her boss, telling listeners to a radio program that despite references to "the so-called empire of Alejandro Toledo, with all due respect, I have never submitted myself to the empire of any man."[26]

Merino soon became disillusioned with President Toledo's interference and refusal to give her a free hand in selecting cabinet members. Despite this conflict she did much to revitalize Toledo's ailing administration threatened with social unrest, teacher strikes, and guerilla activities. The president's approval ratings had dropped to just slightly more than 10 percent, but during Merino's tenure Toledo's approval rose to 18 percent. Polls placed her at 66 percent approval.[27]

Perhaps concern about the greater popularity of his subordinate as well as hints that Merino might seek the presidency in 2006, led Toledo to fire the entire cabinet less than six months after he had installed it. A whispering campaign developed accusing the unmarried Merino of being a lesbian—an accusation that she denied.[28] The issue, however, was a particularly sensitive one in Peru with its large Catholic population.

Leaders of Former Soviet Republics

Kazimiera Prunskiene (1990–1991)

Kazimiera Prunskiene, a 47-year-old economist, was selected to oversee the birth of a new state. The collapse of communism in 1989 led to the breakup of the Soviet Union into its 16 republics, some of which selected women for the top position in the government. Prunskiene had served in various capacities in the Soviet-controlled Lithuanian government, and she was a founding member of Sajudis, the Lithuanian Reform Movement or the principal group pushing for independence in the Supreme Council or parliament. Upon being named in 1990 prime minister of Lithuania, a state that only days earlier had declared its independence from the Soviet Union, Prunskiene resigned from the Communist Party.

Though Soviet President Mikhail Gorbachev proposed greater economic and political openness, he was not prepared to recognize the independence of Lithuania. It fell to Prunskiene along with the chairman of the Supreme Council (the equivalent of president), Vytautas Landsbergis, to chart a course in this delicate situation, but the two clashed over strategy. While Landsbergis took a fairly harsh stand, the more popular Prunskiene urged compromise. She traveled throughout the world, seeking support for her country's independence. Amid an economic embargo on vital oil and natural gas shipments and threats of military action by the Soviets, she negotiated with Gorbachev about Lithuania's future.

Like Suchocka, Prunskiene was not able to sell her approach to creating a more market-oriented economy. When the Supreme Council rejected her plans to increase retail prices sharply, she resigned her post as prime minister although she kept her seat in the parliament. In 2004 Prunskiene, who drew support for her left-leaning party based in the rural areas, sought the presidency, but was defeated by Valdas Adamkus in a runoff election in June. She had won a seat in the European Parliament, the relatively weak legislative body of the European Union, earlier that month but had given it up to seek higher office.

Yulia Tymoshenko (2005; 2007–)

A second woman to reach the top in a former Soviet republic was Yulia Tymoshenko, a 44-year-old economist, who was appointed prime minister of Ukraine in 2005. Almost two decades after "people power" played a role in Corazon Aquino's rise to the top, a similar uprising led to the appointment of Tymoshenko to head the government of Ukraine. As in the case of the Philippines, a corrupt presidential election so aroused the population that pressure was exerted to reverse the results. Following a presidential election won by the incumbent in November 2004, tens of thousands of Ukrainians poured into the squares surrounding government offices in Kiev, virtually closing down the government for several days. Evidence of fraud was attested to by outside observers as some voters in the Russian-speaking areas, where support for the incumbent was strongest, were allowed to vote several times, compiling a 90 percent voter turnout.[29]

In a December rerun of the election ordered by the Ukrainian Supreme Court, Viktor Yushchenko won 52 percent of the vote. He appointed Yulia Tymoshenko, his coleader in the so-called Orange Revolution, prime minister—a position she said she was offered when Yushchenko sought her support before the election.[30] Viewed as a "fiery and unflinching supporter of reform," Tymoshenko, with her signature blond braid that she wore ringing her head, "added an element of passion and charisma that may have proved decisive in Yushchenko's eventual victory."[31] Despite some reservations, her nomination was approved by a parliamentary vote of 370–0 in February 2005.

Tymoshenko's tenure as prime minister was short-lived as she was dismissed, along with her cabinet, by the president later that year. There were serious disagreements between Tymoshenko and President Yushchenko that could not be resolved. Yet the differences between the two paled when compared to those between Yushchenko and Tymoshenko's successor, Victor Yanukovich. In response, the president dissolved parliament in April 2007 and sought new elections with the hope of reviving the Orange coalition.

Tymoshenko's price for cooperation was a return to the prime ministership. Months of negotiation, both before and after the September 2007 parliamentary election, were required before agreement was reached on who would form the new government. Yushchenko reluctantly agreed in December to nominate Tymoshenko for a second term as prime minister. He recognized that keeping her in a political alliance might prevent her from challenging him in the next presidential election.

The Finnish Duo

Tarja Halonen (2000–) and Anneli Jaatteenmaki (2003)

In 2000 Tarja Halonen, a 56-year-old former labor union lawyer and 20-year-veteran of parliament, was elected president of Finland that has a dual system similar to that found in France with a prime minister who handles domestic matters and a president, who in cooperation with the prime minister, is responsible for foreign affairs. With the support of women, trade unions, and urban dwellers, Halonen, who was an advocate of the rights of women and minorities, was able to win a narrow victory in a presidential runoff election over her opponent, Esko Aho, the leader of the agrarian Centre Party. Halonen won a second term of office in January 2006 in another close runoff election in which security policy and the nonaligned country's relationship with NATO were the major issues.

Three years after Halonen's assumption of the presidency, 48-year-old Anneli Jaatteenmaki led the Centre Party to a narrow parliamentary victory, becoming prime minister. Following her negotiation with two other parties, she assembled a three-party coalition government.

Jaatteenmaki's tenure as prime minister was a brief one as she was accused of obtaining secret foreign ministry documents and then lying to the parliament about how she had acquired them. The documents included reference to President George W. Bush's thanking her opponent who was the incumbent prime minister for support in the Iraq War—a sensitive issue in a state in which the voters opposed the war and in which the population takes pride in its neutrality in foreign policy. In fact, the leaked documents may have been decisive in turning the election Jaatteenmaki's way, but the prime minister's governing coalition broke down, forcing her to resign after just 63 days in office. Jaatteenmaki was eventually acquitted on all counts in January 2004 and went on to win a seat in the European Parliament in June.

Leaders of Plural Executives

Milka Planinc (1982–1986), Ruth Dreifuss (1999), and Micheline Calmy-Rey (2007)

Milka Planinc, who was born in 1924, served as chair of the Federal Executive Council of Yugoslavia from 1982 to 1986. She had worked her way up through Communist Party ranks and in 1971 became head of the party in Croatia, one of the six republics into which the country was divided. When Croatians moved to secure greater autonomy, Planinc remained loyal to Josip Broz Tito, helping him purge the party of dissidents. She was rewarded with the position as president of the Central Committee of the League of Communists of Croatia, assuring her an important role in central decision making.

In 1982, Planinc rose to the top as part of a plan devised by Tito to take effect after his death to prevent any single faction within the Communist Party from dominating. A Federal Executive Council, composed of a member from each of the regions within the country, acted as a government steering committee and was elected by the assembly for a four-year term. The chair of the Council, a position that rotated among the members of the council, was the equivalent of a prime minister.

In Switzerland, which also has a plural executive, Ruth Dreifuss rose to the top in 1999. As in Yugoslavia, the members of the Federal Council are selected by the assembly every four years, but the chair of the Swiss Council serves only a one-year term with the presidency rotating among the members of the Council. The 58-year-old Dreifuss was elected to the seven-person Council in 1993 and was chosen to head the ministry of home affairs. She had served as vice president, the steppingstone to the top, in 1998. Dreifuss was not only the first woman to hold the presidency in her country; she was also the first Jew to lead the Federal Council at a time when the behavior of Swiss banks during the Second World War was under increased scrutiny.

A second woman, the 61-year-old Micheline Calmy-Rey, was chosen to serve as the president of Switzerland for the year 2007. Calmy-Rey headed the Foreign Affairs Department at the time of her selection for the top position, and she continued in that post. During her tenure as foreign minister, she pushed for Switzerland to play a more active role in the international arena while retaining its historic role as a neutral state.

Leaders of Micro States

Two small island states in the Caribbean, Dominica and the Netherlands Antilles, along with the island of Sao Tomé and Principe located off the coast of Africa, have also had women prime ministers. The size of these states may have made it easier for the population to become familiar with those women, making the voters more willing to accept a woman in such a role.

Mary Eugenia Charles (1980–1995)

In 1980 a 61-year-old lawyer and businesswoman, Eugenia Charles, became prime minister of the Caribbean island, Dominica, located 300 miles southeast of Puerto Rico. The former British colony that had acquired independence in 1978 was beset by high unemployment, rampant inflation, and saddled with a government led by Patrick John that was mired in corruption. Legislation had been proposed by the John government to curb press freedoms as well as the right of unions to strike. In an attempt to put down protests to this move, the security forces fired on the demonstrators, and the John government was forced out of office.

Having spent five years as leader of the opposition, expanding the base of her party with the help of young volunteers, Charles was rewarded. In the election that followed the government's fall, her party won 17 out of 21 seats. In an interview in which she sought to explain why the John government had been turned out, Charles said: "There was so much mismanagement, the people couldn't take it anymore."[32]

Charles' Dominica Freedom Party won reelection in July 1985 when it took 15 seats in the parliament and, with a reduced majority, she was returned to office again in 1990. She did not seek reelection in 1995.

Maria Liberia-Peters (1984–1986, 1988–1993); Susanne Camelia-Romer (1993, 1998–1999); and Emily De Jongh-Elhage (2006–)

The Netherlands Antilles, a group of islands located just north of Venezuela has had four women serve as prime minister.[33] Three of these women were professional politicians, the first of whom was Maria Liberia-Peters, a 43-year-old educator, who became prime minister in 1984. Amid increasing economic pressure, a conflict had broken out between the prime minister and the speaker of the parliament over the approval of a subsidy from the United States to send a team to athletic games in Puerto Rico. The speaker, who accused the government of moving too slowly, was expelled from his party because of his interference in executive matters, and the government fell. The National People's Party, a right-of-center party that had withdrawn from the governing coalition the previous year, turned to the popular Liberia-Peters who put together a government made up of five parties.

In the election held the following year, the National People's Party won more seats than any other party, but Liberia-Peters was not able to assemble a governing coalition. The government formed by her opponents did not complete the term as conflict over the separation of one of the islands and disagreement over proposals to cut the numbers of civil servants led to its fall. In 1988 Liberia-Peters once again became prime minister. Two years later, following the parliamentary election, she formed another coalition government but was forced to resign in November 1993. She had suffered a defeat on a referendum providing for separate status for Curacao—a measure she had supported but which failed to receive the necessary votes for passage.

Liberia-Peters played an important role in securing the elevation of her protégé, the 35-year-old Justice Minister Susanne Camelia-Romer, to the top position in 1993, but Camelia-Romer was viewed as too inexperienced and remained in the job for only one month. She became prime minister again in 1998, following five months of political stalemate during which no one was able to put together a governing coalition. Camelia-Romer lost the election held the next year as the economy continued to perform poorly despite her introduction of a series of austerity measures and tax reforms.

Following parliamentary elections in 2006, Emily de Jongh-Elhage, a 60-year-old former teacher and realtor, was sworn in as prime minister of the Netherlands Antilles. In addition to serving as president of the Party for Restructuring Antilles (PAR), she had experience in several ministerial positions, including education, public enterprises, and public housing. De Jongh-Elhage may be the last of the Netherlands Antilles prime ministers as the islands have been involved in negotiations to go their separate ways.

Maria das Neves (2002–2004) and Maria do Carmo Silveira (2005–2006)

Although Africa has not had any widows or daughters rise to the top, it has had some professional politicians assume the position of prime minister in dual systems. In October 2002, Maria das Neves was appointed prime minister of the small state of Sao Tomé and Principe with a population of 170,000. Having fired the previous prime minister, President Fradrique de Menzes asked his 44-year-old minister for trade, industry, and tourism, to form a government. Her previous experience had consisted of working as an economist in the civil service, the World Bank, and UNICEF. She was also active in politics as a member of the country's largest political party.

Just months after assuming the position of prime minister, das Neves and some of her colleagues were placed under house arrest in an attempted coup by army officers while the president was out of the country. Although it was largely a bloodless coup, das Neves suffered a mild heart attack. Thanks in part to pressure from neighboring Nigeria the coup lasted only about a week, and a truce was worked out that involved reshuffling the cabinet. Das Neves submitted her resignation in August 2003, but the president refused to accept it, choosing to change other cabinet assignments instead. She continued in the post of prime minister until the following September when the president took a different course and demanded her resignation in light of corruption charges surrounding her. She may have become a scapegoat for others in the government, as she argued that it was all part of a political cabal, asserting that the president was the country's main lawbreaker.[34]

Just two years after de Menzes forced das Neves to resign, the president sought his fourth prime minister following parliamentary elections in 2002. He chose another woman, 44-year-old Maria do Carmo Silveira, in June 2005 to fill the position that she held along with that of head of the planning and finance ministry. Silveira, who had served as governor of the central bank since 1999, was a graduate in economics from Donestsk University of Ukraine and like das Neves belonged to the majority party, the Movement for the Liberation of Sao Tomé and Principe (MLSTP).

Relations between Silveira and the president soon became strained. President Menzes blasted the MLSTP for reneging on a pledge to hold a constitutional referendum governing power sharing—a persistent problem since the parliament was controlled by the opposition. Silveira stepped down as prime minister following parliamentary elections that were held in March 2006.

Elected Executive Presidents

Michelle Bachelet (2006–) and Ellen Johnson Sirleaf (2006–)

The first two professional women elected president were sworn into office in 2006. Previous presidents had either gained the top position as part of a political legacy or they served in a ceremonial role. Although Latin America has had a number of widows such as Violeta Chamorro, Janet Jagan, Isabel Peron, and Mireya Moscoso serve as president, 54-year-old Michelle Bachelet, a pediatrician by training, was elected president of Chile, considered one of the most conservative of the Latin American states. As a single mother and a religious agnostic, she hardly met the expectations for a woman, let alone those required for a Chilean political leader. Her rise to the top had been a rapid one. When she decided to seek the presidency, Bachelet had been a public figure for only about four years, having been appointed first as health minister and later defense minister. She had never held an elected office and had sought public office only once in a municipal council race, winning a mere 2 percent of the vote.

Since Soledad Alvear, a former foreign minister, sought the nomination of the Christian Democratic Party, and Bachelet that of the

Socialists, it appeared that the two women would be competing for the endorsement of the center left coalition, Concertacion. With the polls showing Bachelet to be far ahead of Alvear, the latter chose to drop out of the race several months before the Chilean election, saying that she would thereby "strengthen Bachelet's candidacy."[35] Two men on the center right remained in the contest. The election that was held in December 2005 was not decisive as none of the candidates won a majority although Bachelet led in the vote. Bachelet won the runoff election between herself and the wealthy entrepreneur, Sebastian Pinera.

The voters of war torn Liberia chose 67-year-old Ellen Johnson Sirleaf as president in November 2005. She began her climb up the political ladder when she sought the presidency in 1997 but lost out to warlord Charles Taylor. For her criticism of the Taylor government, she paid a price as she was imprisoned for a time and later forced into exile. The 2005 presidential election afforded her another opportunity to seek the highest office. With 22 candidates in the race, no one contender won a majority of the votes, and a runoff election was necessary. Sirleaf defeated her principal opponent, the popular soccer player, George Weah, taking approximately 60 percent of the vote with a large number of them from women.

Conclusions

Some of the professional politicians who have risen to the top, like many of the widows and daughters of prominent male politicians, were chosen to prop up sagging or divided parties or aid troubled governments. Others actively sought the position as leader of their parties and challenged rivals. For example, Margaret Thatcher and Tansu Ciller risked their future political careers when they made the decision to enter the contest for the leadership of their respective parties. Helen Clark and Jenny Shipley led coups of a sort to capture control of their parties. On the other hand, Kim Campbell, who campaigned for the position of leader, was handpicked by her predecessor to succeed him.

Several women were chosen to aid a faltering party failed in their mission. Tansu Ciller and Kim Campbell led their respective parties to a devastating defeat, leaving them with little representation in the parliament. Edith Cresson's approval dropped so precipitously that she was asked to resign before the parliamentary election.

Although the number of professional politicians who have assumed the highest political office remains small, it appears that women are more likely to rise to the top in a parliamentary system as opposed to a presidential one. A prime minister, who usually represents a single constituency and is chosen by her peers in the parliament, is less likely to suffer the consequences of prejudice because of her gender. Members of the legislative body have worked with her over a number of years and have had the opportunity to become acquainted with her capabilities. Executive presidents, at least in democracies, are often selected by the entire electorate, many of whom may object to having a woman as leader. In 2006, two women who assumed office as president—Ellen Johnson Sirleaf of Liberia and Michelle Bachelet of Chile—defied this marker. Neither of the women was related to a politically prominent male although Bachelet was the daughter of a general, and this connection may have led military interests to be more sympathetic to her candidacy.

Chapter Four

Temporaries, Tokens, and Ceremonial Leaders

Still other women have assumed the top political post on a temporary, acting, or interim basis. In a sense, leaders such as Sirimavo Bandaranaike, Indira Gandhi, and Golda Meir were viewed by the politicians who supported their candidacies as filling temporary positions, but these three stretched their tenure in office much beyond what was expected. Bandaranaike in 3 separate terms served approximately 17 years, Gandhi remained in office for more than 15 years, and Meir served almost 5 years.

Leaders Overseeing Elections

Maria de Lourdes Pintasilgo (1979–1980)

More typical of a temporary leader is Maria de Lourdes Pintasilgo who served only a few months as the Portuguese prime minister, beginning in July 1979. Pintasilgo, who was at the time her country's ambassador to UNESCO, was invited by the president of Portugal to form a caretaker government. The Socialist-led governments created after the 1976 election had failed amidst growing dissatisfaction with a struggling economy, but the president, Antonio Ramalho Eanes, rejected the notion of holding an election so close to 1980 on the grounds that it would be too costly. The constitution ratified in 1976 provided for an election to be held four years after the first one, even if it were necessary to call an interim election. Following the failure of two more governments, Eanes reversed his position and scheduled an election, setting the stage for the creation of a government to prepare for the campaign and conduct the nation's business until a properly elected government was in place.

The 49-year-old Pintasilgo seemed an ideal candidate to perform these tasks. Although she had held several appointive positions, she did not belong to a political party and had never sought elective office. Her appointment ran into some opposition from the right center parties on the grounds that her leftist leanings would provide the parties of the left an advantage in the upcoming election. While in office, she instituted a number of social welfare measures, such as raising the minimum wage and increasing pension and unemployment benefits, but these changes did little to mobilize support for her political views. The Social Democratic Party, a right center party, won a majority of the seats, and many of the measures Pintasilgo put in place were rescinded.

Pintasilgo's experience as prime minister seemed to have stimulated her interest in elective office, as she ran, although unsuccessfully and with no major party backing, for the office of president in 1986. The following year, after Portugal had been accepted for membership in the European Community, she was elected to the European Parliament, serving until 1989.

Lydia Gueiler Tejada (1979–1980)

The same year Pintasilgo rose to the top as a temporary prime minister, another woman, 56-year-old Lydia Gueiler Tejada, who objected to revealing her age, saying "I believe one should consider what age a person appears or acts; age doesn't matter for politics,"[1] was chosen interim president by the Bolivian congress. Unlike Pintasilgo, Gueiler had held elective office. In fact, the popular and well-liked political activist was serving as president of the Chamber of Deputies at the time she was named interim president.

In 1979, following some 15 years of military rule in Bolivia, elections were held to fill the post of president. Since many political parties put forward a candidate out of a sense of frustrated ambition, the results proved inconclusive in that no one candidate received at least 50 percent of the vote as required by the constitution. An interim president, Walter Guevara Arze, was chosen to serve until elections could be held in May 1980, but within days he was ousted by some in the military who felt uneasy with this government that lacked the support of the major political parties. Following talks between the military and congressional leaders, Gueiler was elected to lead her country. Her connections to both right and left wing parties made her an acceptable candidate.

Gueiler's government was repeatedly threatened with coups, and terrorism was rampant. The military sought a postponement of the voting on the grounds that civilian rule was not satisfactory and would lead to a devastating situation for the country in the long-run.

After some hesitation, Gueiler signed off on the election that was held as scheduled in June 1980. The results were once again inconclusive. Before another president could be selected by the congress, the military staged a takeover. Gueiler went into exile in Paris where she lived with her daughter. She later returned to become her country's ambassador to Colombia in 1983.

Ertha Pascal-Trouillot (1990–1991) and Claudette Werleigh (1995–1996)

During the 1990s two women were called upon to supervise elections in Haiti that was undergoing a period of great political turmoil. Forty-six-year-old Pascal-Trouillot became president in 1990 following the ouster of the fourth military-dominated regime to rule that country since the departure of the dictator Jean-Claude Duvalier in 1986. Under pressure from the United States, Lt. General Prosper Avril, who had presided over a particularly brutal regime, agreed to leave the country. According to the constitution, the head of the Supreme Court was the first in line to succeed under these circumstances, but the occupant of that post was rejected because of his close association with Avril. Although other members of the court refused to serve, Pascal-Trouillot, the first woman appointed to the court as well as its most recent appointee came forward, saying that she "accepted this heavy task in the name of Haitian women."[2]

Perhaps because of her lack of political experience, Pascal-Trouillot expected that she would be able to hold the election soon and arrange the turnover of the reins of power to her elected successor with few complications. Instead, on assuming office, she found herself embroiled in political conflict, sharing power with a council with which she frequently disagreed. Many of her initial supporters abandoned her when she was accused of corruption and nepotism as well as incompetence, and her resignation was demanded.

The election was held some nine months after Pascal-Trouillot, who refused to resign, took office. Before the newly elected president, Jean-Bertrand Aristide, a leftist priest, could assume power, a coup led by a physician, Roger Lafontant, was staged. During the rule of Duvalier, Lafontant headed the Tontons Macoutes, the dreaded militia that was used to control the opposition, and he feared for his future under an Aristide government. The coup was foiled by the military, and the preparations for the inauguration of Aristide continued. Lafontant insisted that he did not stage a coup but that

Pascal-Trouillot had turned power over to him. She was arrested after she left office and charged with complicity in the attempted takeover but was released a month later.

Approximately five years after Pascal-Trouillot was chosen to oversee a Haitian election, Claudette Werleigh, who had served as Pascal-Trouillot's minister of social affairs, was appointed caretaker prime minister by President Aristide. The 49-year-old Werleigh, who, at the time of her appointment, was Aristide's foreign minister and a close adviser to the president, was given the task of overseeing the presidential election set for December 1995.

Werleigh's rise to the top came about when her predecessor Smarck Michel, who had serious disagreements with the president over economic policy, resigned in October 1995 following widespread protests. Michel, a businessman, favored privatization of some industries as recommended by the World Bank and the International Monetary Fund, but Aristide and many of his supporters opposed such a plan on the grounds that it would result in a loss of jobs. Werleigh, who favored a national debate on economic issues, served only briefly, for the presidential election took place as scheduled, and approximately two months later Aristide's successor named a new prime minister.

Reneta Indzhova (1994–1995)

Another woman chosen to supervise an election was Reneta Indzhova, who was appointed interim prime minister of Bulgaria in 1994. When the deeply divided Bulgarian parliament failed to produce a government in late 1994, the president dissolved the legislative body and appointed 41-year-old Indzhova to oversee the election scheduled to be held in December. A professor of political economy, Indzhova had little political experience although she had served as the executive director of the government's Privatization Agency. Her experience as a temporary prime minister seemed to have whetted her appetite for politics. Like Pintasilgo of Portugal, Indzhova later attempted to run for president as an independent although her candidacy was rejected by the Central Election Commission.

Madior Boye (2001–2002)

Madior Boye, a former jurist who served as justice minister in her predecessor's government, was selected in March 2001 to lead Senegal temporarily and supervise an election. Her appointment came following disagreements between the president, Abdoulaye Wade, and the incumbent prime minister, Moustapha Niasse. Boye, who did not have any party affiliation, was expected to remain in office until the election that was to be held two months later. She was considered a strong candidate for the post since she was viewed as a technocrat and thus no threat to the charismatic Wade. Her performance as a temporary prime minister so impressed the president that he appointed her to a full term after the election. Although she did not appear comfortable in the role of prime minister, the precipitating event that led to her dismissal and the dissolution of her government the following year was the loss of a ferry with more than a 1,000 people on board. Serious questions were raised about her handling of the situation when she blamed the incident on the weather rather than on the operation or safety of the ferry.[3]

Leaders Chosen to Deal with Civil Conflict

Ruth Perry (1996–1997)

The first African woman to serve as head of state was chosen to implement the peace plan brokered by the leaders of neighboring countries to end the long-running civil war in Liberia. In addition to supervising the conduct of an election, the 57-year-old Ruth Perry, a former senator, community activist, and widow of a legislator, was to oversee the disarmament of the conflicting factions. She was considered a solid choice for the job ahead, because she was acceptable to the leaders of the several warring parties and did not belong to any faction.

Perry, who was confident she could accomplish the task, did not shy away from challenges, for when she was elected to the Senate in 1985, she was the sole member of the opposition to serve. Her colleagues refused to participate since they viewed the election as fraudulent. Perry, on the other hand, believed that one could not "resolve problems by staying away." Describing her role as that of a "stabilizer," she saw her appointment as president as "an upliftment for women in Liberia and Africa as a whole."[4]

Like many of the women leaders, Perry proved to be less manipulable than had been expected although the faction leaders were able to control resources available to her.[5] Viewing herself in the role of a mother overseeing her squabbling brood, she managed, after the factions were disarmed, to bring off an election two months later than originally scheduled.

Sylvie Kinigi (1993–1994) and Agathe Uwilingiyimana (1993–1994)

Two other African women, Sylvie Kinigi of Burundi and Agathe Uwilingiyimana of Rwanda, owed their temporary rise to the top to an attempt to find an accommodation to the ethnic conflicts that plagued their respective countries. The 40-year-old Kinigi, a member of the Tutsi ethnic minority, was appointed prime minister by the first Hutu president, Melchior Ndadaye, in June 1993. During the presidential campaign, Ndadaye had promised to appoint a Tutsi as prime minister. Kinigi, a former civil servant who was working as an economic adviser to the president and prime minister at the time of her appointment, expressed amazement, saying that this "is a good surprise for Burundian women primarily, but for African women too."[6]

Within months, troops of the Tutsi-dominated military attacked the palace and assassinated the president and several other officials. Violence erupted between the ethnic groups. As acting president, Kinigi, who along with others in the government took refuge in the French embassy, was asked by the military leaders to form a new government. When some order was restored, a new president was chosen by the parliament to fill the unexpired term of Ndadaye, and the new head of state selected another candidate to serve as prime minister.[7] Kinigi, whose husband had recently died, took a job with Burundi's Commercial Bank.

Within less than a week of Kinigi's appointment as head of government, the 40-year-old Agathe Uwilingiyimana was named prime minister of neighboring Rwanda under the terms of a power-sharing agreement reached between the president, a Hutu, and several opposition parties. Her government was given the task of working out the specific terms of an accord with the Rwandan Patriotic Front, a Tutsi guerilla movement. An agreement was reached and the slots in the cabinet were assigned to the various parties. Uwilingiyimana was to be dismissed as prime minister and given a minor post in the new government, but before the agreement could be signed, the president was killed in a suspicious plane crash, leading to violence between the Hutus and Tutsis. Uwilingiyimana, who had pressed for cooperation among the warring parties, stayed on as a caretaker prime minister until her assassination in April 1994 at the hands of the presidential guard that held the Tutsis responsible for the death of the president.

Interim Leaders

Rosalia Arteaga (1997) and Nino Burdzhanadze (2003–2004)

In addition to those women whose principal task was to oversee an election or resolve civil conflict, others have occupied the top position for a brief period on an acting or interim basis following the resignation or the removal of a leader from office. Rosalia Arteaga, the 40-year-old vice president of Ecuador, who took over in 1997 after the president was removed from office, remained only a few days in the top post. Abdala Bucaram, who had served only six months of his term, had been declared mentally incompetent and accused of corruption by the Congress. The military withdrew its support from his government that faced labor unrest and inflation.

Controversy surrounded the appointment of someone to fill the unexpired term of the president as the constitution did not provide a clear line of succession, but an agreement was quickly reached which provided that Arteaga would continue as president until the Congress could select a successor. Arteaga argued that a constitutional amendment was necessary to spell out the rules governing the succession and to provide an orderly transfer of power,[8] but it took the Congress only days to complete its task and appoint its president to head the government. In commenting on the decision, Arteaga, who continued as vice president, argued that in part the failure to approve her appointment as a matter of course was because she was a woman. She said, "I believe machismo is very strong in this society." She noted that in the past vice presidents had automatically assumed the presidency, but some of her critics held her responsible for failure to remain at the top, suggesting that she had not moved away from Bucaram soon enough.[9] Arteaga unsuccessfully sought the presidency in the 1998 election as the head of a small right of center party that she had founded.

Another leader whose path to the top was settled by the laws governing the succession was Nino Burdzhanadze who as a child dreamed of some day becoming an ambassador.[10] As the constitutional successor to the president in her position as speaker of the parliament, the 39-year-old Burdzhanadze, one of three politicians who led the movement to oust President Eduard Shevardnadze, in 2003 became acting president of Georgia, a republic of the former Soviet Union. Following the controversial election held earlier that year, Shevardnadze, who headed a corrupt administration and oversaw an economy in shambles, resigned in the face of widespread street protests reminiscent of "people power" in the Philippines and the Orange Revolution in Ukraine.

Burdzhanadze served in the job for approximately three months until an election could be held, but she refused to seek the presidency on the grounds that she was not ready to take on such responsibilities. She may have been influenced by the fact that her opponent in the race enjoyed much popularity as he had played a key role in the street protests.

Irena Degutiene (1999)

In response to a bitter and ongoing feud between the Lithuanian President Valdas Adamkus and Prime Minister Gediminas Vagnorius over a wide variety of issues, the prime minister resigned in May 1999 and the president selected Irena Degutiene to fill the slot temporarily. The second woman to occupy that post in her country, the 49-year-old physician was serving as minister of social welfare and labor at the time of her appointment. She indicated that she was not qualified to lead her country as prime minister, but she had changed her mind by the end of her brief tenure, saying that she was confident enough to lead the government. With the resignation of another prime minister later that same year, Degutiene once again was named to the top post, but remained only a few days as she again refused to accept a full term as prime minister.

Luisa Diogo (2004–) and Han Myung-sook (2006–2007)

Two recent prime ministerial appointments were made by presidents serving out the remaining months of their terms with no intention of continuing in office. The first of these appointments was that of Luisa Diogo, the finance minister of Mozambique. She was named prime minister in 2004 by President Jaquim Chissano to fill the vacancy left by the resignation of Pascoal Mocumbi, a physician who took a position with an international health organization. In selecting Diogo to fill the role until elections scheduled for later in the year, the president suggested he was doing so because of "her competence, her youth, and the fact that she is a woman."[11] Another reason for her appointment was to ensure continuity of government for the remaining nine months of the term, but Diogo managed to turn the temporary post into a permanent position. Her performance was such that the newly elected president invited her to stay on.

Han Myung-sook, a women's rights advocate, was named prime minister of South Korea by President Roh Moo-hyun in April 2006 to serve for the few remaining months the president would be in office. Han's predecessor, Lee Hae-chan, had been forced to resign following a series of missteps. On the first day of a crippling national railway strike, Lee seemed indifferent to the plight of his constituents as he played golf. To make matters worse, one of his golfing partners had been accused of rigging stock prices.

Han was not the first woman to be selected for the post as the previous president had nominated a woman, Chang Sang, to the same position four years earlier, but the National Assembly rejected her. This time President Roh made certain that his nominee would be accepted by the opposition party, and Han was approved by a vote of 182 to 77. Han had ensured her position by going to the head of the main opposition party asking for his help and making it clear to him that she would remain neutral in the upcoming local elections. Rather than serving out the entire term, Han resigned the prime ministership in slightly less than a year of taking office. In doing so, she announced she would remain in parliament but wanted to consider her own run for the more significant office of president.

Nyam-Osoriyn Tuyaa (1999) and Mirna Louisa-Godett (2003–2004)

Two other women were appointed acting prime minister and were given very restricted roles to play. The first was 41-year-old Nyam-Osoriyn Tuyaa, who was serving as foreign minister and became the acting prime minister following the fall of the Mongolian government in 1999. She carried out the duties as head of government for just more than a week until the parliament could agree on a successor. Tuyaa continued to serve as foreign minister in the newly appointed government.

The more unusual ascension to the top political position was that of Mirna Louisa-Godett who became acting prime minister of the

Netherlands Antilles in August 2003. Her rise to the top came as a result of an appointment made by her brother, Anthony Godett. Anthony was the duly elected prime minister but could not assume the position because he was under investigation on corruption charges. He was subsequently convicted in January 2004 and later sentenced to several months in jail. Mirna in the meantime continued as prime minister until April of that year.

It was clear throughout her tenure that her brother retained control of the reins of power. As she assumed the position, he announced publicly that she still had to learn the ropes and that "when you see Mirna, you see Anthony."[12] During her brief time in office she pressed her brother's agenda, which included more autonomy and additional financial aid from the Netherlands along with the replacement of Dutch with English as the primary language.

Tokens

Elizabeth Domitien (1975–1976)

Women have risen to important positions in government as tokens. To placate women's advocacy groups, a single position or series of positions may be reserved for women. Token selections, whose purpose is to enhance a party or government's standing with women, have usually been made to fill lesser cabinet posts. But in January 1975 such a motive may have played a role when Jean-Bedel Bokassa, president of the Central African Republic, appointed his childhood friend, Elizabeth Domitien, a prosperous businesswoman in her mid-50s, as prime minister. He also appointed three other women to the cabinet.

Bokassa, who proved to be a bizarre and ruthless leader,[13] had become president as well as prime minister in 1966 after he led a military coup to oust a cousin. Domitien, who had been active in politics for some years, served as vice president of the country's sole political party, Mouvement d'evolution sociale de l'Afrique noire. She helped mobilize support, especially among women, to proclaim Bokassa president for life in 1972. To boost his sagging power and demonstrate his commitment to women's rights as well as reward a loyal supporter, he created a dual system, separating the duties of president and prime minister. After serving as prime minister for just over a year, Domitien was removed from office following a disagreement with the president. She retained her position in the party until

1979 when she was imprisoned after the ouster of Bokassa by a French-led military operation.

Ceremonial Leaders

In addition to serving in a temporary capacity or as a token, women have also risen to the top as ceremonial leaders. In a presidential system such as that found in the United States, the head of state and head of government are usually one and the same, but in a parliamentary system the head of state generally performs only ceremonial functions and represents the country on formal occasions. In some systems, the head of state may dissolve parliament or appoint a prime minister but usually only on the recommendation of the elected government or when no political leader is able to put together a majority—a role that Vigdis Finnbogadottir of Iceland[14] described as a kind of midwife to political parties that have to agree on forming a government.[15]

In some countries, the head of state is chosen by hereditary succession. Queen Elizabeth II of Britain, for example, became head of state in 1953 when there was no male to succeed to the throne. Among other countries that rely on hereditary succession to select a ceremonial leader are Belgium, the Netherlands, and Denmark—states that have had a woman in this role.

In some of the former colonies that have remained within the British Commonwealth, a governor-general, representing the British Crown, is appointed by the monarch on the advice of the elected government of the member country, to be head of state. A number of women have served in this capacity. Jeanne Sauve, who had a distinguished political career and oversaw the proceedings of the Canadian House of Commons as Speaker, was governor-general from April 1984 until January 1990. Another woman, Adrienne Clarkson, a television interviewer, author, and publisher, was appointed governor-general of Canada in 1999. Clarkson was succeeded in 2005 by Michaelle Jean, an immigrant from Haiti, who was a television journalist. Jean's appointment was seen as an attempt by the prime minister, Paul Martin, to enhance his position with the immigrant community.

New Zealand, which has had two women serve as prime minister, has also had women as governors-general. Catherine Tizard, a tutor in zoology at the University of Auckland and later mayor of Auckland became governor-general in November 1990, serving in that role until March 1996; and Sylvia Cartwright, a lawyer and jurist as well as an advocate for women's rights, was appointed governor-general in 2000.

Vigdis Finnbogadottir (1980–1996)

In other parliamentary systems the president or head of state is popularly elected. Vigdis Finnbogadottir, the 50-year-old director of the Reykjavik Theatre Company, was elected in June 1980, winning approximately 34 percent of the vote in a 4-person contest. In Iceland with its strong literary tradition, she proved to be a popular choice, running virtually unopposed in the next three elections held in 1984, 1989, and 1991.

Though Vigdis Finnbogadottir had lobbied for government grants on behalf of the theater, she had not taken part in political activity before seeking the office of president except to participate in a demonstration against NATO's use of the airbase at Keflavik. While her opponents in her first electoral contest were veteran politicians, she did not even belong to a political party. Vigdis said that when she was first approached by friends about seeking office, she "thought it was a joke."[16] Stressing that she was pushed into running by people and friends "who thought it was time for a woman's face among the candidates," she told a reporter that "it took them sometime to convince me." She said she made the decision to go ahead with the race, because she "wanted to prove that women could do it."[17]

In commenting on her electoral success, Vigdis pointed to the role of the one-day strike organized by the women of Iceland in 1975. By attempting to stress their importance, women created an atmosphere that made their increased participation in politics possible though at the time of her election, there were no women in the cabinet and only 3 women in a parliament of 60 members. When it came time to select a president, she said women were thinking, "Good heavens, why did we organize that [the strike] for a whole year, and nothing has come of it?"[18]

Mary Robinson (1990–1997) and Mary McAleese (1997–)

Unlike Vigdis Finnbogadottir, Mary Robinson, a 46-year-old human rights lawyer, had a record in politics. Robinson, who became president of Ireland in 1990, had served as a representative for Trinity College in the Senate, the upper chamber of the Irish parliament, for a number of years and had unsuccessfully sought a seat in the Dail or lower house on two occasions.

The Irish presidency was thought of as the preserve of the largest party, Fianna Fail. In fact, there had been no contested presidential election for 17 years as the major parties had agreed on a candidate to serve in this post that was viewed primarily as a reward for a politician in the twilight of his career. With the anticipated retirement of Patrick Hillery as president in 1990, the opposition parties, especially the small Labor Party, saw this as an opportunity to improve their standing as well as to debate the issues affecting the country's future. Despite the fact that she had resigned from the Labor Party in 1985 after being passed over for the position of attorney general,[19] Robinson was a perfect fit to seek the post. She was well-known throughout the country, and her appeal would likely go beyond that of the typical Labor Party leader. Since she was young, she would be able to conduct a vigorous campaign. Given her identification with such controversial issues as abortion, divorce, and homosexual rights in her legal practice and in her tenure as a senator, she was associated with the forces for change in her country. Also, as a lawyer with political experience, she would likely be sensitive to the issues raised by a more engaged president and in a position to take advantage of the opportunity to play a more active role in the affairs of the nation.[20]

Following lengthy negotiations, during which she refused to join the party as a condition of her candidacy, arguing that it would compromise her independence, Robinson was named the party's nominee. She had retired from public life the previous year to concentrate on her legal practice, but she believed she could contribute to the enhancement of women's rights by seeking the presidential office.

Robinson was given almost no chance of victory although she believed she could win. While she early on captured the imagination of the voters, her prospects for success increased only days before the election when the front runner, deputy Prime Minister Brian Lenihan was caught up in a minor scandal and removed from his government post. Some sympathy developed for him after he was sacked, but he was not able to overcome the momentum that Robinson's candidacy had built, especially among women. In a speech after her victory, she noted the special role women had played when she said that she was elected "above all by the women of Ireland who instead of rocking the cradle rocked the system, and who came out massively to make their mark on the ballot paper, and on a new Ireland."[21]

When Robinson, who used the presidential office to showcase issues of interest to her, announced that she would not seek another term in 1997 and subsequently accepted the post as UN High Commissioner for Human Rights, the parties had to decide whether to revert to the old system of developing a consensus on a single candidate no longer actively involved in politics or whether to offer competing contenders. In light of Robinson's continued popularity as well as the growing disapproval of politicians in general, it was decided to stage a contest as in the previous presidential race. The majority party, Fianna Fail, chose Mary McAleese, a 46-year-old vice-chancellor of Queen's University in Belfast and a former law professor who specialized in criminal and family law, as its nominee. McAleese who lived in Northern Ireland was eligible to seek the presidency as she was an Irish citizen. More conservative with respect to social issues than Robinson, she had no political experience although she had unsuccessfully run for a parliamentary seat in 1987. Perhaps because she was an outsider and relatively unknown, she may have seemed less threatening to the veteran politicians than some one more like Robinson.

Two other women entered the race with party support and a woman and a man, a former police officer, ran as independent candidates. With the backing of the largest party, McAleese won easily. She proved to be an effective candidate and a good debater as her experience as a television journalist proved useful. She ran unopposed for a second seven-year term in 2004.

Agatha Barbara (1982–1987); Vaira Vike-Freiberga (1999–2007); and Pratibha Patil (2007–)

In some parliamentary systems, the president or ceremonial leader is elected by the legislative body. Agatha Barbara, a 59-year-old former teacher with an extensive record of political activity, was elected president by the Malta House of Representatives in 1982. The opposition party did not participate in the presidential election as it was boycotting the parliament to protest the results of the previous general election. Barbara, who had held cabinet positions such as education and labor and social services in Labor Party governments, would have preferred a cabinet post since from that vantage point she believed she could get more things accomplished.

In 1999, Vaira Vike-Freiberga, a 61-year-old former psychology professor was chosen president by the Latvian parliament. She had spent much of her life in Canada as her family left Latvia shortly after the arrival of Russian troops near the end of the Second World War. Through the years she remained active in the Latvian community abroad and authored several books on Latvian culture. After her retirement in 1998, Vike-Freiberga returned to her homeland to head the Latvian Institute, a nonprofit organization to promote Latvian culture. Political leaders urged her to seek the presidency, and she agreed to enter the race after the first ballot failed to produce a majority for any candidate. With the contest hopelessly deadlocked and displeasure with politicians widespread, the parliament eventually turned to her as an outsider and a candidate who did not have a political base. Her popularity in office soared and she was elected for a second term in 2003 by a vote of 88 to 6.

The next woman to rise to the post of ceremonial president was 72-year-old Pratibha Patil who was sworn in as president of India in July 2007. Having entered politics in 1962 at the age of 27, Patil was actively involved in political affairs, serving throughout the years in a variety of positions at the state and national levels. Before coming to the presidency, Patil was a member of the Lok Sabha and later governor of the state of Rajasthan.

In India, the president is nominated by the governing party or parties and is subject to the approval by the vote of both the national parliament and the state legislatures. Although the position is largely ceremonial, the president is responsible for selecting someone to head a new government when the current government no longer enjoys a majority. Given this power, having someone loyal to the governing coalition in that position is seen as an important asset.

When there was no agreement as to a candidate for the presidency, Patil was proposed by Sonia Gandhi, Indira Gandhi's daughter-in-law, who headed the ruling party coalition. Patil remained close to the Gandhi family, having thrown her support to Indira after the split in the Congress party in 1977.

Conclusions

As outsiders women meet an important criterion for serving as a temporary or interim leader. They are not seen as contenders for the job they have undertaken temporarily. To be appointed, one must have significant achievements in an area of endeavor and some political experience or politically related experience, but only enough to give visibility.

The temporaries are appointed to office to serve until some task is completed. In so far as this study of women political leaders is concerned, there are three types of temporary leaders—those appointed to oversee an election, those chosen to deal with civil conflict, and those who serve while a leader is sought to fill a vacancy. Approximately one quarter of the women who have risen to the top (n=64) have served as temporaries. Each of these women exercised power for less than one year except Madior Boye of Senegal who was later appointed for a full term as prime minister but was dismissed after somewhat over a year. Also, Luisa Diogo of Mozambique was appointed for a full term by the new president after the election as her skills were viewed as critical to the continued growth of her country's economy.

As outsiders women provide a good fit for the symbolic role of the ceremonial leader. In that capacity, they do not threaten those who hold power, and visibility is provided for members of a group that have historically been excluded from the political arena. Ceremonial leaders do not play a critical role in governing. Two of these leaders, Mary Robinson of Ireland and Vaira Vike-Freiberga of Latvia, were active in pushing their agendas.

Chapter Five

The Early Years

In responding to an interviewer who asked when she first became involved in politics, Indira Gandhi said: "It is impossible to say. I do not remember any time when I was not involved."[1] In describing her early life, she later wrote that all the games she played were political, and her favorite game was "to collect as many servants as I could, stand on a table and deliver a speech—repeating disjointed phrases that I had picked up from grown-up talk."[2]

Parental Political Activities

Although Indira Gandhi's early years were overshadowed by her family's role in the Indian independence movement, many of the women who have risen to the top grew up in families that were involved in political activity or community affairs. Although many male politicians have also been reared in households in which the parents participated in public affairs, the family may be especially important in influencing the decision of a woman to enter the political arena. The strong commitment of one or both parents to political action may serve to compensate for any other influences that might discourage her from taking part in political activities. Early exposure to the ways of politics may seal a girl's interest in the political arena, and interaction with the parents may give her the resolve to pursue such a course. A woman who grows up in a family that participates in public affairs has the advantage of being able to make contacts that are useful for molding a political career. She has the opportunity to develop a sense of ease in dealing with politicians, and familiarity with political life may make it more likely that she will be able to put together the confidence to seek office.

Aside from the fact that, for the most part, the fathers of the women who rose to the top were the political or community activists, the specific political experiences to which these women were exposed varied. Gandhi's birth in 1917 coincided with the launching of the struggle for Indian autonomy and her family's embrace of that movement. Her childhood was the one most directly influenced by the family's political activities. In the Nehru household, the personal and the political often seemed intertwined.

Shortly after Indira's father, Jawaharlal Nehru, returned from his student days at Cambridge, he joined forces with Mahatma Gandhi who was engaged in a campaign to broaden the efforts to achieve Indian independence. As the scene of meetings and planning sessions, *Anand Bhavan*, the palatial home of Nehru's father, became the center for the activities associated with the fledgling movement known as the Indian National Congress. The police were frequent but uninvited visitors, coming either to arrest some member of the family or take possessions as payment for fines that the Nehrus had refused to pay. Gandhi, in describing these experiences and their effects on her, said: "This continuous process of despoliation was irritating enough, but to watch it impotently was beyond the patience of a strong-willed child such as I was. I protested to the police and indicated my strong displeasure in every way I could, once nearly chopping off an officer's thumb with a bread-slicing gadget."[3]

From the age of four, Indira was frequently alone in the house with the servants since members of her family were either occupied with politics or confined to prison. Years later she noted that she resented the fact that her parents were away from her so much, but, at the same time, she felt proud of them. Characterizing her early years as lonely, in a BBC interview in 1971, she said: "I was part of the processions and meetings...it was an extremely insecure childhood because we did not know from day to day who would be alive, who would be in the house, and what would happen next."[4]

Eager to be a part of her parents' activities, Indira had her first experience in political organization at the age of 12 when she established a branch of the Monkey Brigade, a group made up of children from families of Congress supporters. These young people were able to perform many useful functions, such as delivering messages and providing food and water, for the Congress volunteers without arousing suspicion.

Like Gandhi, Benazir Bhutto, whose family was also immersed in politics, described feelings of loneliness as a child, but the fact that she had two younger brothers and a younger sister may have made the frequent absences of her parents less painful. Also, like Gandhi, Bhutto viewed her parents' activities with ambivalence, for in her autobiography she noted, in an apparent point of pride, that "I saw my father as much on the front pages of the newspapers as in person...."[5]

As the oldest child, Bhutto felt a special responsibility. The children were left in the care of an English nanny, but when her parents were preparing to leave, they would instruct Benazir to "look after the other children." Bhutto recalled that when her mother was away, she would pretend to review the household accounts each evening.[6]

The political career of Benazir's father, the son of a wealthy landowner, had its beginnings when Zulfikar Ali Bhutto returned from several years of study in the United States and England. He was asked to join the cabinet after the military coup in 1958 and served in several different posts through the years, including that of foreign minister.

Following a disagreement with President Ayub Khan over the acceptable terms of peace ending the 1965 war with India, Zulfikar Bhutto broke with the regime and formed the Pakistan People's Party. In the election held in 1970, the new party performed well in the western part of the country, but the Awami League, which had its base in East Pakistan, won an overall majority of the seats in the parliament. When the leaders of these two parties were unable to reach an agreement on the degree of autonomy for East Pakistan, civil war broke out, leading to a split of the country. The eastern section became the state of Bangladesh under the leadership of Sheikh Mujibur Rahman, and the west became a truncated Pakistan governed by Bhutto.

Like the fathers of Gandhi and Bhutto, Sheikh Hasina's father was away from home for extended periods when his children were young. Sheikh Mujibur, the first prime minister of Bangladesh later served as president of his country. He had been involved in politics since his days as a student, campaigning for Bengali autonomy. Viewed as a troublemaker, he was denied the opportunity to complete his legal studies at Dhaka University and was arrested on several occasions. Hasina, Mujibur's older daughter, experienced first hand the trauma sometimes associated with politics, for it was reported that on one occasion the police forced entry into Hasina's room to arrest her father, breaking her dolls.[7]

By 1963 Sheikh Mujibur, who had been elected to the National Assembly some eight years earlier, had assumed leadership of his party, the Awami League. When civil war erupted, he was again arrested by the Pakistani authorities. At the end of the war, Mujibur was released, and he returned to the newly independent Bangladesh. His tenure as president was cut short as he, along with several members of his family, was assassinated in 1976 by elements of the military. Hasina was spared when her family was attacked as she and a younger sister were traveling in Germany at the time.

The father of Chandrika Kumaratunga, S.W.R.D. Bandaranaike, entered the political arena after he returned from his student days at Oxford. An intensely ambitious man, he held a variety of government posts through the years while campaigning for a greater measure of self-rule for his country. In describing life during the early years of her marriage, Kumaratunga's mother indicated that her home was "a public place, like a hotel, with people casually dropping in at all times and my husband hailing each one most hospitably, inviting all and sundry to stay 'for a bite.' "[8]

Following independence, Bandaranaike became a key actor on the political stage, leading his Sri Lanka Freedom Party to victory in 1956. Before the end of his first term as prime minister, he was assassinated by a disgruntled Buddhist monk. Chandrika was 14 years old at the time, but this did not end her exposure to the vagaries of political life as her mother assumed the leadership of the SLFP and became the world's first woman prime minister.

Two other women who rose to the top had fathers who headed governments—Megawati Sukarnoputri and Gloria Macapagal Arroyo. Megawati was only two years old when her father assumed the presidency of the newly independent Indonesia in 1949. Sukarno, who was trained as an engineer, had joined the independence movement in the 1920s, spending a number of years in jail and living in exile because of his revolutionary activities against Dutch rule. In view of the important role he played in the independence movement, Sukarno was regarded by many as the father of his country. He gradually assumed a dictatorial posture, establishing himself as president for life. A coup in 1965 effectively removed Sukarno from power, but Suharto, who took over, allowed the former president to retain his title and continue to live in the presidential palace.

Diosdado Macapagal, who was described by his daughter Gloria Arroyo as the most influential person in her life, served in a variety of advisory and appointive positions before he began his political career in 1949 as a member of the Philippine House of Representatives. Macapagal, who had earned a degree in law and a doctorate in economics, was successful in his quest for the vice presidency in 1957, but he had to content himself with ceremonial functions as he refused to switch his party affiliation to that of the newly elected president. He traveled around the country, strengthening the base of his Liberal party in the rural areas. In 1961, he was successful in his run for the presidency against the incumbent whom he accused of corruption. Macapagal served as president of the Philippines for only one four-year term and lost his bid for reelection in 1965 to the more charismatic

Ferdinand Marcos. Though Macapagal was reluctant for his children to enter politics, he used his contacts on his daughter's behalf when she sought and won a seat in the Senate in 1992.

Other women who rose to the top were exposed to the workings of national politics during their early years although on a somewhat more modest scale. For example, the father of Gro Brundtland, who described her home as a "political one," held two different cabinet posts. As a reward for his service as personal physician to several Norwegian Labor Party prime ministers, Gudmund Harlem was invited to join the cabinet in 1955 as minister of health and social affairs and later as minister of defense.

Claudette Werleigh's father, a coffee exporter, spent more than 20 years as a member of the Haitian parliament. The father of Corazon Aquino served for a brief period in the Philippine National Assembly shortly after the birth of his daughter in 1933. The well-to-do Cojuangco family had a long history of political involvement, but at the end of the Second World War, with the family's affairs in disarray, Jose Cojuangco concentrated on restoring his family's business though he continued to exercise political influence. As a landowner and banker, the father of Eugenia Charles was a prominent member of his community. In the 1950s while Dominica was still a colony of Britain, J. B. Charles served briefly in the Legislative Council.

Some fathers were active in local politics. For example, Margaret Thatcher's father held a variety of posts in local government, serving as borough councilor, alderman, magistrate, and finally, mayor. Alfred Roberts, an austere and frugal man, operated a store that also housed a post office, and the store became a gathering place where political matters dominated. Sirimavo Bandaranaike's maternal grandfather, and later her father, served as Chief Headman of Balangoda, an administrative district in the Kandyan section of Ceylon. While the island was a colony of Britain, the power of the headman was severely restricted, but the old ruling aristocracy served as an intermediary between the British authorities and the local population.

Golda Meir's father did not hold any office, but he was active in community affairs. Golda was five years old when her father, a carpenter and cabinetmaker, left Russia for America with the expectation that he would return to his family after he made his fortune. But her mother grew concerned about the oldest daughter's involvement with an illegal revolutionary organization and insisted that she and the children move to the United States. The family was reunited shortly after Golda's eighth birthday in Milwaukee where her father had taken a job in the railroad workshops. In describing her new home, Meir said: "The house was always alive with public affairs; our family never limited itself to matters of personal interest. Mama used to help other families. Both she and Papa were members of B'nai B'rith... Papa was active in a society for overseas aid and, later, in the American Jewish Congress."[9]

The father of Ruth Dreifuss was also active in local affairs. During the Second World War he was accused of falsifying documents to aid Jews who were attempting to enter Switzerland. Because of the accusations, he lost his job in a textile importing company located near the German border. The family resettled in Geneva when Ruth was five years old.[10]

The fathers of Tansu Ciller, Edith Cresson, and Kim Campbell worked as civil servants, and the father of Michelle Bachelet served in the military, giving the families of these men more than a passing interest in politics. Ciller's father who served as a provincial governor in Turkey had unsuccessfully sought elected office before becoming a bureaucrat. During his daughter's early years, Cresson's father, Gabriel Campion, who was a tax inspector, served as a financial consultant to the French Embassy in Yugoslavia where he had been assigned in 1940. During her teenage years, he was posted to the embassy in Morocco in a similar capacity. After completing his legal studies, George Campbell took up a general law practice, but in 1966, when his daughter Kim was a teenager, he joined the office of the Vancouver prosecutor, a position he held until his retirement in 1985. Bachelet's father, a popular air force general who worked in the administration of President Salvador Allende, was imprisoned after General Augusto Pinochet led a successful coup in 1973 against the regime of President Allende, and General Alberto Bachelet died while in the custody of the Pinochet authorities.

Although the father of Violeta Chamorro, a well-to-do rancher and an influential member of his community, did not actively participate in politics, he came from one of several prominent families that dominated the Nicaraguan political scene. The political experiences of relatives were discussed at family get-togethers but, if anything, Chamorro's father discouraged involvement in politics. Perhaps because the history of this Central American country was replete with wars and periods of exile for those in opposition, he reminded her when she was leaving home to attend a boarding school in Managua to "never discuss politics or religion, and you will see you will get along with everyone."[11]

The Father/Daughter Relationship

Despite their busy schedules, the fathers of many of the women who rose to the top of the political ladder developed a close relationship with their daughters. Since a father is the one most likely to provide his daughter her first glimpse of the world outside the home, he is in a position to shield her from the effects of the perception of women as weak and ineffective. By conveying to her that she can accomplish her goals, and praising her efforts, he makes it easier for her to take risks and test her mettle.[12]

Gandhi's father who held comparatively progressive views about the role of women, asserting that they should be able to choose among a variety of roles,[13] carried on an active correspondence with his daughter, especially after she went away to school. In responding to her suggestion that he should not write if he were too busy, he replied: "Do not worry about my having time or not to write to you. I always have time for that. I like writing to you and it is a relief to me from care and work."[14]

Although letters cannot take the place of a parent's physical presence, this correspondence, some of which has been published since Gandhi's death, provides a unique glimpse into this father-daughter relationship.[15] Nehru gave his daughter advice about her studies, recommended books for her to read, and discussed current affairs with her. He frequently inquired about her career plans. Nehru urged his daughter to pursue her own interests and pay heed to her own counsel. He wrote: "I want you to grow and develop after your own fashion and only so can you fulfil your life purpose."[16]

Nehru acknowledged in a letter written when Indira was a student at Oxford that he had always been ambitious for her, noting: "Many years ago I used to dream that when you grew up, you also would play a brave part in what is called public life in India... And I wanted you to train and fit yourself in body and mind for this engrossing task."[17]

Nehru's ambitions for his daughter, even if they were not directly expressed, influenced her. When she was eight or nine years old, she became fascinated with the story of Joan of Arc, fantasizing about playing a similar role in India's struggle for independence. She used her dolls to act out the conflict with the British and to stage attacks on the prisons to secure the release of the Congress followers.

Early on Gandhi accompanied her father on some of his travels. When the Nehru family moved to Switzerland to get medical treatment for Indira's mother, Gandhi accompanied her father on his tour of

Europe as she was to do on subsequent visits, and she was exposed to many political and intellectual leaders.

Even if other children are added to the family, a father may remain close to a first daughter, especially if they have common interests. Bhutto, like Gandhi, on occasion traveled with her father, whom she described to an interviewer as a man without blemishes, "the shining star."[18] In her autobiography, she noted that he "always encouraged me to feel a part of the greater world."[19] Believing that the meeting with Indira Gandhi to hammer out the terms of peace that would end the Bangladesh war would represent "a turning point in Pakistan's history,"[20] he took Benazir with him to Simla. Though he disliked Gandhi, the fact that she was a woman may have influenced him to include his daughter in his entourage. Like Nehru, whom he admired,[21] Zulfikar Ali Bhutto had ambitious plans for his daughter.

Although Bhutto grew up in a traditional Muslim household, he rejected such practices as *purdah*, the seclusion of the women's living quarters, and the wearing of veils by the women in his immediate family. Benazir's relationship with her father had always been a close one, but during his stay in prison they developed a special bond. It was during this period that she committed herself to political action.

Although first daughters may have an advantage in getting the attention of the father, in some families, a second daughter may develop a close relationship with a father as she may fill the role of a son who was not to be. Margaret Thatcher, like Bhutto, idolized her father. Even after she became a national political figure, she frequently noted his influence. Following the victory of her party in 1979, Thatcher said: "He brought me up to believe all the things I do believe, and they're the values on which I fought the election…I owe almost everything to my father."[22]

Alfred Roberts showed a keen interest in his daughters' development, especially his younger daughter in whom he saw real potential. In addition to stressing the importance of schooling, he urged Margaret to read, study music, and attend local lectures. Roberts was himself an avid reader, and he often discussed books as well as current affairs with his daughter.[23]

Thatcher, who helped with the chores in the family store and sometimes accompanied her father when he made deliveries, was encouraged to take part in the discussions of the adults. Finding the experience to her liking, years later she told a biographer that she enjoyed the work in the store, because she was able to meet "so many different kinds of people."[24]

In contrast, Helen Clark rebelled against the political views of her father, a New Zealand dairy farmer who was active in the affairs of the National Party, a right of center party. When Helen came home from boarding school on holidays, she would argue with her father about political issues. One of her sisters described the confrontations when she said: "They used to argue terribly.... She was very left-wing and my Dad, at that stage, was very right. And of course he loved an argument."[25] By the time she was in college, Helen had moved further away from her father, participating in protests against the Vietnam War, apartheid in South Africa, and nuclear testing in the South Pacific. She later joined the Labor Party and eventually ran for office on the Labor Party ticket.

A woman who did not have the benefit of a close relationship with her father was Kim Campbell whose parents separated when she was about 12 years old. George Campbell acknowledged that his two daughters who had been sent to a boarding school just before the separation but begged their father to let them return to live with him "raised themselves." He said that he was available to them if they needed him, "but for the most part they got up and went to school."[26] He indicated that he knew little about what his daughters did outside the home.

The fathers of some of the women leaders encouraged their daughters to participate along with them in political or community activities; thereby, reinforcing the daughter's view of herself as capable and making for pleasant memories associated with political action. Thatcher was exposed to the trials of canvassing and electioneering at an early age as her father campaigned for a number of political offices. Her first experience with national politics came during the 1935 election. She folded election literature for the Conservative candidate, and on Election Day she carried the lists of those who had voted from the polling station to the party committee. During subsequent election campaigns, she passed out leaflets door to door.

After she left school, Sirimavo Bandaranaike accompanied her father on his trips around his district. Bandaranaike later said of their work together: "I discovered we were on the same wave length. I began to understand how he felt about the people he had looked after for years and considered his own... It was from him I acquired a sense of compassion for anyone in distress and realized it was not enough to merely sit around and sympathize...."[27]

Although her father S.W.R.D. Bandaranaike did not live to make good on his promise, Chandrika Kumaratunga, who had a close relationship with him, remembers "sitting on the arm of her father's chair, absorbing it all."[28] She told a reporter that he "used to say I was the one who would follow in his footsteps. He intended taking me to meetings and teaching me how to speak in public."[29]

During her teenage years, both Golda Meir and her father participated in a number of relief activities to benefit Jewish refugees. She took part in the People's Relief Committee as the representative of a Labor Zionist literary organization while Moshe Mabovitch represented his trade union. But it was her father's failure to respond effectively to threats that had the greatest influence on her. In recounting one of her earliest memories, Meir described her father's reaction to a threatened pogrom: "Papa reacted to it [the rumor of a pogrom] as I had known him to react all his life—he made no arrangements to hide the family, but tried instead to bolster the doorway by clapping boards on to the door."[30] In discussing the incident years later, she said that at the time she experienced "an angry feeling of impotence."[31] She also observed that the incident provided an explanation for what she tried to do with her life—to save other Jewish children from "a similar experience."[32]

Though most of the women who rose to the top grew up in intact families, the fathers of some of them died while their daughters were still young. Isabel Peron''s father who worked as a bank manager died before Isabel began school. With five children to care for, Peron's mother worked at various jobs. Because of the financial strains on the family, Isabel eventually went to live with a couple who were practitioners of the occult, coming in time to view them as surrogate parents. Mireya Moscoso's father, a teacher and farmer, died when she was a child. Ertha Pascal-Trouillot's father, an ornamental iron worker, died when she was 13, but her mother was able to keep the family of 10 children together by working as a seamstress. Chandrika Kumaratunga was a young teenager when her father was assassinated, Benazir Bhutto was 25 at the time of her father's execution, and Sheikh Hasina was in her late 20s when her family was murdered in a military coup. Kazimiera Prunskiene's father, a forest ranger, was killed in a gunfight when she was an infant. Violeta Chamorro's father died when his daughter was 18 and was attending Blackstone College in Virginia where she was enrolled in secretarial courses. She did not return to her studies, having found English very difficult to master. Instead, she assumed responsibility for many family chores as her mother undertook an extended period of mourning. Jenny Shipley's father, a Presbyterian minister, also died when his daughter was 18, but she was able to attend college despite the fact that her mother had to care for 4 girls on a widow's pension.

The Mother/Daughter Relationship

Serving as role models, mothers also have significant influence on the course their daughters chose to follow. While Kumaratunga was the only leader whose mother held high political office, the mothers of these women were, on the whole, strong-willed women who, in some cases, shared in the task of making a living for their families. Many of them also played an important, if supportive, role in the political or community action in which their husbands participated. By taking part in activities outside the home, the mothers conveyed to their daughters that such behavior was not inappropriate for women. Since the mothers had interests apart from their immediate families, some distance was maintained between them and their daughters, permitting the daughters to look to a variety of persons, including the fathers, to define appropriate behavior for a woman.

Before her husband's death, Sirimavo Bandaranaike, Kumaratunga's mother, concentrated her attention on taking care of household tasks and rearing the couple's three children. Given her husband's preoccupation with politics, Bandaranaike was both mother and father to her children. In describing her husband's role, she said: "He kept himself aloof from the domestic sphere to some extent and other diverse matters were left entirely in my hands."[33] She acknowledged that she sometimes wished "he'd take a greater interest...in our own private affairs for a change, and I was at times a little impatient of his wholehearted dedication to his work."[34]

Though Gandhi's mother, an advocate of rights for women, did not have a career as such, she did take part in the political activities of the family despite the fact that she experienced two unsuccessful pregnancies and tuberculosis was diagnosed in 1925. Since so many of the men in the Indian independence movement were in jail, the women, who were less likely to be arrested, were encouraged to assume a variety of responsibilities. Kamala Nehru helped in organizing meetings, leading processions, and addressing rallies. To her delight, she was arrested for her activities and spent a brief period in prison.

Kamala Nehru was a strong supporter of her husband's decision to join with the Mahatma Gandhi forces. In commenting on her mother's role years later, Gandhi said: "When my father wanted to join Gandhiji and to change the whole way of life...the whole family was against it. It was only my mother's courageous and persistent support and encouragement which enabled him to take this big step...."[35] Kamala, who grew up in a comparatively prosperous but orthodox Hindu family, was more comfortable with the austere lifestyle prescribed by Gandhi than she was with the affluent and Western trappings of the Nehru household.

Kamala's marriage, which had been arranged by the parents of the couple, proved, at least in the early years, not to be a happy one. The young bride experienced some difficulty in adjusting to her new home, and Nehru who was preoccupied with politics had little time for his wife. The conflicts between Kamala and her husband's sisters, especially the older sister who was jealous of the attention focused on the newest member of the Nehru family, were a particular source of pain. Kamala's work in the independence struggle may have provided a diversion from a difficult situation as well as a means for the young wife to please her husband although Nehru expressed concern about the effect a prison stay would have on her health.[36]

Since motherhood enhanced the status of a young Indian woman, it was common for her to lavish attention on her child.[37] In Kamala's case, since she not only had to deal with the stress in adjusting to a new family but also had to cope with the frequent absences of her husband, she concentrated her attention on Indira's care, frequently dressing her daughter in boys' clothes.

As the wife of the Chief Headman, Sirimavo Bandaranaike's mother, who was described as strong-willed, was active in the affairs of the community, intervening with her husband on behalf of the villagers. While Bandaranaike's father was sought out by many in the community for counsel and advice, he was usually approached through his wife. In describing the situation, Bandaranaike, who depicted her home as a very happy one, said: "It was my mother they would usually speak to in the first place. She was able to influence my father. Sometimes it was a little good advice that was needed, a practical suggestion, a straightforward solution to straighten out a problem...."[38] Many in the community also consulted her about remedies for illnesses and injuries as she followed in her father's footsteps and practiced Ayurvedic medicine that makes use of herbs in the treatment of disease.

A mother may also convey to a daughter that a woman can be competent by the role a mother plays within her own family. Many of the women political leaders have described their mothers as the dominant figures in their homes. For example, Eugenia Charles remarked that while her father was "a very, very, very great man" who taught her "much about being tough where it counts and about always being open and honest with people,"[39] her "mother was the boss" and the most important influence in her life.

Corazon Aquino described her mother, who was a graduate in pharmacy and an active campaigner for her husband and later her son, as a forceful figure. When asked whether her own composure came from her family, Aquino said: "I think from my father. He was very calm...He was so quick to forgive...My mother was not so forgiving. She was more the fighter..."[40] Helen Clark's mother, a former teacher, active in community groups, was the disciplinarian in the family. She was described by her daughters as a "strong, no-nonsense, enormously practical, hugely efficient woman."[41] Gloria Arroyo also viewed her mother, who gave up the practice of medicine after her marriage, as a disciplinarian.

Golda Meir saw her mother as more sophisticated than her father in dealing with others and observed that her mother was a bright and energetic woman.[42] After her husband's departure for the United States, Blume Mabovitch moved with her three daughters to Pinsk, Russia, where her family lived. She baked and sold bread to earn enough money to afford her own apartment. Following the move to Milwaukee, she operated a dairy store despite her husband's opposition, in space attached to the family's apartment to supplement the household income.

Maria Liberia-Peters said that her mother, who operated a small grocery store in which Maria helped after school, had little interest in politics, but she "had a very central position" in the lives of her five children. According to her daughter, she was the "director."[43] Violeta Chamorro indicated that since her father was frequently away from home attending to the family's ranch, her mother whom she described as "strong in substance" but "moderate in style of expression" was left "to carry out the task of educating five children."[44] Beatriz Merino, whose father was a dreamer and a thinker, described her mother, in contrast, as "all business," saying that Aida taught her daughter to be tough.[45]

Benazir Bhutto's mother, Nusrat Ispahani, the daughter of an Iranian businessman who had immigrated to India before the partition, grew up in a family that permitted women greater involvement in the outside world than was typical of Muslim households. Nusrat Ispahani and her sisters did not wear veils and were permitted to drive. After the family moved to Karachi, she joined the Pakistan Women's National Guard and learned to drive trucks and ambulances. Her marriage did not prove to be a particularly happy one. Bhutto's father had a reputation as a womanizer, and he and his wife separated at least once. Though she frequently traveled with her husband and was an effective hostess, Nusrat did not share his preoccupation with politics. That role was left for his daughter.

On the other hand, Sheikh Hasina's mother encouraged Mujibur and played a role in the reorganization of his political party. According to Hasina, "[m]y mother never thought of our family's comfort but spent money to support party workers and the movement by selling her ornament and household furniture." She went on to say that "she [Hasina's mother] took a bold stand for the independence of Bangladesh."[46]

A mother may not only communicate the importance of independence to a daughter but may also stress the traditional female role. Gro Brundtland told an interviewer that her mother "never underestimated the female role." She said that her mother, a civil servant who worked as her daughter's secretary when Brundtland was leader of the opposition, "managed to convey both a kind of independence and also the feminine values."[47]

While as a role model, a strong mother may encourage her daughter to explore her own interests and, at the same time, develop the nurturing aspect of her personality. The daughter of a weak mother may look to her father for guidance and resolve to become more like him.

Margaret Thatcher noted that after the age of 15 she and her mother had little to say to one another as her mother was preoccupied with household chores. By her teenage years Thatcher's interests had moved beyond the traditional female concerns. She indicated to one biographer that she believed she was closer to her father than she was to her mother, noting that from her mother she learned practical things, such as sewing and cooking.[48] Thatcher rarely mentioned her mother and would change the subject when asked about her, usually commenting on her father's influence, instead. In her autobiography Thatcher paid scant attention to her mother, reserving considerable space to her father's accomplishments.

Beatrice Stevenson Roberts was a very shy woman who stood in the shadow of her husband although she did work along with him in the grocery store in addition to taking care of household tasks. Also, the money she earned as a seamstress before her marriage helped purchase the original store, and through hard work and saving the Roberts improved their lot in life, moving the young family into the middle class.

While the daughter of a weak mother may suffer from lack of a strong female role model, the daughter who loses her mother through death or divorce may not receive sufficient guidance, especially if she does not have a close relationship with a father who is able to help her deal with the loss. Since adolescents are especially concerned about appearing different, as a teenager she is likely to become preoccupied with minimizing those differences that separate her from her contemporaries. According to one authority, "to be like the rest of her crowd" she may suppress her emotions, dealing with feelings of loss by engaging in a flurry of activity.[49]

When Kim Campbell's parents separated, her mother left the family's home. Lissa Campbell accompanied her future husband to England although the couple finally ended up in the Caribbean where they operated a business crewing sailboats. While she kept in touch with her two daughters by mail, she did not see them for 10 years. In describing his younger daughter's reaction to the loss of her mother, Campbell's father remarked: "Kim had a tender heart. She didn't cry much. But she would feel it just the same."[50]

Campbell, who had been given the name Avril Phaedra, changed her name after her mother left the family. She later said this move was a response to the trauma she felt at the time although she did not discuss her feelings with her friends. Instead, she displayed enthusiasm as she went about a myriad of school activities. By changing her name, she could separate herself from the mother who had "abandoned" her as well as take a step to forge her own identity.

The parents of Megawati also separated when Sukarno made the decision to take a second wife. Megawati's mother moved from the family's home with the oldest child—a son and left the other children with Sukarno. As the oldest daughter, Megawati, who was supportive of her father, became a substitute mother for the other children.

In addition to a mother, other female relatives may influence the choices a young woman makes. Among the political leaders, Mary Robinson and Hanna Suchocka had aunts who pursued careers outside the home. Though Mary Robinson's mother was a physician, she did not practice after the birth of her children, but an aunt—her mother's sister—who was also a physician did have a medical practice.

While in an interview Suchocka indicated that she learned how to work hard from her mother,[51] a pharmacist who plied her skills in the family business located below the living quarters, it is likely her interest in politics was piqued by other female relatives. Her paternal grandmother served as minister of women's affairs in the 1919 government of Ignace Jan Paderewski, and her father's sister, whom Suchocka greatly admired, never married and was actively involved in the movement for equal rights for women in Poland.

Sibling Relationships

The popular wisdom holds that only children are likely to be overrepresented among high achievers as such children receive considerable adult attention early in life. Several of these women, including Indira Gandhi, Vigdis Finnbogadottir, and Tansu Ciller, did not have siblings. Also, it is commonly believed that there are likely to be no sons in the families of female high achievers, with a daughter taking on traditional male responsibilities. Helen Clark, Golda Meir, Margaret Thatcher, Hanna Suchocka, and Jenny Shipley did not have brothers. Clark attributes having certain advantages, such as attendance at a boarding school, to the fact that she had only sisters. If she had had a brother, he, she contends, would undoubtedly have been favored.[52]

A study by Blema S. Steinberg of 41 women presidents and prime ministers who had risen to the top as of the year 2000 "revealed that first-born female leaders, like first-born male leaders, were found to be over represented at the top level of political power."[53] In fact, the ratio of first-born women leaders was higher than that of their male counterparts. The author also found that before 1990, the women who rose to the top were less likely to have an older brother than those who have risen since, suggesting that the feminist movement may have made it more acceptable for women to be assertive and to believe that it is possible for women to reach the top.

But perhaps more important than the composition of the family is the attitude of the parents toward their children. Many of the families of the women leaders not only encouraged their daughters to achieve but also treated them as equal to their sons. Brundtland described the situation in her family when she said: "From when I was very small, both [of her parents] gave me very clear indications that a girl has the same abilities and responsibilities as a boy. So I had this background of equality between the sexes instilled in me from the very beginning."[54] She indicated that she was pleased that her parents let her be a tomboy but also let her outgrow it. She observed: "I think many girls find that they are asked to be so equal they are not allowed to develop those feminine traits which all of us have."[55]

Bhutto noted that there was no preference shown by her parents for her brothers. She wrote in her autobiography that there was no question that "my sister and I would be given the same opportunities in life as our brothers."[56] If anything, she says, as the oldest child, she received the most attention.[57] Mary Robinson, noting that she had been treated no differently than her four brothers, said that she "grew up in an environment of total equality."[58] One of Robinson's brothers told an interviewer that "she [Mary] grew up unquestionably a tomboy. It was 'fight your own battles and fight then hard or be swallowed.' She learned to take hard knocks and stand up for herself."[59]

Although a woman's father may reinforce her sense of confidence, making it possible for her to take risks, and her mother may serve as a role model, siblings also play a part in her training for political leadership. Interaction within the family circle provides experience in dealing with such mainstays of the political arena as conflict, competition, and persuasion.

Conclusions

Although the family played a significant role in the preparation and encouragement of those women who rose to the top in the political arena, the family may become less important in channeling daughters into politics as the participation of women becomes more widely accepted. The personal costs to individual women of active political involvement may no longer be so great. Commenting on the change in women's assessment of their opportunities, Kim Campbell said shortly after she was elected to the Canadian parliament in 1988: "Women in my generation assumed we would have a career. We were products of the 1960s, when the doors were already opening."[60] This is not to suggest that families will not remain important in providing their daughters with the interest and motivation to take an active role in a nation's business. Having parents with considerable interest in politics who participate in political activity at some level, parents who instill confidence in their daughters, fathers who push their daughters to excel, strong mothers with interests outside the home as well as siblings who serve to provide lessons in human relations may point a woman in the direction of a political career.

Chapter Six

Educational Experiences

Golda Meir, who lived with her mother and two sisters in Pinsk after her father immigrated to the United States, did not begin school during that period. Instead, she received some instruction from her older sister. Following the move to Milwaukee, Meir was enrolled in an elementary school where she learned English quickly, made friends easily, and in general made a good adjustment to the new environment. This otherwise satisfying picture was marred by disagreements with her mother who insisted that her daughter work in the family-operated store, forcing Meir on many days to arrive at school late. It was only after the intervention of a truant officer that other arrangements were made for opening the store.

Meir completed elementary school at the top of her class and expressed interest in becoming a teacher, but her parents disapproved of her continuing her education. Instead, they arranged a marriage for her with an older man as the security that marriage could provide seemed to them the best way to ensure her future. Although the marriage never took place, and Meir began high school, this conflict further strained relations with her parents, and she eventually ran away from home to join her sister and brother-in-law in Denver.

Within a few months Meir was reunited with her parents. She resumed her studies and, on graduating from high school, enrolled in a teachers' college; but the increased demands of her work on behalf of Poale Zion, a political group committed to socialism and Zionism, made it difficult for her to continue her academic pursuits, and she withdrew from the program.

Although Meir's educational record did not measure up to what would be expected of a national leader, it closely resembled the experiences of women at that time. As late as the nineteenth century, the belief was widespread that women were innately inferior to men as far as the ability to learn was concerned. Little attempt was made to provide education for women beyond the rudimentary requirements for housekeeping as it was argued that they would be unable to tolerate the stress associated with learning given their fragile constitutions. Concern was also expressed in the developing medical community that serious study might lead to sterility in women—a view resembling such beliefs as those commonly held in India that education would result in widowhood and difficulties for a woman's family. Since the "proper" role for women was viewed as marriage, they were encouraged to leave school earlier than men as parents were concerned that education might jeopardize their daughters' marital prospects.

Admission to graduate and professional schools proved to be a particularly thorny issue with some faculties stubbornly resisting the inclusion of women well into the twentieth century. Apart from beliefs that women were not capable of advanced study, it was argued that such opportunities would be wasted on them as they would marry and not pursue careers.

Even after the attendance of women at universities became widely accepted, women still did not necessarily have the same opportunities as men. In France, for example, as late as 1983 only 21 percent of those attending the prestigious National School of Administration, the training ground for politicians and high-level civil servants, were women.[1] Elite colleges throughout the world were slow to admit women.

Also, women who attended a university concentrated their work, whether because of discriminatory practices or personal preference, in such fields as education rather than in those areas from which most politicians are recruited—namely, law, business, and the other professions. In Poland where 56 percent of those enrolled in higher education in 1980 were women, almost 81 percent were studying education, while in Canada in which approximately half of those attending college were women, 70 percent were in education.[2]

Since women have not historically had access to the same educational opportunities as men, their ability to become active players in the political arena was impaired even when the legal barriers to their participation were withdrawn. By not attending school or by receiving inferior instruction, they were not exposed to the ways of thinking or the kinds of knowledge that would enable them to develop an interest in the workings of public affairs or allow them to acquire the skills necessary to exercise power.

Formal Education

For the most part, those women who have risen to positions of national leadership had the benefit of superior educational experiences and grew up in families that emphasized the importance of education for their daughters. Eugenia Charles of Dominica perhaps best described the role of the family in the education of these women when she told an interviewer about the part played by her own parents. Noting that they had little formal education themselves, she said: "They gave us [her along with her sister and two brothers] a choice of what we wanted to study, but no choice of whether or not we wanted to study. We were expected to make something of ourselves."[3]

The widows are the exception. Only Corazon Aquino of the Philippines, who attended the College of Mount St. Vincent in New York City and studied law for a brief period before her marriage, graduated from college. Janet Jagan of Guyana attended college and later enrolled in nurses' training, but she did not complete either program. Mireya Moscoso of Panama, who was criticized during the 1999 election campaign for not having a college degree, attended a community college in Miami where she studied interior design. Khaleda Zia of Bangladesh enrolled in college, but she attended classes only briefly as she dropped out of the program when she married. Violeta Chamorro attended college in the United States briefly, but she had difficulty mastering English and left after her father's death.

Although Sirimavo Bandaranaike of Sri Lanka did not attend college, her parents were concerned that she as well as her brothers have a good basic education, but they encouraged their daughter to leave school early. When she was eight, she was sent to St. Bridget's Convent, a school established by the Sisters of the Good Shepherd in Colombo. Though she was initially homesick and resented the fact she had been sent away to school, Bandaranaike quickly adjusted to the strict and disciplined life at St. Bridget's and sought to stay on another two years after completing the Junior Cambridge Examination. Though she was a good student, her academic record was not outstanding, but her performance on the examination along with the pressure exerted by her teachers persuaded her parents to let her remain at the school. During the next two years, Bandaranaike concentrated her efforts in areas that would prepare her for household responsibilities in addition to the study of music and painting.

Sensitive about her lack of educational achievement, Bandaranaike insisted during the 1965 election campaign in which she unsuccessfully sought a new mandate for her party that the country had not taken second place at international conferences because of her background. She argued that what was important to govern was honesty and pure intentions and that she had been able to face difficult problems.[4]

On the other hand, the daughters who rose to the top had impressive educational credentials, all of them attending college for at least a time. Their families felt strongly about the importance of education for their daughters. In making arrangements for Indira's education, the Nehrus were concerned that she be able to earn a living although women in preindependence India were not encouraged to pursue educational goals. Kamala Nehru, who had little formal education herself, was a firm believer in the importance of education for women. Perhaps because of her own marital difficulties, she viewed marriages in which the wife had considerably less education than her husband as unsatisfactory and felt that education was the key to freeing women from the restraints of male domination.

In selecting a school for Indira, Nehru was concerned that his daughter have the opportunity to develop her own interests. He was opposed to the more structured style of the European institutions that were boycotted by the families active in the independence movement. Nehru and his father clashed over the issue as her grandfather preferred that Indira attend a more established school. After brief stays at a kindergarten in Delhi, the nationalist-oriented Modern School in Allahabad, and a private school, St. Cecilia's, Indira received instruction at home since there was no agreement on a school for her.

In 1926, because of Kamala Nehru's deteriorating health, the family moved to Geneva where Kamala received medical treatment. Indira attended the International School that had been established by a group of civil servants working at the League of Nations. She was later enrolled in an international school at Bex. It was hoped that the mountainous location would be beneficial to Indira's health as she was prone to respiratory diseases. When the family returned to India at the end of 1927, Indira, who was provided instruction in Hindi at home, was enrolled in St. Mary's Convent School located in Allahabad, but she did not find the cloistered life at the school to her liking.

After the death of her grandfather in 1931, Indira was sent to a school in Poona, the Pupils' Own School and a fairly informal institution that emphasized discussion and encouraged social service activity. On receiving her school-leaving certificate in 1934, she enrolled in the Vishwa Bharati University at Shantiniketan, a school established and operated by Rabindranath Tagore, the Noble prize-winning poet. Though she enjoyed the peaceful atmosphere at the school, a sharp contrast to the style of life she had experienced as a child, she left in 1935 to accompany her mother to Switzerland. Kamala Nehru's health had seriously declined, and she died in February 1936.

After another stay at Bex, Gandhi enrolled in the Badminton School in Bristol, England, to prepare for her entrance to Oxford University as she had failed her earlier examinations. In 1937, she began her work at Somerville College, one of the oldest women's colleges at Oxford, where she studied public and social administration, history, and anthropology. After she failed to pass the qualifying examination, usually taken in the first year, coupled with another bout with respiratory illness and a stay of several months at a sanatorium in the Alps,[5] Gandhi lost interest in academic pursuits. To the disappointment of her father, she did not graduate and, instead, returned to India where she became caught up in the independence struggle.

In contrast to the schooling of Gandhi, that of Benazir Bhutto was quite stable. When she was five years old, the Bhuttos enrolled their daughter in the Convent of Jesus and Mary School in Karachi that was operated by Irish Catholic nuns, and she received instruction at home in Islam from a private tutor. Bhutto remained at the school except for a brief period during her early teens when she attended a boarding school.

Bhutto's father closely monitored his children's progress. In her autobiography, she noted that "in our house education was top priority. Like his father before him, my father wanted to make examples of us, the next generation of educated and progressive Pakistanis."[6] Her father repeatedly reminded his children, "I ask only one thing of you, that you do well in your studies." Bhutto remarked that "luckily I was a good student, for he [her father] had great plans for me to be the first woman in the Bhutto family to study abroad."[7]

At the age of 16 Bhutto entered Radcliffe, graduating cum laude with a degree in comparative politics. At her father's urging, she then enrolled at Oxford, earning a second bachelor's degree, concentrating on philosophy, politics, and economics. She spent an additional year at Oxford studying international law and diplomacy in preparation for a career in the diplomatic corps.

The other daughters of prominent male politicians also had the benefit of solid educational experiences. Chandrika Kumaratunga, whose parents sent her to St. Bridget's despite the criticism of Buddhist supporters, studied political science at the University of Paris where she later did graduate work in economics and law. Sheik Hasina attended Bangladesh's Dhaka University, completing the requirements for graduation after her marriage, and Gloria Arroyo attended Georgetown University in the United States and earned a doctorate in economics from the University of the Philippines. Megawati, who entered college to study agricultural engineering, left school to assist her father when he was overthrown by Suharto. Though she later returned, her stay was brief, and she, like Gandhi, never completed the requirements for a degree.

Aside from Golda Meir, who was the only woman president or prime minister born in the nineteenth century, those women who worked their way up the political ladder had educational experiences similar to those of their male counterparts. For example, Margaret Thatcher earned a Bachelor of Science degree from Oxford, which along with Cambridge trained most of the British political elite. After she married, she studied law at Lincoln's Inn, a special tutorial college.

Although Thatcher's parents had little formal education, they took great interest in their daughters' education and were willing to make financial sacrifices for both daughters to be able to attend the best schools in the community. Thatcher remarked to a biographer that she felt her father, who regretted that he had not been able to pursue his intellectual interests formally, tried to realize his ambitions through her.[8]

At the age of five, Margaret was enrolled in Huntingtower Road Elementary School. Although this was not the school closest to her home, her parents preferred it as Huntingtower had a good academic reputation. Her performance was excellent, and she won a scholarship when she was 10 years old to Kesteven and Grantham Girls' School, a grant-aided grammar school or one in which parents were required to pay a portion of the fees.

At Kesteven, Thatcher stood first in her class every year save one. She concentrated her work in science and math, her interest in these subjects having been piqued by the excellent teaching of her chemistry instructor. Years later she explained her decision: "That was a period when we were dazzled by what it [science] could achieve. We thought there were no problems that could not ultimately be answered by science."[9]

Thatcher early on expressed an interest in attending a university, and she set her sights on Oxford. Gaining admission was no easy task, especially for a woman with her background. She was discouraged from even making an attempt by her headmistress, particularly since Margaret wished to begin her university training at the age of 17, a year earlier than was the custom.

To prepare herself for the entrance examinations, Margaret pressed her father to pay for private Latin lessons since Latin had not been offered at Kesteven, and knowledge of Latin was required for admission to Oxford. She mastered the five-year Latin course in a few months and also took elocution lessons to help overcome her Lincolnshire accent.

The results of various examinations gained her a place to read chemistry at Somerville, the same Oxford College that Gandhi had attended only a few years earlier. At Oxford, Thatcher was considered a thorough but not a brilliant student, earning a second rather than a first-class Bachelor of Science degree. Her tutor, Dorothy Hodgkin, a distinguished scientist who later won a Nobel Prize in chemistry, said of her: "I came to rate her as good. One could always rely on her producing a sensible, well-read essay and yet there was something that some people had that she hadn't quite got."[10]

By the time she received her degree, Thatcher realized that she had studied the wrong subject, for she was more interested in law and politics than chemistry. During a visit to her home while still a student, she attended a birthday party at a friend's house. As the young people were cleaning up at the end of the evening, someone said, "I feel that what you would really like to do is to be a member of Parliament." She indicated at that point it occurred to her that one day she might be able to seek office.[11] Because of her financial situation, the pursuit of a political career had appeared unrealistic. The remuneration received by members of parliament was relatively small while science, on the other hand, offered good employment opportunities.

Thatcher's marriage in 1951 to a prosperous businessman made it possible for her to pursue her interest in law, and she devoted full time to study for the Bar, passing the final examination five months after she gave birth to twins. Her choice of tax law, a male-dominated field, as her area of expertise made it more difficult for her to secure an apprenticeship required to complete her legal training, but her determination to enter politics led her to challenge the prevailing wisdom that clients would not accept a woman tax barrister. It seemed to her that grounding in tax law would be more useful in the political arena than areas such as domestic relations.

In addition to Thatcher, several other professional politicians pursued legal studies. For example, Kim Campbell earned a law degree from the University of British Columbia. While in 1970, she had received a generous fellowship to study for her doctorate in Soviet Studies at the London School of Economics, she failed to complete the requirements for the degree. Instead, she returned to Canada with her husband, Nathan Divinsky, a divorced mathematics professor at the University of British Columbia, whom she had dated while an undergraduate. The couple were married in 1972 when he came to England as a visiting professor at the University of London. Following the couple's return, she taught on a fill-in basis at the University of British Columbia and at the Vancouver Community College, but academia did not have enough action for her and the arrangement proved unsatisfactory. She began her legal studies in 1980. Although she was not particularly interested in the law per se, Campbell said, "I knew that there was a lot that you could do with a law degree. I had in the back of my mind the idea of going into politics some day."[12]

Eugenia Charles of Dominica, who became interested in law after attending court hearings to practice shorthand, pursued her legal studies in Britain after graduating from the University of Toronto. Hanna Suchocka's parents wanted her to follow in their footsteps and take up pharmacy, but she decided to study law at the Polish University of Adam Mickiewicz. A legal career offered the opportunity to leave the communist country to attend international conferences.[13] After a brief stint as a college teacher followed by a period working at the Institute of Small Arts and Crafts, Suchocka returned to teaching and pursued graduate work in constitutional law, earning a doctorate in 1975. Other professional politicians who studied law include Susanne Camelia-Romer who served as prime minister of the Netherlands Antilles; Tarja Halonen who was elected president of Finland; Anneli Jaatteenmaki who served for a brief period as prime minister of Finland; and Beatriz Merino of Peru who earned a degree in economics at the London School of Economics and went on to study for a master's degree in law at Harvard.

Some of the politicians who reached the top prepared for other professional careers. For example, like her father, Gro Brundtland studied medicine, graduating from the University of Oslo. She married while still a student and later came to the United States with her husband, earning a master's degree in public health from Harvard. Another leader who trained as a physician was Michelle Bachelet of Chile. Bachelet attended classes at different schools as she lived in exile for a time following the takeover by Pinochet. She eventually returned to Chile where she graduated from the Universidad de Chile medical school. Bachelet later attended the National Academy of Political and Strategic Studies as she had an interest in military affairs and security issues. She also received a scholarship in 1997 to attend the Inter-American Defense College in Washington, D.C.

Edith Cresson, Tansu Ciller, Kazimiera Prunskiene, Helen Clark, Yuliya Tymoshenko, Ellen Johnson Sirleaf, and Angela Merkel all pursued graduate studies. Following her graduation from a religious school whose strict approach she did not find to her liking, Cresson studied business at l'Ecole des Hautes Etudes Commerciales in Paris. Like Thatcher, she returned to school after her marriage to a business executive, earning a doctorate in demography. For her dissertation, she chose to do an interview study focusing on the lives of women in a rural district of France. Ciller, who attended the American College for Girls, began her academic career at Turkey's prestigious Robert College (now Bosporus University). She then moved to the United States with her husband, her high school sweetheart whom she married when she was 17, and earned a master's degree in economics from the University of New Hampshire and a doctorate in economics from the University of Connecticut. Prunskiene of Lithuania also earned a doctorate in economics at the University of Vilnius. Clark who received an MA in political studies from New Zealand's Auckland University did not complete a dissertation for her doctorate as she became increasingly involved in politics.[14] Tymoshenko of Ukraine earned a doctorate in economics from Dnipropetrovs'k State University after her marriage. Ellen Johnson Sirleaf received a master's degree in public administration from the Kennedy School of Government at Harvard—a fact that worked to her advantage during the election campaign for the presidency of Liberia in 2005—as her opponent, a well-known soccer player, had not completed high school. Merkel, whose mother had been an English teacher, wanted to be a teacher and translator, but because of her father's work as a Protestant minister, she was not permitted by the communist government of East Germany to pursue her goals. Instead, she earned a doctorate in physics and took a job as a researcher at the Academy of Science.

Maria Liberia-Peters of the Netherlands Antilles, who became a teacher and school administrator, pursued graduate studies in education at a college in the Netherlands. Another teacher, Jenny Shipley, graduated from Christchurch Teachers College in New Zealand.

Milka Planinc of Yugoslavia attended the School of Management at Zagreb University to prepare for her work in the communist party while Ruth Dreifuss of Switzerland studied economics at the University of Geneva. Micheline Calmy-Rey, who was a successor of Dreifuss, received a degree from the Graduate Institute of International Studies in Geneva.

Since the selection of a leader to serve on an interim basis is made from among those with a record of achievement, those women selected to lead their countries temporarily were, on the whole, well educated. For example, Maria de Lourdes Pintasilgo was a graduate of the University of Lisbon. As a sickly child she developed an interest in music and literature, but she earned a degree in chemical engineering. She explained her decision to concentrate on science at the university by noting that she wanted to find out whether "women can do the same things as men do,"[15] for she knew young women who had attempted such a course of study but had failed.

Although Erthe Pascal-Trouillot of Haiti wanted to become a physician, she decided to follow the lead of her history teacher and future husband and study law. Nino Burdzhanadze of Georgia earned a degree in law from Tbilisi University—a school where she later taught—and took a doctorate in international law at Moscow University. Claudette Werleigh of Haiti, earned a degree in adult education as well as law, and she also studied medical sciences. Rosalia Arteaga of Ecuador and Madior Boye, who served as a judge in Senegal, studied law while Irena Degutiene studied medicine. Ruth Perry received a teacher training certificate from the University of Liberia and taught for a time before becoming a vice president of the Chase Manhattan Bank. Another teacher, Agathe Uwilingiyimana of Rwanda, earned a master's degree in chemistry. Reneta Indzhova of Bulgaria had a doctorate in economics, Luisa Diogo of Mozambique received a master's degree in economics, and Sylvie Kinigi studied economics. Nyam-Osoriyn Tuyaa completed graduate studies in politics, while Lydia Gueiler of Bolivia trained as an accountant.

The ceremonial leader who is elected is also more than likely to have a record of academic achievement. Before Vigdis Finnbogadottir's birth, her father, a professor of engineering, believed that the proper role for a woman was the care of a home despite the fact that his wife was a nurse who served as chair of the Icelandic Nurses' Association for many years. After his daughter was born, he focused on her education. Vigdis remarked that "nothing was too good for this daughter! He had high ambitions for me."[16] She attended a junior college in Iceland at which she later taught French, and then studied French, literature, and theater arts at the University of Grenoble and the Sorbonne in Paris and theater history at a university in Copenhagen, ultimately graduating from the University of Iceland.

Mary Robinson, who studied law at Trinity College and later received an L.L.M. from Harvard, was drawn to the law because of the influence of her paternal grandfather. She described him as "an old-style lawyer" who had "a passionate commitment to justice."[17] Since the Catholic Church viewed Trinity unacceptable, it was necessary for a Catholic to obtain a dispensation from a priest to attend the Protestant college. Mary's father made the necessary arrangements while her mother purchased a house, which happened to be the birthplace of Oscar Wilde, for Mary and her four brothers in Dublin. The children's nanny was sent along to care for the college students.

Robinson's successor as president of Ireland, Mary McAleese, also pursued legal studies as did Pratibha Patil who became president of

India in 2007. Latvian President Vaira Vike-Freiberga earned a doctorate in experimental psychology at McGill University in Canada and went on to a distinguished academic career of more than 30 years at the University of Montreal. Among the ceremonial leaders, only Agatha Barbara of Malta did not have a college degree.

Extracurricular Activities

In addition to providing students with academic training, the school affords a variety of experiences that are useful in preparing for a career in politics. As a participant in student government, a girl acquires experience in managing conflict, competing with her contemporaries, negotiating differences as well as persuading others to pursue a certain course. By taking part in extracurricular activities, she is able to hone skills in administration as well as public speaking. Pintasilgo, who served as president of a Catholic women's student group and played an active role in the International Movement of Catholic Students during her college years, noted that participation in these organizations helped her develop the ability to speak before groups. She also attributed a budding interest in social concerns to her contact with students of different nationalities.[18]

Institutions have more often than not been assumed positions in coeducational institutions are more often than not assumed by men, the single sex school or college offers advantages for women who are interested in politics in that it provides opportunities to assume a variety of roles. Many of the women political leaders attended a single sex school at some point in their formal education, more often than not at the elementary or high school level. Few attended women's colleges, suggesting that at that level, it may be more important to study at schools that have traditionally trained the political elite and to develop contacts with other potential political leaders.

Many of the women leaders took part in a variety of activities while in school, frequently assuming a leadership role. For example, Gro Brundtland joined the Labor Party's Association for Juniors when she was only seven years old. At the age of 15, she was one of the founders of a socialist club in her school and subsequently served as deputy chair of the Upper Secondary School Socialist Union. While continuing to pursue her interest in politics, despite a demanding schedule as a medical student, she participated in student government and at the University of Oslo served as vice-chair of the socialist students' association that was affiliated with the Labor Party. Helen

Clark joined the university branch of the Labor Party and became vice president. Sheikh Hasina took part in student politics while at the University of Dhaka, and she carried messages between her father and student leaders when he was incarcerated.

It was at Oxford that Thatcher's passion for politics began to mature and her political beliefs took form. She participated in the Oxford University Conservative Association, becoming the first woman to serve as its president. While the Oxford Union was the meeting ground for budding politicians, women at that time were barred from membership.

Many years later, Benazir Bhutto successfully sought the presidency of the Oxford Union that had finally opened its doors to women. According to friends, because she was so intent upon winning to please her father, she waged a vigorous campaign—so vigorous, in fact, that official complaints were lodged against her.[19]

Golda Meir, who became an effective fund raiser for Israel, first organized for a cause when she was 11 years old. Some of the pupils in her class were too poor to purchase books, and after obtaining the cooperation of some of her classmates, Meir organized a public meeting in a hall that had been rented for the occasion. Many in the neighborhood attended the meeting, and Meir explained the reason for the gathering. A fund to provide assistance for the poorer children was established. While in high school, Meir served as vice president of her class.

As a student, Kim Campbell participated in a variety of activities. For example, she organized dramatic and musical presentations. While in high school she showed an interest in politics, serving as president of the student council, and in college she was elected vice president of student government. Chandrika Kumaratunga, who was an excellent speaker, was a member of the debating team at St. Bridget's and also edited the school newspaper. Mary Robinson served as the secretary of the students' union and was active in debate.

Gandhi did not assume an active political role, but she did join the student wing of the British Labor Party and took part in some local party activities as a student in Britain. She worked for Krishna Menon's India League and also participated in the All India Students' Federation; but her contributions, for the most part, were inconsequential. The several bouts of illness she experienced while in college as well as her shyness may have made it difficult for her to play a more significant role.

The school also provides opportunities to take part in competitive sports, activities that may develop skills in working with others to accomplish a task and reinforce values associated with competition. Among men, competitive sports have been viewed as useful preparation for later pursuits in politics and business. Women, on the other hand, were often discouraged from engaging in physical activity as they were seen as too delicate.

Several of the women took part in competitive team sports during their school years. Aquino excelled in volleyball while Thatcher served as vice captain of her soccer team at Kesteven and Grantham Girls' School. Liberia-Peters played center on the girls' basketball team at her school, and Chamorro, who said that in addition to music what she liked most was sports, participated in both softball and basketball. Shipley, a champion swimmer, described herself as a "very sports oriented young person who thought that the world was my oyster."[20] Clark took part in a variety of athletic events, such as netball and, according to her sister, was more than a competent tennis player.[21]

Conclusions

The educational achievements of the women who have assumed positions of political leadership resemble or surpass those of their male counterparts. A study by Jean Blondel of those who served in the top position between 1946 and 1975 found that 68 percent of the 1,028 leaders, all of whom were men save five, attended college.[22] In the current study, 89 percent of the women political leaders (n=64) were enrolled in a college though in some cases their stays were brief. Although the figures would suggest that women may need more formal education to be selected for a position of political leadership than men, the fact that these two studies did not examine the same time period may provide a partial explanation for the discrepancy. More people throughout the world are now attending college with women in many countries surpassing men in the totals pursuing higher education.

Many of the women political leaders earned graduate or professional degrees, even those from countries in which few women attended school. Some 62 percent of the women prime ministers and presidents (n=64) enrolled in a professional or graduate program. Law, which is considered an important stepping stone to high-level political office, was the choice of 17 of the 40 women opting for graduate or professional training. Economics was also a popular choice, with several women rising to the top as a result of their experience in economic or finance ministries.

In selecting a college, many of these women chose to attend the prestige schools that train the political elite within their countries and/or colleges with an international reputation such as Oxford and Harvard. For the most part, these were ambitious women and they early on made wise choices.

Chapter Seven

Balancing Family and Political Career

Gro Brundtland of Norway expressed the challenge facing a married woman who wishes to pursue a career in politics when she said that "there simply isn't time to be a mother, a wife, and a politician at the same time." Noting that "there are not so many women who can put everything into politics," she said that she had "been very lucky. My husband has taken care of everything in the home. By and large, I haven't had to do a thing."[1]

Though Arne Olav Brundtland did not belong to the same political party as his wife, he was supportive of her career. He told an interviewer that it was he who first suggested that she enter politics. While they were both students at Harvard he said "she was doing so extremely well...I told her 'since you're so damned clever, why don't you go home and join the government?'"[2] When she began her political career some years later, he agreed to assume responsibility for their home on condition that the chores be done his way. Olav's schedule as an international relations researcher provided flexibility, making it possible for him to care for the home and the couple's four teenage children. Brundtland also had the support and assistance of her parents who helped with the children.

Nino Burdzhanadze of Georgia remarked to an interviewer that "it's hard to combine home and professional work." She went on to describe how she had managed when she said: "I wouldn't have gotten where I am if it were not for my Mama, who took on all the burdens. She cooks, she does the laundry, she looks after my children, and practically speaking, I am liberated from this work."[3]

Margaret Thatcher laid out more specifically the conditions necessary for a woman to pursue a career and run a home when she said: "First, her husband must be in sympathy with her wish to do another job. Secondly, where there is a young family, the joint incomes of husband and wife must be sufficient to employ a first-class nanny-housekeeper to look after things in the wife's absence. The second is the key of the whole plan."[4] On another occasion, she noted that a married woman who has a full-time job must be "extremely well organised. She has to be able to deal with domestic affairs quickly, make up her mind about household menus and shopping lists. And if she also has children there has to be someone responsible at home to care for them, whether it's a mother-in-law, a sister or a nanny."[5]

Denis Thatcher, who had unsuccessfully sought local political office before he met Margaret but had given up any interest in seeking office himself, was devoted to his wife and encouraged her political ambitions. The fact that the Thatcher family owned a large paint and chemicals firm, which Denis served as managing director, made it possible for Margaret to continue her study for the Bar before the arrival of the children and for the couple to afford household help.

Thatcher met her husband, who was 10 years older than she, during her first political outing when she was chosen as the Conservative Party nominee for the safe Labor Party seat from Dartford in 1950. After the meeting in which she received the nod, she stayed late into the evening to talk with the local party leaders. Denis offered her a ride to London so that she could catch the train to Colchester where she was working as a chemist in a nearby plastics firm. The couple became unofficially engaged the following September just before the parliamentary election in which Thatcher once again sought the seat from Dartford. They were married on December 13 of that year, making their home in Chelsea, an affluent section of London.

Unwavering in his support for his wife and also protective of her, Denis became her best friend and confidant, frequently traveling with her. In addition to looking out for her safety and well-being, on occasion he gave her advice, especially on business-related matters. The fact that he was semiretired by the time she reached the top may have been an advantage in that the burdens associated with a two career family and that of a political career were somewhat reduced.

Though she met the conditions that she had laid out for combining a career and marriage, Thatcher seemed to need an incentive to continue with her career after the birth of her children. In explaining to a biographer her decision to take the final bar examination just a few months after she gave birth to twins, Mark and Carol, in 1953, she said: "I thought that if I didn't do something quite definite then there was a real possibility that I'd never return to work again, so I entered my name for the bar finals."[6] After admission to the bar and with the help of a nanny, she began her work as a barrister when the children were a year old.

A ceremonial leader whose domestic arrangements satisfied the conditions identified by Thatcher as necessary was Mary Robinson of

Ireland. Robinson met her husband, Nick, while they were both students at Trinity College, but the couple did not marry until 1970, after they had been out of school some five years. At the time of their marriage, Mary was teaching at Trinity as well as conducting a law practice and pursuing a budding political career, while Nick, a solicitor, was a political cartoonist for the *Irish Times*. When a daughter arrived in 1974, the first of their three children, the Robinsons were able to afford a nanny.

Nick Robinson, whom Mary described as "a very close friend," was supportive of his wife's political pursuits. During the campaign for the presidency he not only traveled with her but he also took an active role in planning campaign strategy and in serving as liaison with the office in Dublin. One of the professionals who worked in the campaign observed that Robinson "could not have gotten through the campaign without him."[7] Perhaps Nick, like Denis Thatcher, was able to fulfill his own political ambitions through his spouse—ambitions that would have been difficult for a Protestant in a dominant Catholic country to realize.

After his wife's victory, Nick, who described himself as the "First Follower," took a leave of absence from his position at the Centre for European Law at Trinity, a research facility that had been founded by the Robinsons shortly before the presidential election. In commenting on his decision, he told an interviewer: "I'm quite happy to simply make the analogy to the countless able women who have put their support behind male political leaders. If they can do it, why shouldn't a woman expect the same from her husband?"[8]

Included among the husbands who made major changes in lifestyle to accommodate a wife's political career were Pentti Arajarvi, Tarja Halonen's long-time partner, and Burton Shipley. Though she had a daughter, Halonen remained single until after she was elected president of Finland. During the campaign she was criticized for not making the relationship official. Several months after she was sworn in, the couple exchanged vows. Arajarvi, who was counsel for the parliamentary social affairs and health committee, resigned his position before the marriage to avoid the appearance of a conflict of interest.

After Jenny Shipley won a seat in the New Zealand parliament, her husband sold the family farm and took over the care of the couple's two children. He returned to school and eventually got a job as a business development manager for a bank although he continued to accompany his wife to various functions.

Among the domestic arrangements that did not meet Thatcher's conditions was that of Golda Meir, who early on encountered difficulty in meshing career and family. First, she and her husband did not share the same goals; and, secondly, the family did not have the resources to hire household help. In fact, their financial situation was such that Meir had to work to keep the family afloat.

Meir met her future husband, Morris Meyerson, a Jewish emigre from Lithuania who was five or six years older than she, while staying with her sister in Denver. Morris was a quiet, sensitive man who had read widely though he had little formal education and who loved poetry, art, and music. He suggested things for her to read and also took her to concerts when he was able to get enough money from his small wages as a sign painter. His knowledge of things about which she knew very little as well as his gentle manner attracted her. Following a somewhat turbulent courtship, conducted partially by mail after her return to Milwaukee, they were married on December 24, 1917. While Morris was not a Zionist, he agreed to go to Palestine as she made this a condition for their marriage.

When they had saved sufficient funds, the Meyersons left for Palestine, but the romantic visions of the pioneer existence soon gave way to the harsh realities of life in a developing land. Before leaving the United States, the young couple had decided to seek entrance to a kibbutz. Since they had a friend living in Merhavia, they applied to that community and were accepted despite the reluctance to admit an American girl in the belief that she would not be able to manage the hard work.

Life in the kibbutz appealed to Golda, and she responded favorably to its egalitarian thrust. She enjoyed living closely with other people, most of whom shared her views on political and social issues and were just as intense as she was about them. On the other hand, Morris did not take well to the new life with its lack of privacy. As a result of his recurring illnesses, the couple left Merhavia in 1923 and moved to Tel Aviv. Golda worked as a cashier in the Histadrut's Public Works and Building Office, later named Solel Boneh, but neither she nor Morris was happy in Tel Aviv. She wished to return to the kibbutz, but Morris's recovery was very slow. Eventually they moved to Jerusalem where they both worked in the public works office.

Following the birth of their son Menachem in November 1924, Golda and the baby returned to the kibbutz, but they remained only a few months as she still hoped to make her marriage work. In May 1926 a daughter Sarah was born. Meir described the period between 1924 and 1928 as the most burdensome in her life. Morris continued to work as a bookkeeper in the Jerusalem branch of Solel Boneh, but he did not receive anything like adequate wages for his growing family, and Meir was tied down with household chores. In return for her son's tuition at nursery school, she washed the clothes of the other children in his class, and she also taught English in a private school.

Meir was not playing the role she had visualized for herself, and the relationship with her husband became increasingly strained. During one of her frequent trips to Tel Aviv, she was asked to become secretary of the Histadrut's Moetzet Hapoalot (Women's Labor Council). Recognizing that her marriage was a failure and being keenly interested in becoming more involved in the activities of the fledgling Jewish community in Palestine, she accepted the position. She and the children moved to Tel Aviv with Morris joining them for weekends. The final break in the marriage came in 1940 although the couple never divorced.

While the conditions laid out by Thatcher may be necessary for a woman to combine marriage, children, and a career, they are not sufficient to ensure her doing so successfully. Indira Gandhi and her husband, Feroze, shared a strong commitment to the cause of Indian independence, and though the Nehrus had made financial sacrifices for their political participation, they were not without adequate resources. But as Gandhi became increasingly involved in working with her father, her marriage faltered.

Indira early on had made the decision not to marry since she believed that having a family would interfere with her work in the struggle for independence. When she did decide to marry, she said, "I just did not think out things any more. I just got married."[9] She remarked on another occasion that had it not been for her desire to have children she might not have married.

After her mother's death in 1936, Indira found a sympathetic companion in Feroze Gandhi, a self-confident and assertive young man, who first proposed marriage to her when she was 16 because of a fear that a union with someone else might be arranged. Feroze, who was not related to Mahatma Gandhi, had been a friend and political ally of the Nehrus for many years and helped care for Kamala during her final illness. Indira remarked that one reason she chose to enroll at Oxford was because Feroze was a student at the London School of Economics. After she moved to England, she spent considerable time with him, and he courted her seriously.

There was little to keep Indira in England after she quit her studies at Oxford, and in 1941 she and Feroze sailed for India. She was eager to be with her father and take part in the political work. Shortly after their return to India, the young couple, who had become secretly engaged while in Europe, announced their intention to marry.

The Nehru family initially opposed the marriage. Undoubtedly reflecting on the early conflict in his own marriage, Nehru expressed concern that Indira and Feroze came from such different backgrounds. The fact that Feroze was a Parsi[10] while the Nehrus were Brahmin Hindus did not trouble him, but the fact that Feroze had grown up in a modest lower middle-class home did.

Indira persisted in her decision, and the young couple were married in 1942. Both became involved in the independence struggle, spending some time in prison. On their release from jail in 1943 they returned to *Anand Bhavan*, and Feroze sold insurance and did some freelance writing. On August 20, 1944 their son Rajiv was born. In 1946, the family moved to Lucknow where Feroze became the managing director of *The National Herald*, the paper founded by Nehru, and in December of that year a second son, Sanjay, was born. After Nehru became prime minister, Gandhi believed that her father needed her, and her husband did not object to her commuting between Lucknow and Delhi. Initially her primary responsibility was that of hostess for her father. She did not particularly enjoy the duties, for she remarked that she "hated the thought of housekeeping and what I hated most was to be hostess at a party, as I always disliked parties and having to smile when one doesn't want to."[11]

Gandhi became increasingly valuable to her father over the years as his health weakened and her political skills sharpened. In describing this period of her life, she said: "At first it was only a question of setting up a home for my father in New Delhi and coping with the social obligations of the prime minister's house. But gradually circumstances and my own intense interest in the path that the country was trying to follow drew me deeper into public affairs."[12] A friend of the Nehrus suggested that Gandhi was motivated to work with her father as she wished to take advantage of the atmosphere surrounding his office.[13]

While Gandhi refused to seek office herself, saying that her children and her father needed her, Feroze was elected to the parliament from Rae Bareli in 1951. He joined his family in New Delhi and moved into the prime minister's house, but he felt insecure in this setting. His boisterous manner was a sharp contrast to that of the aristocratic Nehrus. Considered a very astute politician, Feroze eventually took up residence in a house provided to him as a member of the parliament although he visited his family daily.

Feroze apparently did not feel threatened by his wife's having a career, for as Gandhi observed to an interviewer: "I wouldn't have gone into public life if he had said no. But I am so intense in whatever I do, he must have been frightened to have it all concentrated on him.

He wanted me occupied." She went on to say that "when I went into public life, and became successful, he liked it and he didn't like it. Other people—friends, relatives—were the worst. They would say, 'How does it feel, being so-and-so's husband?' He would get upset, and it would take me weeks to win him over. To hurt the male ego is, of course, the biggest sin in marriage."[14]

The couple's relationship, which Gandhi described as turbulent, also suffered because of Feroze's romantic involvement with a number of different women through the years.[15] Despite the conflicts, the couple continued to feel affection for one another. In a letter written in 1955, Gandhi expressed some regrets about her strained marriage when she wrote: "I have been and am deeply unhappy in my domestic life. Now, the hurt and the unpleasantness don't seem to matter so much. I am sorry, though, to have missed the most wonderful thing in life, having a complete and perfect relationship with another human being: for only thus, I feel, can one's personality fully develop and blossom."[16]

Feroze suffered a heart attack and died in September 1960. Gandhi later remarked in an interview that "toward the end, we were... becoming very close."[17] In a letter written shortly after Feroze's death, she spoke of feelings of despair and depression. She wrote that "up till now I had somebody to whom I could pour out my thoughts—even if there was a lack of attention and sympathy—and with the removal of that outlet I have to look outward."[18]

Ambivalence about Marriage and Family

Because of the difficulties of combining marriage, a family, and a political career, some women who reached the top expressed doubts about the ability of a woman to handle a job given her family responsibilities. For example, Golda Meir in an article written anonymously in 1930 for *The Plough Woman*, a collection of memoirs, said: "The mother... suffers in the very work she has taken up. Always she has the feeling that her work is not as productive as that of a man, or even of an unmarried woman. The children, too, always demand her in health, and even more in sickness. And... this double pull, this alternating feeling of unfulfilled duty—today toward her family, the next day toward her work—this is the burden of the working mother."[19]

Since women have been expected to bear the major responsibility for the care of children, some of those women who have pursued a political career have reported feelings of guilt. Thatcher acknowledged that she felt guilty about the amount of time she was away from the twins and later remarked that "you live for them as you've never lived for anyone else...and yet, I knew that I had something else to give."[20] When she decided to seek a parliamentary seat, she insisted upon serving a constituency near London to reduce the need for frequent travel, and when she entered parliament, she gave up her legal practice. While many members of parliament hold outside employment, she did not believe that it was appropriate to have what would amount to a third career given her domestic responsibilities.

Gandhi who had initially planned to devote full time to her family in view of her own unstable childhood indicated that "to a mother her children must always come first, because they depend on her in a very special way. The main problem in my life was, therefore, how to reconcile my public obligations with my responsibility towards my home and my children."[21] In an apparent attempt to deal with the dilemma, she observed: "It was not the amount of time spent with the children that matters as much as the manner of spending it...No matter how busy I have been, or how tired or even unwell, I have taken time out to play and read with my sons."[22]

Since Meir represented the Histadrut Council at international conferences and also took part in fundraising activities, she often found it necessary to be away from home. In her autobiography, she commented on the effect of these absences on her two children when she wrote: "I am not sure that I didn't harm the children or neglect them, despite the efforts I made not to be away from them even an hour more than was strictly necessary. They grew up to be healthy, productive, talented, and good people...But when they were growing up, I knew that they deeply resented my activities outside our home."[23] In a biography of Meir written by her son, he described the bitterness he had harbored toward his mother as a child.[24]

Occasionally Meir left Menachem and Sarah in the care of her sister Sheyna and her mother, as her parents had immigrated to Palestine in 1926, but, for the most part, her family provided little support. Instead, they argued she was neglecting her children. In the article for *The Plough Woman*, Meir perhaps described herself when she wrote that "there is a type of woman who cannot remain at home...In spite of the place her children and her family take up in her life, her nature and being demand something more; she cannot divorce herself from a larger social life. She cannot let her children narrow her horizon. And for such a woman, there is no rest."[25]

Lusia Diogo of Mozambique acknowledged that she was so involved with her work that she spent little time with her three children. In speaking about her feelings of guilt she stressed a single episode. It seems she left her three-month-old daughter in the care of others to attend a two-week meeting in France in 1995 with officials of the International Monetary Fund—a gathering that was critical for her country's future course.

Even women who have not married and do not have the responsibility for the care of a home and children are subject to doubts as to their suitability for political office. By not marrying, a woman fails to pursue the course expected of her, and she is likely to be viewed with some suspicion. Commenting on the reason for the repeated inquires by journalists as to why she was not married, Benazir Bhutto, who remained single until she was in her 30s, indicated that she thought their curiosity reflected a belief that there must be something wrong with a woman who was not married, especially "in a Muslim society, where marriage was regarded as the fruition of a man and a woman's life."[26]

Bhutto was concerned that the fact she was not married would hurt her political career, but since she was the subject of considerable public scrutiny, it was difficult for her to establish a serious relationship. Like Sirimavo Bandaranaike of Sri Lanka and Khaleda Zia of Bangladesh as well as many young people in South Asia, she followed a tradition that had been recognized for centuries and consented to a marriage arranged by her family.

Asif Zardari, who had attended school in England, was the son of a prominent land-owning family. Like the Bhuttos, the Zardaris had a record of political activity. Asif's father had served as vice president of a small political party closely associated with the Bhuttos' Pakistan People's Party, and Asif had intended to seek office in the election scheduled for 1985 although it was boycotted by the opposition because of a ban on political parties.

An issue that had to be resolved before an engagement could be announced was whether Asif would support a wife's political career. Following conversations between various members of the two families as well as meetings between the couple, a decision was made to go ahead with plans for a wedding despite Asif's reputation as a playboy. The 1987 wedding that took place only a few months after the attractive young couple became engaged was a lavish affair. The political advantage to be garnered from such a celebration was not overlooked, and the elaborate, lengthy Muslim ceremony was followed by a large reception for Bhutto's political supporters.

Helen Clark eventually accepted the notion that the fact she was not married would damage her political career. She did not want to marry and was not interested in having children, but she gave into the pressure from the leaders of her party and married her partner of five years, Peter Davis, a medical sociologist. Though Davis encouraged his wife, he made few appearances with her, and the couple lived quite separate lives. Clark remarked a number of years later that had civil union been an option, she would never have married.

It took a bit of persuading from the archbishop of Cologne to the effect that Angela Merkel's political career might suffer if she did not formalize her relationship with her partner, Joachim Sauer, a chemistry professor at Humbodlt University. The two married in 1998. It was the second marriage for both who had met while working at the Academy of Sciences in the former East Germany.[27] The couple did not have children, but Merkel's husband had two sons by his previous marriage.

Among the leaders who remained single were Eugenia Charles of Dominica, Maria de Lourdes Pintasilgo of Portugal, Ruth Dreifuss of Switzerland, Hanna Suchocka of Poland, Agatha Barbara of Malta, and Beatriz Merino of Peru. Charles, who was criticized because she did not have children, said, "I just never found anybody I could imagine spending the rest of my life with."[28] She noted an advantage to her being single when she said that "it's harder for women who have families to take the flack, because it spreads out to their husbands, to their children, and so I think I'm fortunate to have so few relatives."[29]

Pintasilgo, who remarked that her aides did not like the fact that she was single,[30] said that as a young woman she believed that she would eventually marry. She pointed to an advantage of the single state when she observed in an interview that since she had chosen the celibate life, it was possible for her to have "relationships with many different persons, not tied up to a privileged relationship with one person."[31] Dreifuss pointed to another advantage of being single when she said: "I managed to obtain a good education over the years and could compete with men because I didn't have to prove I was a good mother and a good housewife at the same time."[32] When asked whether she had any regrets about not having a family, Agatha Barbara replied "none at all. I realized I couldn't have everything, but I also knew that whichever path I took there would be ups and downs. I accepted that."[33]

Husbands as Political Liabilities

There was much joy surrounding Bhutto's marriage, but she was soon to discover that a husband may become a political liability. When her government was dismissed in 1990 on grounds of incompetence and corruption, it was widely believed that her husband had taken advantage of her position to foster his business interests. Zardari was known as "Mr. 10 Percent" because of the cut he allegedly got for facilitating deals made with the government. In the midst of the election campaign that followed Bhutto's dismissal, her husband was arrested and charged with, among other things, kidnapping and extortion. Though he was acquitted after his wife was reelected in 1993, he had spent close to two and one-half years in prison, only to return on a variety of charges after she was again forced out of office in 1996.

Despite Zardari's assertions that he intended to be less visible during his wife's second term, he continued to be a lightning rod for criticism leveled by the opposition as well as by many within Bhutto's own party. Zardari sought to answer his critics when he told an interviewer that "by nature I am an active individual, so I feel I get more in the limelight." But he went on to say, "the fact that I happen to be the husband of the prime minister gives me some stature...for instance, in protocol I am No. 4. Whether somebody likes it or not, there is nothing you can do about it."[34]

The military offered on several occasions to release her husband if she would remove herself from the political scene, but she refused to agree to such a bargain. In an interview, she commented on these overtures when she said that "this is the view that I have spent a quarter of a century fighting. They think women are extensions of men and they think that a woman can be got through her husband."[35]

In private, Megawati Sukarnoputri of Indonesia described her husband as the "Bhutto factor."[36] Taufiq Keimas, who along with his wife owned a chain of gas stations, drew suspicion because of his role in business deals in which government contracts were involved. He had a close relationship with troubled companies seeking government assistance, but he vigorously denied engaging in any improprieties. A savvy politician and an effective power broker in his party, Taufiq was Megawati's third husband. Her first was an air force lieutenant who was killed in a plane crash, and a brief second marriage to an Egyptian diplomat was annulled. Taufiq, who had been a student activist in support of Sukarno, had spent some time in jail. He was supportive of his wife's decision to seek political office and helped pave the way for her move up the political ladder by using his party connections.[37] He had successfully sought a seat in parliament at the same election that marked Megawati's entry into politics.

As the presidential election of 2004 neared, Taufiq Kiemas played an active role in building bridges with leaders of other parties, including Wahid whom Megawati had replaced after his impeachment. To make up for her lack of attention to party business, the executive committee of the Indonesian Democratic Party (PDIP) suggested that Taufiq assume the role of deputy party leader. Although he declined, he continued to hold a seat in parliament.

Mike Arroyo, President Gloria Arroyo's husband, was accused of extensive interference in his wife's administration, including involvement in questionable business dealings with government agencies. Perhaps sensitive to her husband's propensity to involve himself in politics, President Arroyo announced at the onset of her term of office that if one were "looking for a job in my administration don't course it through my husband because what ever he promised would go directly to the trash can."[38] Despite her initial resolve, Arroyo appointed some of her husband's business associates to government positions.

Mike Arroyo, who initially forbade his wife to work outside the home but later used his considerable wealth to help finance her campaigns for political office, said that it was time for him "to remain on the sidelines and preferably disappear from the public scene."[39] He defined his role by indicating that he would devote himself to charity work. Despite these intentions, Arroyo, a lawyer who oversaw the family business, served as a lightning rod for his wife's administration. Among a variety of scandals in which it was rumored he played a role was one in which he was accused of accepting a bribe in exchange for getting his wife to rescind her veto of a telecommunications franchise bill. In view of insufficient evidence, this matter was dropped after the president ordered an investigation into the matter.

Although he promised to stay out of politics, Arroyo remained active on his wife's behalf, engaging in grass roots organization of *Kaibigan ni* (Friends of) GMA as well as in talks aimed at a new coalition of regional parties to provide her a platform for the 2004 presidential election.[40] But President Arroyo announced that unlike her 1998 campaign for vice president, Mike would not accompany her on the campaign trail.[41]

When allegations were made in 2005 that Arroyo's husband as well as her son, who held a parliamentary seat, had received kickbacks from gamblers, both were sent abroad. Arroyo already had too much on her plate in dealing with claims of fraud in the 2004 presidential election. Secretly recorded tapes had revealed the president appeared to be trying to influence an election official before the release of the results.

The business dealings of Tansu Ciller and her husband came under scrutiny after she entered politics. Ozer, who assumed his wife's surname, since she was an only child and her father was concerned to perpetuate the family name, amassed a fortune valued at $50 million in a variety of business and financial dealings over the years. In attempting to explain the source of their wealth, the couple said that they inherited money from her mother—an explanation rejected by many who insisted that her mother was a relatively poor woman. More specifically, after Ciller became prime minister, questions were raised about steps she took in awarding government contracts that served to benefit companies in which the couple had an interest. Also, there was concern expressed about investments the Cillers made in the United States at a time when it was the policy of her government to encourage investment in Turkey.

In contrast, Margaret Thatcher's husband was determined to stay in the background. He noted shortly after Margaret was elected leader of the Conservative Party in 1975 that many regarded him as "the most shadowy husband of all time. I intend to stay that way and leave the limelight to my wife."[42] Although on one occasion, Denis Thatcher used official stationery to write to a Welch official seeking special treatment for a business friend, for the most part, he stuck to his determination to remain outside the political fray and avoid controversy.

There were times when Denis felt overwhelmed by the demands on Margaret, especially when she first became prime minister. Though he continued to be supportive of her, he pursued his interests in sports and maintained his own circle of friends to keep a life separate from that of his wife.

Denis Thatcher's approach to his responsibilities as the husband of a political leader has become the standard, so much so that when his wife became prime minister of France, Jacques Cresson, a retired automobile executive, indicated that he was joining the Denis Thatcher club.[43]

The husband of Angela Merkel, Joachim Sauer, proved to be the most detached from the political life of his wife, having made it clear that he had no intention of playing the usual role of a political spouse.[44] It took eight months following her election before he made his first public appearance with his wife, having failed even to attend her inauguration. The two chose to live in an apartment in Berlin rather than in the official chancellor's residence.

Even minor indiscretions on the part of a husband may prove detrimental to a political leader. The husband of Luisa Diogo,

Albano Silva, who was a lawyer, was accused of bribing a team investigating a fraud case involving the Mozambique Commercial Bank. Silva had been hired by the bank to monitor the investigation, and he allegedly gave approximately $1,000 to the team, a gift that he described as a Christmas present.

Although he was preoccupied with his career as an academic and remained out of the political limelight, Peter Davis, Helen Clark's husband, created a minor embarrassment for his wife when on two occasions, if nothing else, he used poor judgment. In early 2001, he sent an e-mail message for a friend via his wife's office to the health ministry about an appointment as a reviewer. Later that same year he received a contract from the Health Research Council to study the effects of recent health reforms. Though he was qualified to conduct the study, there was an appearance of impropriety. Clark was not only prime minister at the time of the award but had served as health minister during a portion of the period that was to be examined. The opposition took the government to task for permitting these lapses in judgment. Clark was especially vulnerable to such attacks as she had promised to run a government above reproach.

Sheikh Hasina's husband also created an embarrassing situation for his wife when he went public with the couple's marital difficulties. Though there were rumors pointing to serious disagreements in the marriage, it was only after Hasina refused to extend her husband's term of office as head of the Bangladesh Atomic Energy Commission that relations became severely strained. Wajed Mia said that his wife, whom he described as half educated, was not fit to lead the country. He held her responsible for the country's poor showing and bemoaned the fact that she did not even listen to him.[45] The conflict led to a separation, with Wajed Mia moving out of the official residence, but the couple was eventually reunited.

Ertha Pascal-Trouillot discovered that even after a husband has died, his actions may affect her political career. When she completed her legal studies, Pascal-Trouillot married Ernst Trouillot, her former teacher and mentor, who was 22 years older than she. She joined his law practice and the two of them coauthored several books, including one on the judicial status of the Haitian women in social legislation. After she became provisional president, questions were raised about the connection of her husband, who had died some three years earlier, to Duvalier, the former dictator of Haiti. The speculation about possible benefits he may have derived from his association with Duvalier undermined support for her, making the task of overseeing the election more difficult.

Divorce and Widowhood

Although divorce has been viewed in many settings as an obstacle to a political career for a man as well as a woman, some of those women who have risen to the top were divorced. In fact, Lydia Gueiler of Bolivia and Kim Campbell of Canada had been married and divorced twice before they assumed the top post. Gueiler's first husband was a Paraguayan rancher, and her second, Edwin Moller, was a political activist. Gueiler followed Moller's lead and became a founding member of a leftist political party, but she eventually separated from this second husband whose interest in politics had begun to wane.

Kim Campbell, whose first husband was her mentor during her days as an undergraduate at the University of British Columbia, was in the process of getting a divorce from her second husband when she was appointed to head the Canadian defense ministry in 1993. Howard Eddy, an attorney, had moved to Ottawa with his wife after she was elected to a parliamentary seat in 1988, but the couple separated approximately three years later. In a speech made shortly before her appointment to the position at defense, Campbell commented on the difficulties in combining marriage and a political career when she said: "[I]n the course of my life in Ottawa my marriage has ended and I'm very far from home. I find life here often unspeakably lonely and very difficult."[46] She noted that the problem was widespread as most of her female colleagues were single or divorced.

Also divorced was Vigdis Finnbogadottir, who had married a college friend. After approximately nine years of marriage, the couple separated in 1962. In commenting on why it was possible for her to be elected president despite the fact that she was divorced, Vigdis said that she thought the people of Iceland were able to accept a single woman since there had always been so many widows in a country dependent on the seas.[47]

While she did not have a husband, Vigdis did have a young daughter whom she had adopted several years after separating from her husband, but little mention was made during the campaign of the fact that she was a single parent. In an interview, she remarked to a reporter that she thought "people liked it that I had the eccentricity to adopt a child as a single woman."[48]

Both the women who assumed the presidency in 2006 without the benefit of a relationship to a prominent politician were separated. Ellen Johnson Sirleaf, whose ex husband died after the couple was divorced, had four children with her husband. Michelle Bachelet married an architect whom she met while the two of them were living in East

Germany. The couple had a child, and Bachelet had two more children, the last of whom was a result of a relationship with a fellow physician.

The widow of a politically prominent male is not likely to be subjected to the same scrutiny as a woman who has never married or one who is divorced since it is the widow's marital status that made her an asset to her party. But she is likely to face questions concerning the effect of her situation on her ability to lead her country, especially if she has young children. During Bandaranaike's first election campaign, opposition spokesmen argued that as a woman her place was in the home with her children. The widow has another advantage in that the sense of duty to a husband's work may serve to absolve her from the guilt she might otherwise feel about her family.

Conclusions

Combining marriage, children, and the demands of a political career with its long and irregular hours is difficult, particularly for women, who have been expected to take the major role in child rearing and housekeeping. The tasks of caring for a home and young children tend not only to be all-consuming but also isolating from the affairs of the community. The problem associated with finding a way of balancing these responsibilities is often given as to why so few women have entered the political arena. In addition, those women who pursued a political career have historically entered politics when they were somewhat older than the male politicians, making it more difficult for them to acquire the experience necessary to rise to the top.[49]

A supportive family, especially a husband who shares his wife's goals, is important for a successful political career, but a husband may also be a liability if he has political ambitions of his own. The business interests of husbands may also clash with their wives' responsibilities.

The husbands of Bhutto, Ciller, Diogo, Arroyo, and Megawati, who shared an interest in politics with their wives, were at the peak of their own careers when the wives reached the top. Several of these men were charged with corruption and Bhutto's husband spent time in jail. A husband who is retired and has interests that are not threatening to the wife's position may be ideal for a woman with political ambitions.

Chapter Eight
Early Political Experience

While attending the annual Conservative Party conference in 1948 as a representative of the Oxford Graduate Association, Margaret Thatcher met a friend from her days at the university, John Grant, who remarked that she must be interested in being a member of parliament some day. She responded by noting that there was little chance of that happening and that she had not even made an effort to get on her party's list of approved candidates. Later Grant, while sitting next to the chairman of the Dartford Conservative Association, observed that the district was still looking for a candidate, and the chairman responded by asking if Grant had any suggestions. As Thatcher tells the story, Grant replied, " 'Well, there's a young woman, Margaret Roberts, that you might look at. She's very good.' 'Oh, but Dartford is a real industrial stronghold. I don't think a woman would do at all.' 'Well, you know best of course. But why not just look at her?' "[1]

After several interviews Thatcher was chosen to represent Dartford, defeating more than 20 men. Although some of the members on the committee responsible for making the choice argued against the selection of a woman, the constituency had been unable to persuade those men it would have preferred to stand.

After she was selected, Thatcher moved to Dartford, taking a job at J. Lyons as a food research chemist, so that she would have more time to solicit votes. She launched a vigorous campaign, spending most evenings canvassing or attending meetings and preparing for the next day's activities despite the fact that the seat was safely in the Labor Party column. Because of her gender and age, Thatcher received considerable press coverage, and although she lost the election in 1950, she succeeded in increasing the Conservative Party vote by 50 percent while reducing that of the Labor candidate by a third. The Dartford constituency was so impressed with her efforts that she was asked to seek the seat again in the 1951 general election.

Thatcher, who began her search for a safe seat following the completion of her legal studies, had to wait another eight years before she was able to secure the nomination for a safe Conservative seat. In the meantime, she made appearances on behalf of the Conservative

Central Office. As a fairly attractive woman, she was considered useful for television as well as speech-making engagements despite the fact that she seemed a bit stiff in her television performances and had a high pitched voice.

In 1959, Thatcher was nominated for the seat from Finchley, a prosperous suburb northwest of London. The selection committee weeded through some 200 candidates, leaving four finalists. Despite the fact that some on the committee believed she should stay at home and take care of her children, Thatcher, who had the support of the younger members of the party, was chosen on the second ballot. She easily won the seat in the October general election, polling more than 53 percent of the vote.

Getting Started in Politics

Although women historically played a role in the work of political parties, their efforts were not often rewarded as were Thatcher's by an opportunity to run for a safe, or at least a winnable, seat in the national legislative body. Within the larger party their responsibilities were confined to clerical tasks and fund raising, making it difficult for them to develop the skills important for elective office or to make the contacts necessary to facilitate a successful run for office. Their activity was more often than not channeled through special divisions, and few women were able to parlay such participation into a candidacy for high public office.

An exception was Golda Meir who began her public career in 1928 with the Women's Labor Council. She served as secretary of the council that was concerned with the training of young immigrant women for agricultural work. Four years later, she and her children went to the United States to represent the Council with the Pioneer Women—an assignment she requested to obtain medical help for her daughter who was quite ill at the time. Meir remained in the United States for two years, making speeches and spreading the story of Palestine in an attempt to raise funds and recruit new members for the Pioneer Women, but a separate role for women in the labor movement was difficult for her to accept. She took the equality of the sexes for granted, especially in so far as work was concerned—a view that formed a part of the ideology of the Jewish pioneers in Palestine.

After her return to Palestine in 1934, Meir's work with women's political organizations came to an end as she was asked to join the Executive Committee of the Histadrut, the governing body for Jews in

Palestine. During the years that followed, she held a variety of posts, ranging from director of the tourist department to head of the mutual aid department and, finally, to head of the political department.

Another woman who early on in her political career participated in a women's division was Helen Clark of New Zealand. Clark joined the Labor Party in 1971 and took part in a variety of party activities, serving for a brief period as secretary of the Labor Women's Council. Her first run for parliament, like that of Thatcher, was in a district that was safe for her opponent's party. In 1981, some six years later, she was successful in her bid for a parliamentary seat.

For Edith Cresson the performance of menial tasks on behalf of a candidate eventually led to public office. Cresson got her start in politics during the 1965 presidential contest when she worked in the campaign of Francois Mitterrand. While Mitterrand was not successful in his efforts to capture the presidency, Cresson acquired a mentor. Mitterrand was impressed with her energy and intelligence and brought her into his circle of advisers. Following a second unsuccessful run for the presidency in 1974, he sponsored her nomination for membership in the Socialist Party. Shortly thereafter she was named secretary for youth organization, but she served in this capacity only a few months before beginning her career in elected political office.

It is not surprising that several women who rose to the top got their start in local government since much of the work at this level is related to "women's issues," such as education and health. Also, the fact that these positions were not paid particularly well may have made them less attractive to men.

In 1980 Kim Campbell, as a first year law student, successfully sought a seat on the Vancouver school board. After she graduated, she joined a law firm, promising to give up her seat on the board, but her political ambitions held sway and within weeks she entered the contest for a seat in the provincial legislature. She lost her bid for office, but the practice of law was no longer of interest to her. At the invitation of the premier of British Columbia she joined his staff. In 1986, she made a second and this time successful run for a provincial legislative seat. At the urging of party leaders, some two years later she entered the parliamentary election campaign. Since she had recently married for a second time, she was reluctant to seek higher office, but when she heard the opposition party candidate criticize the pending trade agreement designed to bolster trade between the United States and Canada, she decided to enter the contest. She waged an aggressive campaign and won the seat by a narrow margin.

Another woman who got her start in local politics was Jenny Shipley. As a young New Zealand homemaker, who had a record of activity in community service, Shipley ran for the county council in 1983 and was victorious. Some four years later she successfully sought a seat in the parliament. Ruth Dreifuss of Switzerland, who worked as a journalist and had some experience as a civil servant as well as a trade union official before she entered the political arena, also began her career in politics at the local level as a member of the Municipal Council of Bern.

Despite the reluctance of party leaders to nominate women for high office, some of the women leaders, like Thatcher, got their start by winning a seat in the national legislative body. As a member of the Democratic Party (SD), a political organization tolerated by the communist government in Poland, Hanna Suchocka was elected to the *Sejm* or lower house in 1980. She had refused to join the Communist Party, because, as she later told an interviewer, she wanted "the freedom to go to church" since she "was authentically raised in this."[2] Following the collapse of communist rule in 1989, Suchocka was chosen to seek a parliamentary seat by the political division of Solidarity. She was reelected in 1991 as a member of the Democratic Union, a small left of center party.

With a successful career in business behind her, Yulia Tymoshenko, who was appointed prime minister of Ukraine in 2005, successfully sought political office in 1996. She had founded a video rental chain and served as director of several energy-related companies, attaining considerable wealth. In her initial venture into politics, she won a seat in the parliament and was reelected in 1998 and 2002. Tymoshenko was motivated to enter politics to work against government interference in corporate affairs. An oil company she owned was fined more than $300 million for violating currency legislation.[3] While in parliament she chaired the budget committee and served as deputy prime minister for fuel. But her career was not without its bumps. She was dismissed and arrested on corruption charges in 2001 but was later released. She argued that the accusations were politically motivated, saying that the coal industry had felt threatened by her attempt to deal with corruption.

Nino Burdzhanadze got her start in politics when she sought a seat in the Georgia parliament in 1995. She held a number of important posts before she was selected as speaker of that body. Among these were the chair of the committee on cooperation with the European Community, chair of the committee on foreign affairs, and chair of the committee on legal affairs.

Beatriz Merino, a latecomer to politics, achieved her first elected political position in her early 40s when she served as a senator (1990–1992), and subsequently as a member of Congress (1995–2000). She came to office as a technocrat, from time to time practicing tax law. Just before her appointment as prime minister she headed Peru's tax collection agency, receiving plaudits for her success in raising revenue and for her management of a generally corrupt and inefficient organization.

Unlike most of the women who served as ceremonial leaders, Agatha Barbara began her career in politics when she successfully sought a parliamentary seat in 1947, having joined Malta's Labor Party the previous year. Mary Robinson got her start by winning a seat in the Irish parliament, but in the upper or less powerful of the two houses. Though she did not have a record of service to a political party, she was elected by the graduates of Trinity College to represent the college in the Senate. A few years later she joined the relatively small Labor Party and in 1977 and again in 1981 unsuccessfully sought a parliamentary seat.

Other women got their start in politics because they possessed knowledge or skills important for a government and were called upon to consult on specific issues or serve in an appointive position. For example, Tansu Ciller, an economics professor who had taught in both the United States and Turkey, made her debut on the periphery of the political arena by serving as a consultant to various governmental entities, such as the State Planning Organization and the Istanbul Metropolitan Municipality. She first captured the attention of political leaders when she prepared a lengthy report commissioned by the Turkish Association of Industrialists and Businessmen critical of the economic policy pursued by the government led by the Motherland Party. The leader of the opposition True Path Party took advantage of Ciller's visibility and invited her to join his party. She accepted and became a member of the executive board and its deputy chair.

The civil service provided yet another entree to higher office as those trained in business, economics, law, and science were recruited because of their skills. Before she entered the political arena, Maria Pintasilgo worked as a researcher with a government agency and later, an industrial complex. She took a leadership role in various Catholic organizations such as the Graal, a movement of Catholic women concerned with rural development. Pintasilgo's political career got underway on a controversial note. Before the 1974 revolution that ended dictatorial rule in Portugal, she was appointed to a quasi-legislative body, many of whose members were selected by the regime. She was able to overcome this blemish on her record, serving as secretary of state for social security, minister of social affairs, and ambassador to UNESCO in subsequent governments.

Luisa Diogo of Mozambique began her career in the finance ministry where she worked for a number of years. A brief stint as a World Bank official followed, and she ultimately returned to head her country's finance ministry. Sylvie Kinigi of Burundi held a number of civil service posts, eventually becoming senior consultant in the prime minister's office. Maria das Neves of Sao Tomé and Principe worked as an economist for the national civil service, the World Bank, and UNICEF. She was also active in politics and later joined the cabinet, becoming minister for trade, industry, and tourism.

After Anneli Jaatteenmaki of Finland completed her legal studies in 1980, she held a number of civil service positions. In 1987, she became a member of parliament, serving as speaker when she was elected prime minister. Jatteenmaki's only cabinet experience was as head of the ministry of justice in 1994–1995.

Some women began their political career as heads of government departments. For example, Gro Brundtland, whose political career began in 1974 when she was appointed Norwegian minister of environmental affairs, came to the attention of the leaders of her party while a member of the public health service. She had become caught up in family planning issues and had spoken out in favor of liberalizing the abortion laws. She later told an interviewer that she "became furious...and I just felt an obligation as a professional, and as a woman and a politically concerned person, to start writing in the press...I used the true stories of all the women I had been seeing [who needed abortions]...those conservatives' arguments could not stand against reality."[4]

Despite the attention she attracted, Brundtland noted she was surprised when asked to join the cabinet, saying that she had not seen herself as a politician before becoming one.[5] She acknowledged that her gender played a role in her appointment when she said "it was quite clear that the Prime Minister [who was a friend of her father's] was looking for a woman...because the Minister of Health and Social Affairs who had been a woman had died that summer...."[6]

Two other women who began their political careers as ministers were Ellen Johnson Sirleaf of Liberia and Michelle Bachelet of Chile. Sirleaf, who had extensive experience as an international civil servant, got her start in politics in the 1970s, serving as finance minister in the government of President William Tolbert—a position she resigned over what she considered excessive government spending. She was also highly critical of the Samuel Doe government that came to power after the 1980 coup. Following her arrest and subsequent release, Sirleaf went into exile, returning to seek the Liberian presidency in 1997, but she lost out to the controversial figure, Charles Taylor.

Bachelet was working as a pediatrician in a clinic in 2000 when she was invited by the popular President Ricardo Lagos to serve as health minister. Two years later she was appointed defense minister, a move that put her in line for consideration of a run at the top post. Bachelet was a beneficiary of the president's quota system in which he had called for the naming of five women as cabinet ministers.

Some women inadvertently laid the groundwork for a political career by participating in community affairs. As a school administrator, Maria Liberia-Peters organized parents' groups for political action. Given the visibility this effort provided, she was approached by leaders of her party, urging her to become more active and suggesting that it was through politics that she could "really bring about changes." At first she was skeptical of their overtures, indicating that she could do her best work "away from politics," but after further reflection she decided to "see what it's all about."[7] She entered the political fray in 1976 by successfully seeking a seat on the council of Curacao, one of the islands that made up the Netherlands Antilles. In 1982, she won a seat in the *Staten* or national legislative body.

Beginning in the 1950s, Eugenia Charles, who did not belong to a political party, attracted attention when she wrote letters to the local newspaper challenging government actions. Some years later, the Dominica government moved to curtail such provocations by passing sedition legislation. Charles responded by joining with other protesters to form the Freedom Fighters, and she addressed numerous gatherings. When the group failed in its mission, the members founded the Dominica Freedom Party (DFP). Because of her skills in public speaking and debate, Charles was asked to lead the right-of-center party, and she reluctantly agreed.

Despite intense campaigning in the months that followed, the DFP did not fare well in the election held in 1970, winning only two seats. Charles herself was defeated, but she joined the House of Assembly as an appointed member. In the election held five years later, her party made few gains, but Charles won a seat and became leader of the opposition.

Finally, some women got their start in politics by taking part in a revolutionary or resistance movement. By placing her livelihood and, in some cases her life, at risk, a participant is likely to ensure herself a role in any newly created political structure. Among those leaders who took part in such movements were Lydia Gueiler of Bolivia and Milka Planinc of Yugoslavia. Gueiler participated in the underground movement, the precursor to the 1952 revolution.[8] Following a strike at the Central Bank where she had worked during the early 1940s, Gueiler lost her job, because it was believed she was a member of a leftist political party. She denied any such affiliation but noted that "when I was accused of being a militant, I was motivated to find out what it was all about, and that is how I got started."[9]

Following the three-day-long insurrection orchestrated by the left, Gueiler served as the secretary to the president. She gradually moved into a leadership position, and in 1956 she became the first woman to be elected to the Bolivian congress. The military returned to power in 1964, and Gueiler spent much of the next 15 years in exile, working with dissidents and laying the groundwork for her future in politics.

Milka Planinc in 1943, at the age of 19, joined the Partisans, a group led by Tito, the general secretary of the Yugoslav Communist Party, to resist the German occupation. These guerrilla forces, which were ill-equipped, operated from the mountains, harassing the enemy troops. When asked by an interviewer many years later about her experiences, she said: "Those were dangerous times; I vividly recall very hard, very dramatic moments that left deep scars."[10]

After the war, and with Tito in control, a government patterned after that of the Soviet Union was put in place. Planinc, who had joined the Communist Party in 1944, began her career following a period of formal study, specializing in agitation, propaganda, and education. In 1959, she became a member of the party's executive body, the Croatian Central Committee.

Climbing the Political Ladder

Service in a cabinet is a steppingstone to higher office, especially in a parliamentary system. Cabinet posts such as those dealing with foreign affairs and finance are believed to provide useful preparation for the top post. To be singled out for advancement, a politician must first demonstrate her competence, and perhaps just as important, her ability to work with her colleagues.

Thatcher had the good fortune to get her parliamentary career off on a propitious note when she drew second in the ballot for private members' bills, permitting her to introduce her own legislation. She chose to focus on a bill that provided for the opening of local council meetings. During the debate on the measure, Thatcher delivered a

27-minute speech without notes, and one newspaper described it of Front Bench quality.[11] She steered the measure through committee and to final passage, gaining a reputation for thoroughness, hard work, and effective speaking. Having attracted the attention of her party's leaders, Thatcher was offered the post of parliamentary secretary for the ministry of pensions and national insurance in 1961 when a woman left the government.

In the years that followed, Thatcher held a variety of minor government posts. The first opportunity she had to get a cabinet-level position came after the defeat of the Conservatives in 1966. In his memoirs James Prior, who served as Edward Heath's parliamentary private secretary and was a member of the first Thatcher cabinet, said that he was asked who should be the "statutory woman" in the shadow cabinet. Prior indicated that he recommended Thatcher. In responding to this suggestion, Heath, replied, "Yes, Willie [Whitelaw] agrees she's much the most able." But in a prophetic note, he went on to indicate that Whitelaw "says once she's there we'll never be able to get rid of her. So we both think it's got to be Mervyn Pike."[12] When the shadow minister of education retired the following year, Thatcher was appointed to replace him, and after the Conservative Party's victory in 1970, she became minister of education.

The years as education minister proved to be difficult for her. A strained relationship with her cabinet colleagues, negative public response to her, and criticism from the press took their toll. Her husband urged her to leave politics, but she believed strongly in what she was doing and would not be kept from her course.

Thatcher's most controversial move was the decision to end free milk for 7- to 11-year olds. She fought vigorously for increased expenditure for education, but there was pressure within the government to reduce overall spending to keep the party's promise to cut taxes. She wished to protect education programs, and she did not view the provision of milk as education. The policy was greeted with protests in which she was taunted with cries of "Mrs. Thatcher, milk snatcher." In a poll conducted in 1972, she was rated the least popular member of the government.

These years served as a learning period for Thatcher although she never managed to penetrate the inner circle of the party. Although she got along well enough with the civil servants, she blamed them for not warning her of the strength of the opposition. She later spoke out about the quality of the advice she received, indicating that she did not believe she had been quick enough to question the prevailing views. Thatcher expected the members of her staff to keep up with her pace, but, at the same time, she was considerate of them. One civil servant noted that "she was what we think of as a good minister: she took what we gave her and fought for it. She did cross-examine and hector, but she was open to persuasion."[13]

Like Thatcher, many professional politicians who rose to the top served only in minor cabinet posts. For example, Gro Brundtland held the portfolio for environmental affairs, but she made effective use of her position to build up a base of support. She traveled extensively, promoting various environmental issues. Among them was a program for the establishment of nature preserves that proved to be quite popular.

When the cabinet was reshuffled in 1979, Brundtland was informed by the prime minister that she was to leave the cabinet and enter parliament. Since ministers in Norway are not permitted to occupy a seat in the parliament, a proxy had been serving in her stead. This move was designed, according to the prime minister, to prepare her for the day when she would head the government, and the fact that she served on the important committees concerned with finance and foreign affairs give some credence to this explanation. Brundtland, on the other hand, argued that the Labor Party leader Reiulf Steen, who joined the government in the reshuffle, viewed her as a competent rival and was behind her ouster from the cabinet.[14]

Edith Cresson held several different cabinet posts. In 1981, French President Mitterrand asked the prime minister to appoint her minister of agriculture. While she had experience in dealing with such issues since she had served on the agricultural commission of the European Parliament, she faced a hostile constituency that labeled her "the perfumed one." In commenting on the generally negative response to her, she said that French farmers were "such conservatives and woman-haters that giving them a woman as minister, and a Socialist on top of it, nearly amounted to a provocation."[15]

Following her stint at agriculture, she moved on to the ministry of tourism and trade, the ministry of trade and industry, and, finally, the ministry of European affairs. In these positions, she concentrated her efforts on improving the position of French industry, even personally escorting business executives abroad to market their products. Her support of protectionist trade practices as well as tax incentives for investment gained her high marks with some in the business community. When she was named prime minister, Mitterrand remarked that her experiences made her especially qualified to prepare the country for the forthcoming implementation of the single market in Europe.[16]

Angela Merkel, who was elected to a seat in the *Bundestag* in 1991, was quickly brought into the cabinet by Chancellor Helmut Kohl. Her rapid rise can be attributed to the fact that she lived in what was the former East Germany, and Kohl was concerned to bolster his party's support in that region. She was first assigned to the ministry for women and youth and later became environment secretary. In the latter position, she failed to gain favor with environmental groups since she backed the nuclear industry.

Jenny Shipley entered the New Zealand parliament in 1987, and three years later when her party formed the government, she was named minister of social affairs. In this role she overhauled the welfare system, making cuts in benefits. In 1993, she was asked to head the health ministry where she also sought to trim government spending although she did give special attention to the interests of women by providing for the distribution of free birth control pills in hopes of reducing the abortion rate. Perhaps anticipating a move to the top, she asked for an appointment that would be less controversial and was given the ministries of transport and women's affairs.

Shipley's rival, Helen Clark, served as minister of conservation, housing, and labor as well as minister of health. Like Shipley, she sought to reform the health system and gained a reputation as a fiscal conservative although she was viewed as too liberal by some. In 1989, she became deputy prime minister, and following the Labor Party's defeat that same year, she led a successful fight for the post as leader of her party. Though initially she was unpopular, by 1996 she had improved her standing and that of her party and had become a favorite of the media.

The fact that women initially were more likely to serve in those posts concerned with education or social and cultural affairs may stem from the belief that they are incapable of handling matters related to finance and foreign affairs or it may reflect the preference of individual women. Golda Meir, for example, requested the post of labor minister following the elections for the first Knesset in 1949. Later she indicated that she enjoyed the work of the labor ministry "because there you can get something done that people need and see the results."[17]

During Meir's tenure as minister of labor both housing and roads were expanded. Given the influx of refugees at the close of the Second World War, a major responsibility of the ministry was to provide training for immigrants and create jobs to accommodate the recent arrivals. Public works programs in the form of road building were developed, and later immigrants were channeled into agriculture. The labor ministry was responsible for the institution of many new programs such as disability and unemployment insurance, maternity leaves, and benefits for widows and orphans.

Unlike many of those women who early on rose to the top, Meir[18] held a key cabinet post. She was appointed as foreign minister in 1956, becoming the first woman to serve in that position. Her appointment was a response to a disagreement between David Ben-Gurion and his foreign minister over defense policy. In looking for a replacement for Moshe Sharett, Ben-Gurion wanted someone who would do his bidding and would take a hard line stance on the Arab-Israeli conflict. Since Meir shared many of the prime minister's views and had little experience in foreign affairs, she appeared to be the perfect candidate for the post as she would likely defer to Ben-Gurion.

During her tenure as foreign minister Meir often consulted with Ben-Gurion and usually yielded to his wishes. Officials in the defense department worked closely with him, also, and Meir believed the defense ministry assumed some of the responsibilities usually reserved to the foreign ministry. The stormy relationship that developed with Moshe Dayan can be traced to this period, for Meir was not one to forgive slights.

On the whole, Meir did not enjoy her work at the foreign ministry, particularly since she felt uncomfortable with much of the senior staff. British-educated and schooled in the art of diplomacy, they found her manner difficult. One writer observed that some who worked with her noted that she responded on the basis of intuition rather than reason and that she did not respect the expertise of the professional diplomats. Her speeches were written by a staff member, and she did not read extensively.[19]

In some respects Meir's stature was enhanced after Levi Eshkol became prime minister in 1963 as the two politicians were fairly equal in political power. Meir remained an important actor in the dominant party, Mapai, and Eshkol needed the party's support. One aide to Eshkol observed: "Eshkol was more dependent on Mrs. Meir, for party reasons. Moreover, at the beginning he had no knowledge of, or pretensions about, foreign policy."[20]

Two other women who reached the top served as foreign minister—Tarja Halonen of Finland and Nyam-Osoriyn Tuyaa of Mongolia. Halonen, who had also headed the ministry of social affairs and health as well as the ministry of justice, was serving as foreign affairs minister when she made the decision to seek the presidency in 2000. Tuyaa, who served as prime minister for only a little over a week, resumed her duties as foreign minister in the new government.

Just two months before Canadian Prime Minister Brian Mulroney announced his intention to step down, Kim Campbell, who was serving as justice minister, was appointed head of the defense ministry. Unlike Meir, Campbell was pleased with the appointment to the foreign policy arena, for she had a long-term interest in international relations. Her father noted that at the age of 14 she announced that she wanted to become head of the United Nations,[21] and she focused her graduate studies on Soviet government. The move to defense would not only give her the opportunity to acquire experience in foreign relations but would also remove her from responsibility for such volatile, and potentially damaging, issues as abortion and gun control.[22]

Campbell, who, like Thatcher, tended to speak out in cabinet meetings on subjects that were not within her portfolio, was not able to avoid controversy. During her brief stay at Defense, she found herself embroiled in a conflict over the purchase of submarine-hunting helicopters. The opposition argued that with the end of the cold war these very expensive helicopters were unnecessary. Even Campbell acknowledged that at one point she shared such misgivings, but she moved to go ahead with the purchase, thereby enhancing her appeal with the prime minister's supporters.

In addition to those ministries whose focus was foreign relations, those that dealt with economic policy provided experience believed to be important for a national leader. Among those women who had direct exposure to the workings of this critical policy area was Liberia-Peters. She was chosen to head the economic affairs ministry of the Netherlands Antilles during a particularly difficult time following her election to parliament in 1982. The residents of the larger islands believed they were bearing more than their share of the financial burdens and sought independence while the businesses that ran the oil refineries, key elements in the islands' economy, were on the verge of threatening to end operations.

Tansu Ciller was appointed minister of state for the economy sometime after her first electoral contest in 1991. She faced an economy hobbled with high unemployment and a high inflation rate. Despite elaborate plans that included the privatization of state enterprises and the curtailment of government spending, she had relatively little success in improving economic conditions. When she left her post to seek the position as leader of her party, inflation was still running at more than 60 percent—far short of the 40 percent she had promised—and the national debt was increasing rapidly. Her concern to decrease interest rates as a means of reducing inflation led to a highly publicized confrontation with the governor of the Central Bank as bank officials preferred to stabilize the national currency.[23]

Starting at the Top: Widows and Daughters

Although the lack of high-level political experience may have the effect of excluding women from the top position, it has not proved to be a disadvantage for the widows of prominent male politicians. As a wife and hostess to a politician, a widow is viewed as standing in the shoes of her late husband. In addition, she has unique experiences that may be useful for a career in politics. For example, she is likely to be acquainted with other politicians, and, if she were so inclined, she may have acquired knowledge of political maneuvering. Also, she is likely to have assisted with campaigning, for wives of politicians are expected to make appearances on behalf of their husbands.

Sirimavo Bandaranaike had her first experience with electoral politics when she canvassed for her husband during the 1952 campaign. In 1956, she worked in the Ratnapura-Balangoda area for her husband's party and managed the campaign in his constituency of Attanagalla. When Isabel Peron ran as vice president on the ticket with her husband in 1973, she made most of the public appearances as General Peron was suffering from heart disease and was unable to travel extensively. Earlier she had made several trips to Argentina on her husband's behalf, laying the groundwork for his return to the country he had led during the 1950s.

Despite the extensive involvement of her family in political action, Corazon Aquino had little interest in politics, merely tolerating her husband's work. She preferred to watch from the sidelines, fearing that if she even sat on the podium with him, she might be asked to speak. In an interview she remarked that her family had "always been in the thick of things...usually opposed to the government.... As far as I was concerned, having seen it from the inside, I was perfectly happy to take a back seat...."[24] Noting the limits of her own political experience, Aquino said that the "only time I had ever been active politically was when Ninoy was campaigning to be governor or senator. I went the usual rounds of shaking hands with people in the market, farms and factories asking them to vote for Ninoy. But beyond that I was simply a politician's wife."[25] After her husband was incarcerated, she played a role similar to that performed by Isabel Peron, serving as the link to her husband's supporters. She carried messages from prison, conducted press conferences, and coordinated his unsuccessful race in 1978 for the National Assembly.

Violeta Chamorro did not participate in her husband's political activities. She described her role when she said that "my work was to be his wife—to take care of my children, take care of the house, accompany him on his trips, and take food to him in prison...."[26] In her autobiography Chamorro paints a somewhat different picture, that of a strong woman who advised her husband.[27] Perhaps she felt it less politically damaging to speak of her role at the end of her political career, or perhaps she perceived her relationship to her husband differently after her own success in the political arena.

A wife may also have developed political skills as well as built up political support by participating in community and/or volunteer organizations. Bandaranaike attributed her ability to become prime minister to her work in the Samiti, an organization whose mission was to improve conditions in the rural areas and in which she served as president. Stressing the importance of this experience to her personal development, she said:

> I owe my own beginnings as a public speaker to the Samiti. At the time I was overcome with shyness and I would actually find myself covered with a cold sweat, even stuttering and stumbling and rattling off the briefest possible speech in the most abrupt manner! But increasingly I gained confidence and ceased to think of myself—but only of what I wished to convey to the women present who seemed to look up to me for guidance.[28]

She also noted that it gave her "a deeper insight into the life of the average villager,"[29] an asset that proved especially useful when managing her husband's political campaign.

Three of the widows engaged in political activity after their husband's death and before their own rise to the top. Mireya Moscoso of Panama, who reluctantly entered politics, played a role in creating her political party and subsequently served as its president. She became principal leader of the opposition in 1991 and also served in such minor government positions as executive secretary of the social security agency. Khaleda Zia spent several years as leader of her party before becoming prime minister. Her leadership of the Bangladesh Nationalist Party was not without its missteps, for the party suffered splits when some left to join the government. By offering jobs to selected leaders of the BNP, President Ershad sought to exploit the differences within the party.

Violeta Chamorro traveled extensively following her husband's assassination, making speeches and giving interviews to hasten the opposition's fall from power, and she served in the provisional government that took over following the resignation of the dictator Somoza in 1979. As the widow of a martyred hero, her support was particularly beneficial, but she left within months of taking office over policy differences with the Marxist-oriented Sandinista leadership. She described her duties as "strictly confined to public relations matters."[30] Chamorro departed quietly because she did not wish to jeopardize the negotiations over aid from the United States. Having been successful in keeping the members of her immediate family on comparatively good terms by forbidding political discussions in her home, Chamorro was, also, eager to avoid confrontation with a daughter and a son who were strong Sandinista supporters.

Two other widows held public office before they assumed the presidency. Isabel Peron became vice president when the ticket headed by her husband won the 1973 election. Janet Jagan, who had considerable political as well as administrative experience, served in the Guyana parliament for many years and held the posts of minister of labor, health, and housing as well as that of minister of home affairs. She had played an active role in her political party and was named interim prime minister following the death of her husband.

Like the widows, most of the daughters of prominent politicians had relatively little political experience, but they had the advantage of early exposure to politics. While Sheikh Hasina headed her party for several years and served as the leader of the opposition, Benazir Bhutto's early experience was confined to political organization. Chandrika Kumaratunga got her start in politics in the Sri Lanka Freedom Party's Women's League, and also held the position of director of the Land Reform Commission, an appointive post, during her mother's second term. Kumaratunga got her first experience with electoral politics at the regional level when in 1993 she successfully sought a seat on the Western Provincial Council. She was subsequently selected as chief minister of the council, a position that served as a steppingstone to national office.

Indira Gandhi, who served on a number of committees of the Congress Party and was elected president of the party in 1959, held a cabinet position before becoming prime minister. She was chosen by her father's successor to head the ministry of information and broadcasting. There was speculation at the time that she would have preferred the ministry of external affairs, but Lal Bahadur Shastri, who believed she would bolster support for his government, wanted her in a less important post although he did give her fourth rank in the cabinet and included her in the Emergency Committee, a powerful inner circle of advisers.

Gandhi's lack of administrative experience proved to be a handicap although she got the work done quickly. She gave priority to the development of regular television programming and encouraged its use for educational purposes such as the dissemination of birth control information. Her tendency to seek advice from experts outside the bureaucracy did not sit well with the civil servants. The 1965 war with Pakistan provided Gandhi an opportunity to show that she was an effective problem-solver. She was in Kashmir recuperating from a recurring problem with a slipped disc when the Pakistani military raiders infiltrated. She attended the meetings of the Kashmir cabinet and offered her assessments of the situation, persuading the cabinet to organize citizens' committees to improve morale by providing the people with a sense of participation.

Gandhi traveled extensively throughout India, taking the opportunity to visit military encampments. She, also, continued to take part in Congress Party affairs and served as a member of the Congress Working Committee. She played a mediating role in local party disputes. As one official in the ministry said, "she gave a lot of time to doing things which weren't part of her duties, because she was mainly interested in building her public image."[31] Although Shastri appreciated Gandhi's initiatives, for the most part, his interaction with her was marked by tension and distrust. The prime minister sought to isolate her politically, for he was concerned that she was attempting to construct a national power base. He did not consult with her and checked those assignments that might enhance her political position. Gandhi resented this attempt at political isolation, and in private interviews made her dissatisfaction with government policies known. The tension between the two politicians mounted, and Gandhi began to work more closely with Kamaraj, the president of the Congress Party, who also had his disagreements with Shastri. The stage was set for a more important role for Gandhi following Shastri's death in 1966.

Both Gloria Arroyo and Megawati Sukarnoputri served as vice president of their respective countries before rising to the top. Arroyo had her first taste of politics as under secretary of trade and industry in the Aquino administration. She told an interviewer that she had not contemplated going into politics and was quite content being a college professor until she was asked in 1992 by a brother-in-law of Aquino to run for the Senate.[32] Arroyo was successful in her first bid for a

Senate seat and was elected for a second term in 1998, the same year she was elected vice president. Though Arroyo did not belong to the same party as President Estrada, she joined his cabinet, heading the social welfare and development department.

The chair of the Partai Demokrasi Indonesia moved to get members of the Sukarno family involved in the party. Megawati, a homemaker, responded positively to his overture and sought a seat in the parliament on the PDI ticket in 1987. She said that she had "no thoughts of becoming a leader. At the time I felt that since my children were already independent, I might as well become active in politics."[33] As to her experience for high-level office she noted that people "forget that I participated in the struggle for independence with my father. I met a lot of heroes...as well as many world leaders."[34] She was successful in this first bid for public office and was reelected in 1992, becoming chair of her party in 1993.

A Push up the Ladder: The Role of Mentors

A mentor can be especially helpful to a politician who is beginning a career, but a woman has difficulty in contrast with her male colleagues in seeking help. Such contacts may signal suspicions of a sexual relationship. In anticipation of a negative reaction, Edith Cresson, shortly before she was appointed prime minister by her mentor of longstanding, President Mitterrand, said in an interview: "Every time a woman gets nominated or elected somewhere, it is customary to hear that she made it by her physique or by providing favors to some man. Not one woman has ever been selected without the explanation that she slept with so-and-so. Unfortunately, we're still at that stage."[35] Described by the leader of the far right National Front, Jean-Marie Le Pen, as "a lady of the harem who marks the end of the reign," Cresson responded after her appointment to questions as to whether she had an affair with Mitterrand by saying: "I am perhaps the favorite, but the favorite of my voters."[36]

A woman who has separated from her husband is especially vulnerable to being the subject of such rumors. As Golda Meir rapidly moved up the ladder, assuming ever more important positions, there was much speculation that she was involved romantically with several Israeli officials, and she herself acknowledged that she was not a nun. Whether there was any truth to the rumors, several Israeli leaders played an important role in advancing Meir's career.[37] In addition to arranging her appointment to positions that made use of her abilities, these men saw that she got publicity for her accomplishments and provided support for her during times of unusual stress. But Meir had much to contribute, for she was a talented woman whose knowledge of English made her a real asset in dealing with the many problems associated with the creation of a new state.

The politically prominent father who encourages his daughter to pursue a political career and helps prepare her for a life in politics serves as a mentor. While the daughter is able to avoid the sexual innuendo, she must deal with suggestions that she got her position only because of the influence of her father.

When Indira Gandhi moved to New Delhi in 1948 to be with her father, her duties were essentially those of a hostess. Gradually she began to take part in the affairs of the Congress Party, concentrating on local activities. She was called upon to resolve disputes as she proved to be an effective mediator. Such tasks were appealing to her, for she seemed at ease in working with small groups and in relating to those who had less power than she.

Gandhi suggested to an interviewer that the fact she was a woman may have made this apprenticeship possible. In response to a question concerning the course of her career had she been a male, Gandhi said: "I think there probably would have been more difficulties, because, firstly, I could not have really remained with him and helped him in the way that I have. I would have had to make a living.... I think the political world also would have been much more sensitive to the situation and wary of it."[38]

In 1959 when Gandhi was elected president of the Congress Party, some believed that her selection was part of her father's plan to make sure that she would succeed him. Though Nehru did encourage her public career, it is doubtful that he could have forced her on the party despite his dominant position. Although Gandhi was reluctant to accept the position of Congress Party president, her brief term in office established her as an important political figure. She showed a measure of independence, on occasion disagreeing with her father as well as her husband, but she did not seek to continue as Congress president after the completion of the term.

With Nehru's deteriorating health, Gandhi assumed ever more responsibilities. For example, she took over the management of the 1962 election campaign in the midst of speculation that her involvement in decision making was considerable. The Congress leaders resented her influence with Nehru, but they found her advice useful when meeting with the prime minister.

Another daughter whose father played a mentoring role was Benazir Bhutto. She had the support and encouragement of her father to pursue a career in the diplomatic corps, but the military coup that marked the end of Zulfikar Ali Bhutto's rule disrupted his plans to bring her into the government. Instead, after her father's arrest she was thrust into the role of opposition leader to the military regime. As the daughter of the former prime minister, she was acceptable to the leaders of her father's party although some of his colleagues still saw her as the "little daughter."

Conclusions

The paths taken to the top by the women political leaders have varied. Some women have begun their political careers in the parliament, in the cabinet, or in an advisory capacity, while others have started up the ladder by serving at the local level of government or been active in community affairs. Still others have made their move to the top by following in the footsteps of fathers or husbands.

The fact that so many women politicians have not had experience as ministers provides a partial explanation as to why so few of them have risen to the top, especially in parliamentary systems. In July 2007, the number of women serving as cabinet members worldwide was minuscule, only 15.2 percent of the total.[39] The importance of ministerial experience to a political career was alluded to in the Blondel study that found that of the top leaders who served between 1945 and 1975 nearly two-thirds of them had been ministers when the first leaders of new states were excluded.[40] In the present study, 55 percent of the women who rose to the top (n=64) had ministerial experience.

Those women who rose to the top did not have well-developed career plans. Despite her expressions of interest in becoming Chancellor of the Exchequer, Margaret Thatcher indicated that she did not have specific goals but took advantage of the opportunities that came to her.[41] Tarja Halonen said that she did not make the decision to go into politics. "It just happened" after she began working for a former prime minister.[42] Gro Brundtland said that she was surprised when asked to join the cabinet. Hanna Suchocka said that she had not prepared herself for the top post as she never dreamed she would become prime minister, but she remarked that "maybe for man, such a situation wouldn't be so unexpected." She noted that one of her colleagues said: "Every man in politics dreams of being prime minister."[43] Golda Meir said that she never had specific positions in mind, but rather she took on the tasks that were asked of her. Gloria Arroyo stressed that she had not made plans for her life, leaving the mapping of the details to Divine Providence.[44] It was only after she was overwhelmingly elected to the Senate that she began to think about higher office. Some of the daughters such as Benazir Bhutto and Sheikh Hasina represent the exception as they were intent upon avenging the deaths of their fathers. The widows, on the other hand, were reluctant to seek office, but they pursued a political career out of a sense of duty to their late husbands.

The failure to develop a career plan may reflect the fact that historically the prospects for women in the political arena have not been promising, and making plans appeared futile. Or, it may reflect a difference in the experiences of and thus the way men and women view the world. Because they confront conflicting responsibilities in their daily lives, women tend to be more patient and comfortable with ambiguity, thereby making them less predisposed to set out a plan, relying instead on opportunities that come their way.[45]

It might be expected that women would reach the top at an older age given their traditional domestic responsibilities, but women who have become presidents and prime ministers have done so at an age comparable to that of men, if not at an earlier age. It was found that 55 percent of the women (n=64) were less than 50 years old when they reached the top. The Blondel study, on the other hand, concluded that only 40 percent reaching the top were less than 50 years of age. As the barriers to women's participation began to crumble, the political parties may have concentrated on younger women to fill slots as these women were more likely than the older generation of women to have the required education and professional experience.

Chapter Nine

Running for Office

While Margaret Thatcher's victory in the 1975 contest for the leadership of the British Conservative Party came as somewhat of a surprise to many, it became a cause for celebration for her party's opponents. One insider described the opposition Labor leaders' assessment of their party's electoral prospects with Thatcher in the race when she wrote: "I arrived at the House of Commons just as a meeting of senior Cabinet Members was breaking up. I remember they were all laughing, joking and slapping each other on the shoulders with remarks to the effect that all was now well. 'That's it, we're home and dry,' was the general tenor. 'No need to worry about the next election. It's a foregone conclusion. Well, how could the Tory Party—the Tory Party—possibly win with a woman at the head?'"[1]

The Labor Party leaders proved not to be particularly adept at prediction, for Thatcher led her party to an impressive victory in the 1979 parliamentary election as well as in two subsequent electoral contests. Opinion poll data suggest that there was some justification for doubts about the ability of a woman to garner the support necessary to ensure her party a victory. A poll conducted in 1975 for the Commission of the European Communities in the member states found that more than one-third of the respondents believed that politics should be left to men.[2] The figure for the British respondents was a slightly more modest one-quarter but still large enough to have an impact on the outcome of an election. In another poll conducted before the 1979 election in which the respondents were asked whether they would prefer a man or a woman as prime minister, 52 percent said they would prefer a man while only 16 percent said they would prefer a woman, and 29 percent indicated that it would make no difference.[3]

Despite the picture painted by these polls, one analysis of the results of the 1979 British election revealed that there was no evidence that female candidates were penalized by the voters because of their gender.[4] Party loyalty appeared to have snuffed out any qualms individual voters might have had about the qualifications of women.

Responsibility for the paucity of women in politics, the study concluded, lay with the candidate selection committees.

In contrast, some 16 years after Thatcher's victory in the contest for the head of the British Conservative Party, opposition leaders in France became uneasy when Edith Cresson was appointed prime minister by President Mitterrand. They were concerned that women might be energized to work for the Socialist Party, thereby improving the party's prospects in the upcoming election. In criticizing the choice of Cresson, some opposition leaders suggested that "Mitterrand shows that he prefers sensuality over consensus." Others, such as Jacques Chirac, who was to become president of France in 1995, took a more mollifying tone, for opinion polls showed that almost three-fourths of the population were pleased that a woman was serving as prime minister. He noted that "[i]n our country, as in others, women should be able to occupy the most important positions."[5]

Physical Characteristics of Leaders

Although there has been a change in attitudes toward women in politics, women continue to be at a disadvantage when it comes to seeking political office. They do not look like leaders or sound like them as most positions of political leadership have been occupied by men. In speaking to a group of women journalists while she was serving as Canadian justice minister, Kim Campbell stated the problem when she noted that the portraits in her office of her predecessors reminded her that "physically, women do not correspond with some people's ideas of what a politician is." She went on to say that "gradually we are getting to the point where people get beyond the shock of seeing this untypical person who is not wearing a suit and tie and is not greying at the temples and walking around with that wonderful, assertive, confident look men have, whether it's justified or not."[6] A woman's smaller stature, as well as her feminine gestures, does not project an image of confidence and decisiveness associated with a leader. The pitch of her voice tends to be higher than that of a man, a trait sometimes linked to emotional behavior.

Despite the shortcomings their physical attributes conveyed, several women who rose to the top possessed characteristics that compensated for these "handicaps." Although short in stature, Golda Meir, had a deep husky voice that bore the effects of many years of cigarette smoking. Most convincing in extemporaneous discourse, she was an effective speaker with an ability to move her audience. The gift of persuasion proved to be critical to her long but steady rise up the political ladder, for she would charm her country's benefactors in the United States as well as the voters in Israel with her straightforward but emotional style.

Benazir Bhutto, a tall, attractive woman, whom one fashion writer said "blended Islamic attire with Western chic,"[7] also had a comparatively deep voice and was a moving speaker. Her style, which she adjusted to fit the give-and-take characteristic of communication in a Pakistani election campaign, was honed in debate at the Oxford Union during her days as a student. Known for her fiery style of address, Yulia Tymoshenko of Ukraine was able to stir large crowds to action.

It was the effectiveness of Eugenia Charles of Dominica as a speaker that influenced her party to select her as leader. In commenting on Chandrika Kumaratunga's first national campaign in 1994, one reporter described her as a "formidable speaker, giving a theatrical flourish to campaign tours."[8] Referring to the 1999 campaign in Sri Lanka, another reporter said that she was "a natural politician, whose speeches, delivered without notes, are punctuated with laughter and peppered with audience participation."[9]

To improve her public speaking, Thatcher, who was a bit stiff, especially in her television appearances, early on worked with a theater coach to lower the pitch of her voice and slow her delivery. During her first election campaign as party leader she employed a media director, Gordon Reece, a former television producer, who remained at her side and assisted her in improving her communication skills.

Before the 2005 debate between the two contenders for the office of German chancellor, Angela Merkel sought the advice of a television presenter who taught her to smile more as the candidate's appearance was rather severe, and she did not show emotion. Merkel was also encouraged to put more inflection into her voice as she was predisposed to speak in a monotone.

Although a deep voice may inspire confidence, it may prove to be a disadvantage for a woman. Taking a note from the Thatcher campaign, some of Tarja Halonen's advisers suggested that she seek help to lower the pitch of her voice, but others rejected the plan, especially since her opponents reminded the voters that Halonen had chaired the gay and lesbian association as a student. Helen Clark's husky voice combined with the fact that she had made the decision not to have children led her opponents to raise questions about her sexuality, but she resisted suggestions that she take lessons to modulate her voice, make changes in her hairdo, and select more fashionable attire. During the 1996 election campaign, she heeded the suggestions of advisers and agreed to a modest "makeover."[10]

Other women did not have to be concerned about the disadvantages that their being female posed, because the assets they brought to an election campaign far outweighed the handicaps. As the daughter of Nehru, Indira Gandhi, a petite woman who had a small, relatively high pitched voice and was not a particularly good speaker, was viewed as an effective vote-getter. The rallies at which she appeared attracted crowds numbering in the tens of thousands. Often greeted at her stops with garlands and colorful displays of flowers, she spoke in a simple, conversational style, making frequent use of analogies with which her audiences could identify.[11] Megawati, who was a bland speaker, also attracted large, enthusiastic crowds, but her campaign appearances were brief and her speeches devoid of substance.[12]

The widows of martyrs—Corazon Aquino, Sirimavo Bandaranaike, Violeta Chamorro, and Khaleda Zia—were also not particularly good speakers, but they were able to move the crowds with their tearful messages. Their very presence stirred in the voters memories of an idealized past and hopes for a better future dashed by violence.

Coping with the Rigors of a Campaign

In addition to the fact that women do not look like leaders or sound like them, other concerns about their electability stem from the long-held belief that women are by nature delicate, thereby raising doubts about their ability to meet the strenuous demands of a political campaign. In the 1979 British election, Thatcher's opponents built their campaign strategy on the expectation that she would not physically be able to cope with the demands of a national campaign. In scheduling the election, the official period for soliciting votes was extended by almost two weeks beyond the usual three as additional time was allowed for celebration of the intervening Easter holiday. The Labor Party leaders anticipated that the length of the contest would work to their advantage. Pinning their hopes on Thatcher's making a serious mistake, given her propensity to speak out, or her health failing under the stress of the campaign[13] proved to be a disappointing strategy. Except for some problems with hoarseness, she seemed to thrive on the rigors of the campaign.

Thatcher's advisers did take steps to ensure that she would be protected from some of the tensions associated with contesting an election. She was urged not to begin her campaign appearances in earnest until after Easter. The assassination of Airey Neave, the shadow spokesman on Northern Ireland, just before the contest got underway provided justification for the delay. Her advisers were also concerned not to overexpose her to minimize the effects of any weaknesses she might display during the campaign.

The physical demands of a political campaign are considerable, and the experience of leading a party in a national election can be grueling. During Thatcher's first campaign as leader, a typical day began with her presiding over a morning press conference. She would then travel to meetings and speaking engagements in various parts of the country, returning to London each evening. During the last two weeks of the campaign, she visited 30 cities and traveled 3,000 miles.[14]

As candidates with relatively little chance of success, both Mary Robinson of Ireland and Vigdis Finnbogadottir of Iceland conducted long, strenuous campaigns, traveling throughout their respective countries, speaking to numerous groups. Robinson, who began her travels several months before her opponents were even selected, covered approximately 30,000 miles by road in 6 months.[15] The demanding schedule took its toll on her, and her performance at some speaking engagements during the last days of the campaign suffered because of the fatigue she experienced.

Since Vigdis had no political experience and did not even belong to a political party, she had to make effective use of the campaign to introduce herself to the voters. Describing her hectic schedule, she told an interviewer she was "jumping into airplanes and like an ogress covering the country in three steps."[16] She said that while she was campaigning, she "always spoke about the place I was in...I came up with stories and legends pertaining to that particular place. And people liked that."[17]

The physical demands on the candidate were even greater in developing countries as travel was more arduous. During her first campaign as leader of the Sri Lanka Freedom Party in 1960, Sirimavo Bandaranaike made an appearance in every constituency in which there was someone from her party seeking a parliamentary seat. Traveling by car and helicopter, in 1977 she again crisscrossed the country, touring more than 130 electorates. In 1986, Corazon Aquino visited 68 of her country's 73 provinces, addressing more than 1,000 rallies in the campaign for the Philippine presidency.[18]

During the 1967 Indian election campaign that lasted approximately two months, Indira Gandhi toured virtually every state, traveling more than 35,000 miles via airplane, helicopter, car, and, on occasion, a jeep. In 1971, she addressed more than 400 meetings, stressing that her party alone could provide a strong government. In addition to making it possible for her to get to some of the more hard to reach areas, the helicopter offered another bonus. By arriving from out of the sky, she became identified in the minds of some with the Hindu goddess Durga, who had come to earth in a variety of forms. During the 1980–1981 electoral contest in which she staged a political comeback, she traveled more than 40,000 miles and addressed more than 1,500 meetings despite a painful inflammation of the nerve endings in her face.

During her first election campaign in 1991 that lasted slightly more than two months, Khaleda Zia of Bangladesh spoke to 1,800 meetings and rallies, addressing 38 meetings in one day.[19] Her rival Sheikh Hasina visited most of the constituencies and spoke at hundreds of meetings.[20]

Benazir Bhutto, who suffered a kidney infection after the birth of her son, traversed Pakistan via train during the election campaign of 1988 while in 1990 she relied on the motorcade, addressing five or six rallies each day. In 1993, following the lead of her principal opponent, Nawaz Sharif, she used a helicopter that made it possible for her to cover more territory.

In her first national campaign in 1994, Chandrika Kumaratunga sometimes addressed 30 meetings in a day,[21] but in her second campaign for the presidency in 1999 she was urged to curtail her travel. Out of concern for her security, she was advised to make use of satellite TV conferencing to reach the voters. The assassination attempt carried out against her in the last days of the campaign served to make the threats against her credible. She told a reporter that she "never gets used to it [security]. My kids hate it, they hate me doing politics but it's a sacrifice I've had to make."[22]

Violeta Chamorro, who shattered a kneecap in a fall two months before the 1990 election, cleverly managed to use this misfortune to her advantage during the campaign. Accompanied by several members of her family, she traveled to her speaking engagements in a pickup truck with a white canopy. With the candidate usually dressed in white, there was a similarity to the likenesses of the Virgin Mary carried in religious processions; and to ensure that the connection was made, she was introduced as the "salvation of the country," Nicaragua's "Maria," the "white dove of peace."[23]

Meeting Her Family Responsibilities

In running for public office, women face challenges that their male counterparts do not encounter. Since women have traditionally been expected to nurture and care for their families, those who seek public office must establish that they are meeting these responsibilities and that their families are supportive of their political ambitions. Women candidates have sought to assuage the voters about their credentials as a woman by having themselves photographed in homey settings or while engaged in such "feminine activities" as cooking and sewing. When she was seeking the party leadership post in 1975, photographers were permitted to take pictures of Thatcher preparing breakfast for her husband. Robinson, while at first resisting the use of her family for political purposes, eventually agreed to be the subject of a number of magazine stories in which she was featured in such domestic settings as the kitchen, surrounded by her three children. Her advisers believed that this exposure was necessary to counter her identification with such controversial issues as divorce and abortion in her legal practice.

A leader may take other steps to assure the voters that she takes her domestic responsibilities seriously. During a television interview after she was selected to lead her party, Tansu Ciller remarked that "of course at home my husband is the head of the family."[24] Since the Islamic Welfare Party was expected to be a formidable opponent in the upcoming local elections, she likely felt it necessary to stress that though she held the top position in the government, her family was a traditional one.

To signal their support, family members may appear with the candidate or address meetings on her behalf. While campaigning, Thatcher was usually accompanied by her husband who would walk a few feet behind her, often expressing concern about her safety as well as leading the cheers for her. Robinson's husband remained at his wife's side throughout her long, arduous run for the Irish presidency while Mike Arroyo served as his wife's campaign manager in her races for a Senate seat and later for the vice presidency.

Divorced and single women face special problems in attempting to shore up their feminine credentials. Since they have not followed the path expected of a woman, they may be viewed with suspicion. Kim Campbell's two failed marriages became an issue during the contest for the leadership of her party. Backers of her opponent, Jean Charest, argued that some Canadian voters would not support a woman for prime minister and pointed to her marital status as a reason for concern about the viability of her candidacy. To remind the delegates of the contrast with his own situation, Charest was frequently pictured with his wife and three children. One commentator suggested that in the end this approach worked to Campbell's advantage, for a backlash developed in response to the strategy of her detractors, ensuring her victory.[25] Tarja Halonen's principal opponent, Esko Aho, focused on "family values" and held up "his children and stay-at-home wife as a model,"[26] subtly bringing to the attention of the voters his opponent's status as a single mother.

In an interview during the 2005 campaign, German Chancellor Gerhard Schroeder's wife referred to the fact that Angela Merkel, who was divorced but remarried, did not have children as evidence that the candidate would be unable "to further the cause of women," for "she was of 'another world.'"[27] Schroeder was put in the embarrassing position of having to explain his wife's response.

Vigdis Finnbogadottir, who was divorced, attempted to deal with concerns of the voters about her marital status when she observed: "If a man is president and he loses his wife, would you ask him to resign? Everybody can become single again."[28] In a subtle challenge to her ability to perform in office, Vigdis was repeatedly asked how she would handle the job of president without a husband though Icelanders do not, as a rule, focus on the personal lives of political candidates. She responded somewhat flippantly to these queries: "If I were married, I wouldn't be standing here," suggesting that she could not imagine that a man of her age would want to be an "escort" for his wife.[29]

Even a popular widow may be subjected to questioning about her family responsibilities. Especially if she has young children, she may be criticized for entering the political fray. Bandaranaike's opponents argued that she should have stayed at home to care for her three children. With what was to become a typical response to criticism, she pointed to the importance of carrying on with her husband's work, saying in a speech, "what greater service can a widow perform than to remain faithful to the ideals of her dead husband and endeavor to put them into practice...."[30]

Is She Competent?

Since women have traditionally been viewed as less competent than men, those women who seek election must assure the voters as well as party leaders that they are capable of dealing with the complexities of public office. Those skills that have served women well in caring for a home have not been viewed as relevant to the conduct of public affairs although Thatcher sought to make a connection between the traditional chores of a woman and those of a political leader when she said that bringing up a family provides experience in coping with crises. Child rearing "teaches you that you have to keep calm when everyone else isn't."[31] On another occasion in comparing the budget of a family to that of a nation, she pointed to the relevance of a woman's traditional duties: "I know what it's like to live within a budget and I know what it's like having to cope."[32] In a more humorous vein, Maria Liberia-Peters, in addressing the relevance of her training in education, remarked that "there is basically no difference in the behaviour of a four, five, six-year old or a forty, fifty, or sixty-year old."[33]

To the irritation of her opponent, Helen Clark, who had chosen not to have children, Jenny Shipley stressed the relevance of her experience as a mother.[34] In commenting on the role her family played in her development as a politician, she said: "If you have children, you anticipate things constantly. You are all the time teaching them to be risk averse, but you still want them to blossom and grow. A mother who understands how to draw the best out of her child I'm sure can contribute to the future of this country."[35]

Doubts about the competence of a woman may be alleviated if she has substantial academic credentials, and, as noted in chapter six, those women who rose to the top, for the most part, had extensive formal training that equaled and sometimes surpassed that of their male colleagues. Women may also show that they are competent to hold public office by discussing a broad range of issues during a campaign, for a candidate seeking a position of national leadership must exhibit some familiarity with "men's issues"—those related to the economy and foreign affairs. Stress on "women's issues"—education and welfare—may only serve to enhance the doubts about a woman's ability to handle a high-level political office.

A campaign poster with a picture of Prime Minister Hanna Suchocka and the slogan, "First the Economy," signaled the focus of the 1993 Polish election. As Poland's economy was transformed from a socialist one to one dominated by market forces, the economic problems facing the country were the central concern of the electorate. Suchocka, who was a bland speaker at best, spent much of the campaign defending the "shock therapy" reforms that included budget cuts and anti-inflationary measures. At a campaign meeting she said: "You have to tell people the hard truth. You can't tell people you'll give the pensioners seven million zlotys [$350] a month, because that's impossible. My main political task is to educate people on the truth about the economy."[36]

Although women are viewed as more honest, and Suchocka very likely won the respect of the voters for her candor, this approach did not improve the prospects of her party. The voters were already disturbed with the effects of the reforms on employment prospects. Attempts to provide an explanation may have only served to remind the electorate of their problems.

Like Suchocka, Angela Merkel sought to tell the voters what she believed needed to be done to solve Germany's economic problems. She filled her stump speeches with details about policy proposals. Merkel gave a clue as to why she did not stick to the vague pronouncements that politicians favor when she said, "We're telling you before the election what we will do after the election. We don't want people to be afraid, so that's why we're telling you in clear terms what we plan to do."[37] The experiences of these two women in communist-led regimes may account for their sensitivity to the importance of candor though they both paid a price with dwindling support for telling the voters about the harsh realities facing their respective countries.

Gro Brundtland dealt with economic issues by coupling them with "women's issues." For example, during her first election campaign in 1981 as leader of her party, she criticized her opponents for their zeal to reduce taxes and government spending, arguing that they were dismantling the welfare state and discarding the historic emphasis on greater equality.

A candidate for national office, especially an incumbent, may also show that she is competent to handle the affairs of state by demonstrating her ability to influence other world leaders. Faced with a deteriorating security situation as well as an economy beset with a severe balance of payments deficit, Golda Meir turned to the United States for military and economic aid. In the midst of the 1969 campaign she spent 10 days in the United States meeting with American Jewish leaders and government officials, including President Richard Nixon. On her return to Israel, Meir set about exploiting her achievements.

Just days before the 1995 election in Turkey, the customs union with Europe was approved. Ciller was quick to remind the voters of her role in negotiating this agreement that enjoyed considerable popular support. She also sought to reassure the doubters that the agreement did not adversely affect the status of Islam when she noted that "[w]e will enter Europe with our flag, our call to prayer and our book [the Koran]."[38]

The international conference provides another venue for an incumbent to meet with foreign leaders, thereby demonstrating her ability to handle foreign affairs. Thatcher obtained favorable coverage during both the 1983 and 1987 campaigns when she participated in the G7 (Group of Seven) economic summits.

During a campaign a woman may make mistakes that give the voters pause. When asked about her intention to reorganize social programs, Campbell, who led an error-plagued campaign, observed that a 47-day campaign was no time for a discussion of serious issues.[39] In her speeches Violeta Chamorro tended to focus on the larger picture, referring specific questions to her advisers. On one occasion when asked about her economic model for the future of Nicaragua, Chamorro, a stilted speaker who relied on note cards when addressing a campaign rally, responded by saying, "we have one but it is a secret."[40] During an encounter with the press in which she was asked how her own political ideas differed from those of her husband, Aquino, noting that she could not "differentiate anymore where it is Ninoy and where it is Cory," said that she could not do everything Ninoy did, but "I promise I will try my best." She stressed that she would get 50 dedicated men and women to help her run the government.[41] Such gaffes appear to have often been forgiven by electorates eager for change.

Is She Tough?

A major concern about women as leaders since the days of ruling queens is whether they are tough enough to deal with international crises and security matters. To make the case that she is able to handle such situations, a woman running for high-level political office is likely to place emphasis on crime and defense issues. The supporters of Ellen Johnson Sirleaf of Liberia sought to allay the doubts of the voters by stressing their candidate's toughness, sporting a campaign pin that read: "Ellen, she's our man."[42]

Although concerned to reduce the size of government and cut spending, Thatcher indicated, in her first campaign as leader, her opposition to any cuts for the police or the military. During the 1983 campaign, her leadership credentials were bolstered by her forceful and determined actions against the Argentinean invasion of the Falkland Islands in 1982. To remind the voters of her handling of the crisis, she spent a portion of the last day of the campaign on the Isle of Wight, landing against the backdrop of the British flag. In responding to hecklers about her record, she noted: "We've done a damn sight better than the Labor Party did in office. We're the only party in the country that not only has the right policies but the guts to carry them out."[43] While polls showed that she was not well-liked, her firmness in dealing with the international crisis had a positive effect on the public's perception of her, and her approval rating doubled to almost 60 percent.

When she first came into office, Tansu Ciller appeared willing to make concessions to the Kurdish minority that had been fighting for a separate state for approximately a decade. By the time of the 1994 local elections, faced with an economy in decline, a serious opponent in the Islamic Welfare Party, and an increase in Kurdish terrorist activity, she had assumed a hard line. To highlight her law-and-order approach, during the 1994 campaign she used the slogan, "a vote for the DYP [her True Path Party] is a bullet to the PKK [Kurdish Workers' Party]."[44] Campaign advertisements showing her in a flak jacket during a visit to Bosnia were designed to remind the voters of the success of her government in dealing with Kurdish forces.[45]

Although it is important for a woman seeking office to demonstrate that she is strong to persuade the voters that she is capable of handling the demands of public office, there are limits on the measure of toughness she may prudently display. Since women are expected to be compassionate and nurturing, an attempt on the part of a woman to appear tough may alienate some voters. Women who seek public office are confronted with a dilemma: If they do not appear strong, they are likely to be rejected by the voters as unqualified, especially for national leadership; but if they are forceful, they may offend the sensibilities of certain voters. Concerned about their candidate's tendency to be impatient, especially with aggressive interviewers, Thatcher's advisers steered her away from certain reporters during her first campaign as leader. They also urged her to reject the opportunity to debate her opponent although she would have liked to accept Prime Minister James Callaghan's challenge. To provide a foil for her combative tendencies, Thatcher's adviser's recommended clothing and a hairstyle to achieve a softer look.

A carefully choreographed set of appearances was scheduled—a strategy that was aided by the assassination of Airey Neave by the IRA as the police restricted the movements of the candidates during the campaign and threw up tight security arrangements. The itineraries of the candidates were not announced until the last minute, and the events at which they spoke were open only to ticket holders.

Thatcher, who had honed her skills as a street campaigner during her early days as a parliamentary candidate, made every effort to create a connection with people, especially women, as well as produce effective pictures for the evening news. She was filmed engaged in activities associated with the traditional role of women such as shopping, wielding a broom during a factory tour, using a sewing machine, packing chocolates in a factory, and holding a newborn calf during a visit to a farm.

The results of voter surveys suggest that the electorate appeared to be wary of Thatcher's candidacy not because she was a woman but because she was seen as too harsh. One reporter compared her performance as a campaigner to that of "a teacher, explaining crisply and clearly where we have gone wrong."[46] Another said that "there is an air of the sixth-form seminar at her press conferences as she patiently outlines economic policy to the rows of pupils/reporters."[47] In a poll taken before the 1979 campaign, she was described as sometimes having extreme views. It was believed that she talked down to people and was out of touch with ordinary people. At the same time, she was rated as high as her opponent on such characteristics as toughness and straightforwardness.[48] Interestingly, she was also viewed as more compassionate and emotional than her opponent—traits viewed as characteristic of women.

A woman who seeks public office must be cautious when attacking her opponents as well as in fashioning a response to her critics. As a candidate for political office, she is expected to confront those who run against her and to defend her actions against the barbs of her adversaries. She must attack her opponents, persuading the voters that there is a better way to conduct the public's business, but in doing so she runs the risk of alienating voters. There is some evidence to suggest that a woman may be more successful if she confines her attacks to issue positions as opposed to personal criticisms.[49]

During the waning days of the 1993 campaign in Canada, it became clear that Kim Campbell's push for office was in serious difficulty. Perhaps out of a sense of desperation she led an attack against her opponents delivered with a personal edge.[50] Campbell's campaign also aired a political ad in which the appearance of her principal opponent Jean Chretien was ridiculed because of a birth defect that affected his face. While such a move would have been self-defeating for any politician, for a woman, who is expected to be more considerate, it may have been even more damaging.

The Special Case of Widows and Daughters

Those women related to politically prominent men brought advantages to the electoral contests as they were able to develop rapport with the crowds and were able to mobilize the support of the voters. To remind her audiences of her connection to a popular leader, Mireya Moscoso began her speeches with a Latin refrain used by her late husband—*vox populi, vox Dei*—("the voice of the people is the voice of God").[51] By incorporating into her campaign speeches the phrase with which her late husband had begun his speeches—"in the name of Allah, the Beneficent and the Merciful"—Khaleda Zia was not only able to make the voters aware of her connection to General Ziaur Rahman but also to solidify her support among Islamic interests.[52]

The widows and daughters were not able to escape questions concerning their capabilities and toughness as their opponents focused on their lack of political experience. Philippine President Marcos painted a bleak picture of his country's future if his inexperienced opponent were successful, arguing that her election would lead to civil war and a takeover by the communists. Alluding to the president's record in office, Aquino responded to his predictions with sarcasm when she said: "I admit that I have no experience in cheating, stealing, lying or assassinating political opponents."[53]

Violeta Chamorro's opponents, who used her maiden name, argued that a government headed by a woman with so little experience would result in chaos. Painting herself as a conciliatory mother figure, she responded to this criticism, somewhat naively, by suggesting that "there's no need to study how to govern a country. I have accepted the challenge to revive this country with love and peace, according to the dictates of my conscience."[54]

Playing up the relationship to a dead husband and promising to pursue his program may have been an inexperienced widow's only viable option, particularly since she did not have a base of support of her own. Associating herself with a late husband's work may also have provided an effective means to deal with the insecurity she likely experienced in assuming leadership responsibilities. Her bid for office was made not for "selfish" reasons but on behalf of a loved one.

In contrast, a daughter was more likely to be concerned to assert her independence of family influence. As a young adult, Indira Gandhi assumed the role of the dutiful daughter, serving as Nehru's hostess and apprentice and later as his confidant. After she became prime minister, she put some distance between her policies and those of her father as she had done while serving as Congress Party president in 1959. During her first election campaign as leader, though noting her connection to her father, she did not stress her intention to adhere to his policies. Signaling her independence not only from Nehru but from the party leaders as well, she said in a speech before the start of the campaign that although his policies must be pursued, if it were necessary to chart a different course, she was "quite capable of changing them."⁵⁵

On the other hand, Benazir Bhutto, who reminded her listeners of the extended periods she had spent in prison and in exile because of her political activities, spoke of her father at virtually every stop during the 1988 election campaign, and his image appeared on posters alongside those of his daughter. While pointing to the benefits of his program for Pakistan, she did stray from his socialist-oriented agenda, indicating that she would not make use of nationalization schemes to redistribute resources.

During the 1993 election campaign, Bhutto again stressed her connection to her father. At the same time, she cleverly intertwined this message, as she had in her earlier campaign, with a litany of her sacrifices. On one occasion she remarked: "We have faced the terrors of the army, of jails and torture and now Nawaz Sharif, the heir apparent of General Zia ul-Haq who killed my father, your father, dares to come to Sindh and ask for votes."⁵⁶ The difference in emphasis in the election campaigns of these two daughters may reflect the extent of their political experience. Gandhi had acquired considerable political insight while serving as her father's confidant. She had seriously pondered a career in politics and had built up a cadre of supporters, apart from those of her father; whereas Bhutto had just begun her political career at the time of her father's arrest and removal from office. Also, since Nehru did not die a martyr's death, Gandhi was not able to generate the sympathy by the mere mention of his name that Bhutto was when referring to her father.

Another daughter with relatively little political experience referred to her father often and used his portrait in her campaign literature. Sheikh Hasina of Bangladesh described the rule of her father as the "golden era and vowed to punish the killers of the 'Father of the Nation,'"⁵⁷ In contrast, Kumaratunga of Sri Lanka, who along with her husband, had established a political party and had successfully sought elective office did not invoke the names of her famous parents in her bid for high office. Instead, she focused on her intention to find a solution to her country's civil conflict, using doves on her campaign posters to remind the voters of her commitment. The conflict had been set in motion by her parents when they pitted the majority Sinhalese and minority Tamil communities against one another. As a relative newcomer to national politics and a woman, she may have been seen as particularly suited to find a resolution to this deadly dispute.

If the opponents of a widow or daughter are linked to the death of a politically prominent male relative, she is likely to be especially forceful in dealing with them. In such instances the voters are unlikely to punish a woman for aggressively attacking her opponents. Aquino, who believed that Marcos had ordered the assassination of her husband, referred to the president as a coward and urged him to "stand up like a woman and answer charges of his cowardice with truth...if he dares."[58] Bhutto attacked her opponents, accusing them of collaborating with Zia ul-Haq who had led the coup against her father and was responsible for his execution.

While the relative of a politically prominent man may be useful to a party in garnering support, she does not enjoy immunity from the wrath of the voters if her rule proves ineffective. In the Sri Lankan electoral contest of 1965 Sirimavo Bandaranaike once again played the role of the sacrificing widow, but this time her pleas fell on deaf ears. The cost of living was at an all time high, and there were shortages of some goods and frequent strikes. Unemployment was high. The result was a disastrous defeat for the governing party, with the SLFP winning only 39 seats out of a total of 157.

In the 1970 election Bandaranaike led her party to victory, but there were no more tearful appeals although she frequently mentioned her late husband to remind the voters why it was in their interest to support her party. Projecting what one author described as "a charismatic mother image,"[59] she appeared more confident and spoke with a deep and strong voice. In addition to providing her time to reflect on her experiences in office, the period as leader of the opposition gave her the opportunity to work more closely with the local party organizations in preparation for the election.

When Bandaranaike faced the voters again in 1977, the credits of her martyred husband seemed even less relevant than they had been in 1970 as she was a seasoned politician, accountable for her own record. She sought to stir the sympathies of the voters by arguing that her government had done everything possible to find a solution to the economic problems plaguing the country but that it was not an easy task.

When Bandaranaike unsuccessfully attempted a comeback during the 1988 elections, having been stripped of her civic rights for a period of years, she no longer expressed support for the socialist policies of her late husband. Her opponents had introduced market-oriented economic reforms that enjoyed considerable popularity. Reminiscent of her approach as the sacrificing widow, she stressed that she had come forward to save the nation from disaster at the request of the people, and one of her more interesting campaign posters showed doves of peace leaving her hands.

Running against a Woman

In running against a woman, a man may not feel comfortable attacking her as he may be fearful that harsh treatment will create sympathy for her, assuring her of substantial support. Jean Chretien, Kim Campbell's successful opponent in the 1993 parliamentary election in Canada, expressed uneasiness when he acknowledged that he felt more comfortable opening doors for women than running against them. The Bloc Quebecois leader Lucien Bouchard, another Campbell opponent, said that in campaigning against a woman, "you have to be a little more guarded—you can't be rough." He expressed concern that the voters would consider attacks leveled against her as a sign that he was picking on her because of her sex.[60]

During Thatcher's first election campaign as head of her party, the Labor leaders were concerned that criticizing her personally would work to their detriment, but they felt compelled to go on the offensive as Labor was running behind the Thatcher-led Conservatives in the polls. While few personal attacks were leveled against her,[61] Thatcher's proposals were portrayed as extremist. Her name was rarely used and, instead, she was referred to as the "leader of the Conservative Party." In an interview former Labor Prime Minister Harold Wilson echoed his approval of the strategy when he said that "Jim's [Callaghan] been absolutely right in forbidding personal attacks. You see, while she might put off some people from voting for her there are others who will vote for her because they just want to see a woman succeed. I can see the force of that argument; it's just because she is a woman that my wife would vote for her."[62]

During her first electoral contest after becoming prime minister, Golda Meir was also spared personal attacks—something that a leader of the governing party in Israel could not expect. Menachem Begin, the leader of the right-oriented electoral alliance, Gahal, who had a reputation as a feisty opponent, announced that he would not attack her. Although the fact that she was a woman and an older one at that probably influenced her opponents' strategy, her considerable popularity also served to reduce her appeal as a target. It was widely believed that the National Unity Government, which had been assembled by Meir's predecessor on the eve of the 1967 war to give the appearance of national unity, would continue to rule following the election. It was imperative to maintain good relations with the government leaders, for the best the opposition parties could hope for was to influence policy as a participant in the new government.

During the 1973 electoral contest, Meir again escaped personal criticism despite the fact that her reputation had been tarnished. Her government had made what she described as a "fatal mistake" in failing to determine the intentions of the country's Arab neighbors before the attack on Yom Kippur by Egyptian and Syrian forces. While the opposition was quick to exploit the situation, disparaging the leaders of the Labor Alignment for failing to prepare adequately for the attack and mishandling the conduct of the war that followed, the brunt of the criticism was leveled at Finance Minister Pinhas Sapir. It was believed he would take over the leadership of the Alignment after the election.

In contrast to the constraint shown by many men when running against a woman, Corazon Aquino's opponent personally attacked her when she ran for the presidency of the Philippines in 1986. Perhaps Marcos was acting out of a sense of desperation, for the public response to Aquino since her husband's assassination had been nothing short of astonishing. The large enthusiastic crowds who attended the people's power gatherings appeared mesmerized by her.

In an attempt to discredit Aquino, the Marcos campaign literature stressed that she was "only a woman," and therefore not capable of serving in "a man's job."[63] Marcos himself addressed the issue of her gender, saying that it was "kind of embarrassing to be running against a woman"[64]; and in a play on the expression, "women's place is in the home," he said that women should confine their preachings to "inside the bedroom."[65] When Aquino challenged him to a debate, Marcos said: "My conversations with ladies have always been pleasant; I presume I will survive this encounter," but he never agreed to the debate.[66]

Benazir Bhutto's opponents accused her of smoking and drinking as well as dancing in violation of Muslim law. To counter the charges of the religious leaders, who persisted in their objection to a woman leader, she stressed her personal commitment to Islam. In her autobiography that was published before the 1988 election, she emphasized her dedication to her religious beliefs. Though her interpretation of Islamic teachings differed from that of her opponents, she adhered to certain traditional practices, such as keeping her head covered in public.

Although Violeta Chamorro was personally attacked by her Sandinista opponents as a mere figurehead whose understanding of the issues was superficial at best, some of the most severe criticism was leveled against her by two of her own children who were staunch supporters of the Sandinista regime. Her younger son Carlos, the editor of the Sandinista newspaper, *Barricada*, expressed doubts about his mother's ability to govern, while her older daughter Claudia, an official of the Sandinista government, accused her mother of being a traitor to her father's memory. In response, the family newspaper, *La Prensa*, which was edited by her younger daughter, frequently included photographs of the Catholic cardinal blessing Chamorro.

A direct link has been made between the personal attacks leveled against Mary Robinson and her electoral victory in 1990.[67] During the closing days of the campaign, Robinson and her chief opponent, Brian Lenihan, were running almost even. The turn in the fortunes of the two candidates seems to have occurred on the day before the election with the appearance on a radio program of the minister of the environment. Padraig Flynn had instructions to attack Robinson's socialist leanings. Instead, he accused her of "changing her image to suit the fashion of the time and having a new-found interest in the family." He went on to say that "none of us who knew Mary Robinson well in previous incarnations ever heard her claiming to be the great wife."[68] An apology failed to reverse the damage, especially among women. While her campaign advisers exploited the incident, Robinson herself did not give her opponents further cause for argument as she wisely responded to the criticism by making light of it. She said that because of her strong family ties she could "laugh it [the incident] off."[69]

A similar experience awaited her successor Mary McAleese, who was portrayed in her election posters as a bridge-builder. Government documents were released alleging that she was sympathetic to Sinn Fein, the political arm of the Irish Republican Army. In an attempt to make the most of her connection to Northern Ireland, the leader of the major opposition party described McAleese as an outsider and said that she should "stay out of politics in the south."[70] As she had predicted, there was an outpouring of sympathy for her, and her position as the front runner, which was never really in doubt, was solidified.

The political advantage that a woman appears to get when she is attacked by a male opponent may disappear when she levels personal insults against him. Tansu Ciller and Mesut Yilmaz viciously attacked one another during the 1995 Turkish election campaign. During the debates Yilmaz railed against Ciller, referring to her harshly as "that woman." While one observer said that Yilmaz was better prepared, Ciller remained calm but goaded her opponent.[71] The electorate was turned off by the display, and the results of the election were a surprise as the two secularist center parties ran behind the Islamic Welfare Party.

In those electoral contests that took place after a woman had served in public office for an extended period, there seemed to be less reluctance to attack her. In 1983, during Thatcher's second election campaign as leader, her opponents were not so cautious when it came to dealing with her as they had been during the 1979 contest. Perhaps out of a sense of frustration with their own poor showing in the polls or in an attempt to goad her into an angry response, the Labor leaders struck out at Thatcher. Denis Healey, deputy leader of the party, criticized her for her handling of the aftermath of the Falklands War. He remarked that "she wraps herself in the Union Jack and exploits the sacrifices of our soldiers, sailors, and airmen in the Falkland Islands for purely party advantage—and hopes to get away with it."[72] He went on to say that "this Prime Minister who glories in slaughter has taken advantage of the superb professionalism of our forces in the Falkland Islands."[73] While the leader of the Labor Party refused to endorse the statement, and Healey made a partial retraction the following day, saying that he regretted using the word "slaughter," the damage was done. Not only was the statement viewed as excessive but the opposition had introduced the issue that worked to Thatcher's advantage as she owed much of her support to her handling of the war.

Even those women related to politically prominent men were likely to be the subject of increased criticism after they had served in office for a time. When Bandaranaike faced the voters in 1977, after her second term in office, she was taunted at meetings. Charges of corruption were leveled against her in the midst of allegations that she had ignored the restrictions in the land reform law to her personal advantage. Her opponents also accused her of nepotism. Among her relatives who occupied government posts were her two daughters as well as her four brothers. She was also criticized for overreaction to the 1971 student-led insurgency, and her handling of the period of emergency rule that followed was faulted. Her opponents also reminded the voters that she had extended her second term by two years with the adoption of a new constitution in 1972.

Gandhi already had a record of service when she faced the electorate, for her first election campaign took place after she had been in office approximately a year. The opposition parties, frustrated by many years of election failures, staged demonstrations to discredit the ruling party. Encouraged by the unpopularity of her decision to devalue the rupee, opposition groups sought to disrupt her meetings. At a rally held in Bhubaneswar near the end of the campaign, student protestors shouted "Indira Gandhi go back," and she was hit by a stone that broke her nose.[74] By continuing the tour with her face wrapped in bandages, she won the sympathy of the voters and subsequently the election.

It was in Gandhi's third campaign that criticism of her reached its peak. The election had been postponed for more than a year because of the Emergency that she declared in 1975 in response to growing economic difficulties and political unrest. During the campaign, the opposition focused on the actions of the government, criticizing the arrest of fellow politicians as well as the unpopular sterilization program. Gandhi was also subjected to personal attacks. Opposition campaign signs read "End dictatorship, dethrone the Queen!" While she did not draw large crowds, there was considerable heckling at her meetings.

During Bhutto's second campaign as leader, her principal opponent made a connection between the corruption charges leveled against her and the deteriorating economic conditions, accusing her of looting "the country like a conqueror treats a defeated country."[75] Given the severe unemployment as well as the high inflation rate, this proved to be an effective argument.

There have been several electoral contests in which women were pitted against other women in the contest for the top political position. Three women led parties in the 1993 election in Norway, and the campaign was a comparatively mild affair. In contrast, the conduct of the Bangladesh races of 1991, 1995, and 2001 stirred up the hatred that existed between Sheikh Hasina and Khaleda Zia. Both women linked their opponent to a role in the assassination of a political prominent male relative—in the case of Hasina, her father and in the case of Zia, her husband. After the elections they found it difficult to cooperate to push out Ershad's military government, blaming each other for the nation's ills. In the first campaign in 1991 Hasina was viewed as arrogant, while Zia appeared to be more serious, putting forth a 19-point program to deal with the nation's economic woes. In the second campaign held in 1996, Zia was the more negative, "attacking the AL as anti-democratic, politically incompetent, and a pro-Indian stooge."[76] Hasina apologized for "mistakes made by her father and made a number of promises, such as provision of financial assistance for farmers, elimination of corruption and nepotism, and repeal of repressive laws."[77]

The squabbling between the two women outlived the campaign itself. In each case, the party that lost the election claimed that the results had been rigged and boycotted the new parliament, calling for general strikes to disrupt the economy. The campaign of 2001 was the most peaceful of the races as the caretaker prime minister who had been appointed to oversee the election used the military to ensure order.[78]

The two New Zealand women who led their respective parties in the 2001 election did not like each other. Helen Clark resented her opponent Jenny Shipley for the role she played in keeping alive the discussion of Clark's unorthodox marital arrangements. But the campaign was relatively bland with personal attacks confined to the period near the end of the campaign.

In the Finnish election for president that took place in 2000, four of the five leading candidates were women. In commenting on campaign strategy, one observer wrote: "None of the women candidates drew attention to their own roles as mothers and wives, preferring instead to focus on foreign policy and other less personal issues."[79] The concentration on foreign policy in this instance may be explained by the fact that it is the president who is responsible for foreign relations in the Finnish system.

After the assassination of Gamini Dissanayake during the Sri Lanka presidential election campaign of 1994, the UNP chose his widow, Srima, to succeed him as the party's candidate. During the campaign Srima, a lawyer, took issue with the way the government was handling the investigation into the murder of her husband, while Kumaratunga accused her opponent of stirring up communal tensions.

Conclusions

The paucity of women at the top of the political hierarchy is linked to the concern of party leaders about a woman's electability. Since men have historically been dominant in politics, women do not fit the traditional image of a leader. The fact that women are smaller in stature and have higher pitched voices has created concern about whether they can cope with the rigors of public office. Some women have sought to compensate for these deficiencies with elocution lessons and the services of media advisers, while others have been able to dispel the apprehensions as they brought special assets to the job such as being a close relative of a prominent male politician.

Despite their image as weak, the women leaders who have made it to the top have shown great stamina in coping with the rigors of campaigning—an exercise that requires that they address hundreds of rallies and travel thousands of miles.

Women who are married must communicate their ability to take care of their families. Divorced and unmarried women have added burdens in showing that they are "adequately feminine." Women must also demonstrate their competence since they are seen as less capable than men. In selecting campaign themes and plans of attack, women political leaders are caught between the need to show that they are tough and can meet the rigorous demands of public office, while, at the same time, not behaving in a manner that would be considered inappropriate.

The male politician faces a similar dilemma when his opponent is a woman. Should he vigorously attack her, or is he likely to be seen as behaving inappropriately toward a woman? If he treats her more gently, is he likely to be seen as patronizing? The problem loses some of its sting after the female politician has established a record, for her actions in office become an acceptable target for criticism.

Chapter Ten

Forming Governments

Gro Brundtland once told an interviewer that, while traveling in a plane with Margaret Thatcher, she asked the British prime minister why there were so few women in her cabinet. During her 11 years in office, Thatcher included only 1 other woman who served for less than 2 years. In contrast, Brundtland appointed several women to the Norwegian cabinet, with the number reaching almost one-half of the total in her 1986 and 1990 cabinets.

In response to this challenge to her record, Thatcher, according to Brundtland, replied: "We have so few women in our Parliament in Britain. I have no choice."[1] This statement was accurate in so far as the number of women was concerned, for during Thatcher's tenure women made up only approximately 6 percent of those serving in parliament. Brundtland indicated that she thought this a poor excuse and said that she told Thatcher of her own efforts to include women, arguing that "it takes political will and direction."[2]

Brundtland did have an advantage in that women numbered 35 to 40 percent of the total membership of the Norwegian parliament. In making her selections, she was also able to spread her net broadly, for, unlike their counterparts in the British cabinet, those chosen to serve in the Norwegian cabinet are not required to be members of the parliament. In fact, they must give up their parliamentary seats when appointed to the cabinet.

Maria de Lourdes Pintasilgo of Portugal took a more charitable view toward Thatcher's failure to include women in the cabinet. In commenting on her own experience, she noted the difficulties she encountered in persuading women to join her government. While some may have been reluctant to assume a position in the cabinet because Pintasilgo's own appointment was a temporary one, she argued that the rejection of her offer in many cases could be attributed to a lack of self-esteem. A number of the women who turned her down indicated that they were not competent to assume such responsibilities, while men who rejected her invitation gave other reasons for their refusal to join the government.[3] Pintasilgo also observed that women are concerned they will have "to make compromises on an intellectual or moral level" when they enter the political arena.[4]

Cabinet Selection

It is somewhat surprising that those women who have risen to the top have not included more women in their governments. Holding a cabinet post can be important in building confidence as well as in demonstrating that women are capable of performing the duties of high office. In selecting members to serve in their cabinets, political leaders must take into account a number of considerations that have worked against the inclusion of women. First, a leader, if she is prudent, will reward those who backed her candidacy. Second, a leader is likely to appoint some with extensive experience, especially if she herself is a newcomer to high-level office, and, finally, she must include representatives of the various interests in her political party or coalition of parties as she is dependent on their support.

During an interview given shortly before the date for the 1979 British election was announced, Thatcher told a journalist that in putting together a government, she would not attempt to assemble a cabinet of "people who represent all the different viewpoints within the Party.... We've got to go in an agreed and clear direction," she said. "As Prime Minister, I couldn't waste time having any internal arguments."[5]

Despite her resolve to pursue her program with minimal resistance, Thatcher, in assembling her cabinet, took into account those very characteristics she had rejected only weeks earlier. Having led a back-bench revolt and challenged a sitting prime minister for the leadership position, she opened wounds that did not readily heal. Her unwavering commitment to her agenda made it even more difficult to bring the different interests within the party together. Though she had waged a successful election campaign, the Conservative Party won only a plurality of the popular vote, and the strength of her base had yet to be tested in the rough-and-tumble of parliamentary maneuver.

In choosing those who would serve with her, Thatcher had to include some who had a record of service, especially since she had relatively little cabinet experience herself and had never held a key cabinet post. The party leaders, who, for the most part, had supported her predecessor, were keenly aware of their pivotal position, and during the election campaign they reassured the voters who found Thatcher's program too radical that moderates like themselves would be represented in the cabinet.[6]

Despite these limitations on her power to appoint, Thatcher was careful to reserve those ministries that dealt with the economy—the area with which she was most concerned—for those who shared her views. For example, her longtime friend and ally Keith Joseph, whom she believed would resist requests for government aid, was named secretary of state for industry. Later she transferred him to education as she was disappointed in his proposals to aid British industries that were losing money. Other allies in her drive to cut back government included Geoffrey Howe, who became Chancellor of the Exchequer, and John Nott, a Heath appointee, who was named secretary of state for trade.

In the months that followed, Thatcher made a number of changes in her cabinet, removing or transferring doubters to less important posts and bringing more supporters into the cabinet. In January 1981 she moved Francis Pym, who had refused to make the cuts she viewed important, from the defense ministry to the position of leader of the house. In September she sacked three "wets," a slang term meaning weak-willed applied to those who disagreed with her.

With an approval rating of less than 30 percent, Thatcher replaced every minister who dealt with the economy or industry within a short period of time except Geoffrey Howe who remained a strong supporter of her policy to reduce inflation through control of the money supply. In reviewing the record, a British political science scholar concluded that Thatcher "became the first prime minister in British history to sack cabinet members on a large scale, not because they were incompetent but because they disagreed with her. Previous prime ministers sought to keep recalcitrant cabinet colleagues on board; Thatcher consistently threw them overboard."[7] Thatcher did include some in the cabinet who disagreed with her economic policies but whom she viewed as a threat as backbenchers. In her autobiography, she said that Peter Walker who served as minister of agriculture and later as energy minister would have "caused more trouble outside...because he fought his corner hard."[8] The replacements she brought into the cabinet were men such as Norman Tebbit and Cecil Parkinson with whom she felt more comfortable and, for the most part, like herself came from modest backgrounds but had made their way in the professions or business.

Following her party's impressive election victory in 1983 and with her record of leadership in the Falklands War in tow, Thatcher had even greater latitude in selecting the members of her cabinet. She was able to give all the key posts to her supporters, promoting some of her most loyal followers and eliminating her most outspoken critics, such as Francis Pym.

Despite her strong support for Cecil Parkinson, a most trusted adviser, Thatcher was not able to save her secretary of state for trade and industry. On Election Day in 1983 Parkinson acknowledged the paternity of the child his mistress was carrying. Though Thatcher was reluctant to accept his resignation as she had him pegged for the post of foreign secretary, she eventually decided that it was necessary to separate herself from him, particularly since she had stressed the importance of Victorian values during her election campaigns. Following her unprecedented election to a third term in 1987, Thatcher, who made changes in half of the ministerial posts, returned Parkinson to the cabinet, naming him energy secretary.

In 1985 unemployment remained high in Britain. The coal miners' strike was entering its second year and the pound had fallen. The Conservative Party was ranked third in the polls behind its rivals and had not performed well in recent by-elections. To deal with the deteriorating situation, Thatcher made a number of changes in her government, naming new ministers to about one-third of the departments. In an interview, she said that the changes were designed to introduce some "fresh faces" to make it clear she was "putting great emphasis on enterprise and employment" and to enable her to "get our policies across a bit more cogently."[9] In an effort to solve the unemployment problem that was hurting her politically, Thatcher appointed Lord Young of Graffham, a self-made millionaire whom she had brought into politics a few months earlier, as employment secretary. She also brought in two "wets," strengthening this wing of the party.

In 1989 Thatcher moved Howe, who had made no secret of his interest in succeeding her, to deputy prime minister, a position with no duties. To make matters worse, she did not tell him of the change until the morning in which she made the announcement. Though Howe, who had been named foreign secretary after the 1983 election, was among her most loyal supporters, he had sided with the Chancellor of the Exchequer, Nigel Lawson, at a European Community summit meeting, urging her to say when Britain would formally tie the pound to the German mark and other European currencies in the European Monetary System. Thatcher had reservations about closer economic ties with Europe, but a compromise was eventually reached by which Britain would agree to join the system but would set no definite date for the formal union. Despite her anger with the two men, Thatcher kept Lawson on to preserve confidence in the anti-inflationary policy. In October 1989 he resigned.

Like Thatcher, Tansu Ciller, who had relatively little high-level political experience and did not have the support of her party's leadership, expressed resolve to start afresh during her bid to head the True Path Party. She told an interviewer: "I am brave, I have no time to lose. Turkey is at a critical point. We are up against a wall. We will either climb over it or be crushed at the bottom."[10] In forming her first government in 1993, she did not take the opportunity to mend divisions in her party as Thatcher had. She retained only three former ministers from her party in the cabinet and signaled her dominance by including a number of new faces.[11] Her unwillingness to use the resources of her office to unite the various factions within her party may have worked to her disadvantage in the long term as the True Path Party lost seats in the election held two and a half years later.

To reduce criticism of her plans to privatize government-owned businesses, Ciller appointed her opponent, Mumtaz Soysal, foreign minister in the belief that he would be reluctant to attack her if he were in the government. Their differences proved too great, and he resigned only months after taking office.[12]

In selecting those who would serve with them in the cabinet, two other newcomers to national politics, Kim Campbell and Gro Brundtland, at least initially, turned to those who had worked with their predecessors. As part of an overall assault on the budget deficit, Campbell eliminated several cabinet posts, but more than one-half of those remaining were staffed by those who had served in the previous government. Four of those she named were women, and she gave her chief rival for the prime ministership, Jean Charest, responsibility for several ministries concerned with the economy. Brundtland appointed three ministers who had not been members of her predecessor's government, and she included only three women in her first cabinet. In the government she put together in 1986, Brundtland, who remarked that "a natural balance of men and women makes prejudiced decisions less likely and gives the greatest breadth of experience," appointed 7 women to a cabinet of 18.[13] Among the most constrained in making cabinet appointments was Angela Merkel of Germany. Despite her substantial lead in the preelection polls, Merkel's party, the Christian Democratic Union (CDU) and its sister party, the Christian Socialist Union (CSU), failed to win enough seats in the 2005 election to put together a parliamentary majority. Her principal opposition was also unable to form a government. After several weeks of intense negotiations, the CDU/CSU and the Social Democratic Party (SPD) agreed to form a national unity government, known as the "grand coalition." Merkel paid a price to ensure her position as chancellor. Each of the two principal parties were given an equal number of cabinet positions. She also agreed that the SPD would fill the position of vice chancellor as well as hold the important ministerial positions of finance, foreign affairs, and labor.

Presidential Systems

The leader in a presidential system generally has greater latitude than her counterpart in a parliamentary system in choosing the members of her cabinet. She may go outside the legislative body to make her selections, although she, too, is likely to reward those interests that supported her and include some with experience.

In filling the important portfolios concerned with the economy, Corazon Aquino turned to the Catholic business community that had financed her campaign, naming former corporate heads, Jaime Ongpin minister of finance and Jose Concepcion minister of trade and industry. To the consternation of her running mate, Salvador Laurel, who was given the foreign affairs portfolio, she reserved only a few posts for members of Unido, the political organization that Laurel had put together and on which she relied during the election campaign. Aquino kept on two military leaders—Fidel Ramos as armed forces chief of staff and Juan Ponce Enrile as minister of defense—who had paved the way for her to assume the presidency by leading the rebellion in opposition to President Marcos. To round out her cabinet, she turned to those who had been close to her husband, such as Aquilino Pimentel, to fill the sensitive post of local governments' minister.

To satisfy the various interests in her governing coalition, Aquino was quick to make changes in her cabinet with only one member serving throughout her six year term.[14] The first casualty of the Aquino administration was Defense Minister Enrile, who turned out to be a divisive influence within the cabinet, disagreeing with the president on a variety of issues including how to deal with the communist insurgents. Aquino favored a negotiated settlement with the communists, while the military preferred the use of forceful measures. The supporters of Enrile, who was dismissed in 1986 after he was linked to a coup attempt, believed that given the key role as leader of dissident military forces he had played in the ouster of Marcos, he was entitled to the presidency. To placate the military for the loss of Enrile, Aquino was forced to accept the resignation of some in the cabinet who were viewed as left-leaning following another coup attempt in 1987. Others in the cabinet viewed as pro-left were dismissed, including Aquino's closest adviser Joker Arroyo, to reduce the risk of more coup attempts by disgruntled military forces.

Michelle Bachelet who was elected president of Chile in 2006 kept her promise to appoint women to one-half of the cabinet positions, naming 10 women to head key posts in her government. Among the positions given to women were those of defense minister and economic minister. Bachelet's cabinet selections were unusual in other ways as well since she included only two members who had ministerial experience and several did not belong to a political party. The Bachelet cabinet also had more PhDs, MBAs, and those with business experience than did its predecessors.[15]

Dual Systems

In a dual system, consisting of a president and a prime minister who share power, the two sometimes find themselves in disagreement over who should be appointed to the cabinet. In Poland, for example, cabinet selection served as a point of conflict between the two leaders. To improve relations with President Lech Walesa, Hanna Suchocka chose to defer to him in filling certain high-level posts such as that of defense and foreign affairs while she assumed responsibility for the economy.[16]

As prime minister, Edith Cresson had little to say about who would serve with her. In the French system the two leaders are encouraged to work together in selecting a cabinet, but since the president usually has the more developed power base and can dismiss the prime minister, he tends to have the greater influence. In putting together her cabinet, Cresson, at Mitterrand's request, included a number of his closest advisers, some of whom had served in the previous government. Despite the limitations on her ability to choose, she included a number of women in her cabinet, but only 1 more than her predecessor or 7 out of 46 ministers.[17] Cresson, who was viewed as a demanding boss, did not get along well with her ministers, especially those with whom she did not agree.[18] She tried to persuade Mitterrand to allow her to reshuffle the cabinet and bring in ministers with whom she would be more comfortable, but he refused.[19] She later told an interviewer that it was important to be able to choose advisers whom one knows very well. She also spoke of the importance of being able to select people one trusts.[20]

In the dual system in Sri Lanka, the president is authorized to select a cabinet and preside over it, but it must be a cabinet that has the confidence of the parliament. When Chandrika Kumaratunga became prime minister in the summer of 1994, the fact that the sitting president belonged to a different political party than she had little impact on cabinet selection. The president chose to play a nominal role in the state affairs as his days in office were numbered. To fulfill her campaign promise to reduce the costs of government, Kumaratunga put together a cabinet, drawn disproportionately from the political elite, that was considerably smaller than that of her predecessor.[21] When she was elected president some months later, she appointed her mother, Sirimavo Bandaranaike, prime minister but made few other changes in the cabinet.

To ensure a solid victory in the 1994 presidential election, Kumaratunga not only solicited the support of the minority communities but also sought the backing of groups such as the Ceylon Workers' Congress. To seal the arrangement with this union that represented estate workers, she took the leader, S. Thondaman, into her cabinet shortly before the election. Thondaman had been a supporter of her principal opponent, the United National Party (UNP).

When the UNP again won control of the Sri Lanka parliament in 2001, serious disagreements among the contending parties surfaced. In a fit of pique, Kumaratunga allowed the new prime minister, Ranil Wickremesinghe, to choose those who would serve in the cabinet, ushering in a period of conflict between the two leaders. Later she reversed course and assumed the ministries of defense and finance—positions to which she as president was entitled under the constitution. A bit of levity overshadowed the conflict when Kumaratunga brought her dog to cabinet meetings over which she presided, allegedly to improve security. Her opponents responded by bringing along their dogs and telling the press: "The president unleashes her dog on us and we cannot go for cabinet meetings if we are being set upon by a dog."[22]

Following her party's parliamentary election victory in 2004, Kumaratunga was free to make her own cabinet selections. She named some of those who had served with her earlier as well as others who were new to the cabinet. She also included three women[23] and reserved four positions for her alliance partner, the People's Liberation Party (JVP).

Plural Executive and Multiparty Systems

The plural executive system also imposes restrictions on the latitude a leader has in selecting the members of her cabinet. Milka Planinc of Yugoslavia, who made many changes in her predecessor's government, consulted with the other members of the Federal Council before naming her cabinet. Switzerland's Ruth Dreifuss and Micheline

Calmy-Rey had virtually nothing to say about who would serve with them, as the members of the Federal Council assumed the various cabinet portfolios after reaching agreement among themselves on the specific distribution.

In a multiparty system, particularly one in which there is no dominant party, it is likely that several parties will be required to assemble a government, and portfolios must be reserved for members of these parties. In appointing her cabinet, Hanna Suchocka included men who represented the parties that made up the coalition she had put together as well as some who had served with the previous Solidarity-backed governments. In responding to the question as to why there were no women in her cabinet, Suchocka noted: "None of the coalition parties presented a woman candidate." She went on to say: "If I could, I would propose a few women because it is easier to work with women. They are reliable and conscientious." She quickly added: "I am not afraid of working with men. I have always moved in a man's world."[24]

Jenny Shipley of New Zealand inherited a cabinet that included no women. She was able to shuffle the portfolios, placing those who shared her market-oriented approach to head such critical spending departments as health, welfare, education, and commerce.

Shipley dismissed the deputy prime minister in August 1998 after he criticized her during question time. Winston Peters, leader of the New Zealand First Party and the governing party's coalition partner, had walked out of a cabinet meeting along with some of his colleagues during a discussion of the sale of the government's share of the Wellington airport. Shipley had approved the plan to privatize the airport, whereas Peters opposed the scheme. Though the government's future was in doubt, Shipley was able to weather the storm. With the support of some minor parties, she staved off the threats to her government and remained in office until the end of the term.

Shipley's successor, Helen Clark, was also dependent on a coalition, but one of her own making as she reunited the Labor Party with a faction, the left-leaning Alliance Party, that had broken away some years earlier.[25] As Clark had accepted most of the market-oriented reforms introduced during the 1990s, she also reserved the ministries associated with high-spending social programs for her supporters.

While the leader of the New Zealand Labor Party distributed the portfolios, the party caucus selected those to serve in the cabinet. Clark expressed support for the members of her government but acknowledged that she would have made different choices for some of the appointments if the decision had been hers alone. As it was, almost one-third of the cabinet, including the finance minister, came from an academic background as did Clark. Also, some with experience in trade unions as well as 7 women were appointed to a cabinet of 20.[26]

Clark appeared to have gained more latitude in appointing her cabinet after her successful reelection bid in 2002 and again in 2005. By relying on floating coalitions to maintain her parliamentary majority, she was freed from having to include any of the minority parties in her government. Clark also appointed Winston Peters as foreign minister. In that position Peters continued to occupy opposition benches, but he did not attend cabinet meetings. When questions were raised about this arrangement, Clark argued that it was an innovative device "designed to make the Parliament work and the government work in an inclusive way."[27] She went on to suggest that her differences with Peters in the past had been "on other issues," not foreign policy.

Military Dominated States

In a country in which the military is dominant, a leader may be forced to make certain concessions in putting together a government. In Pakistan in 1988, it was only when Bhutto agreed to keep Foreign Minister Sahabzada Yaqub Khan, a member of an opposition party, in his post, that the military signaled its support for her to form a government.

A significant role was given to the military by Megawati as she appointed no fewer than five current or former military officers to her cabinet. Among the ministries led by military leaders were interior, intelligence, and transportation. Her appointment of General Susilo Bambang Yudhoyono as minister of political and security affairs was later to haunt her, for it was he who defeated her in 2004 in Indonesia's first presidential election.

Selection by Widows and Daughters

Since they did not have independent power bases and usually no agendas other than to pursue the policies laid out by their late husbands, the widows who rose to the top had self-imposed limits on their cabinet selections. They were likely to rely, at least initially, on those who served with their husbands. Relatives and friends with whom they felt comfortable rounded out the cabinets.

Heeding the advice of those who had persuaded her to lead the Sri Lanka Freedom Party (SLFP), Sirimavo Bandaranaike selected 10 men, one-half of whom had worked with her husband, to serve as ministers in her first cabinet. She included her nephew, Felix Bandaranaike, the secretary of the SLFP, as minister of finance. Though she was no longer the tearful, semidetached politician when she assumed office for a second term in 1970, Bandaranaike again chose her cabinet from among those who had been close to her husband, asking many who had previously served with her to join the government. In contrast to her first cabinet, she included representatives of the various ethnic and religious groups in an attempt to improve her party's relations with the minority communities. To accommodate those interests as well as the small leftist parties that were a part of the electoral coalition, she increased the size of the cabinet.

In putting together her government in 1990, Violeta Chamorro turned to friends and relatives. For health minister, she chose the pediatrician who treated her grandchildren, while to head the government ministry, she selected a relative, and for education minister, an ally of the cardinal who had at least implicitly lent his support to Chamorro's campaign.[28]

Conspicuous in their absence from the cabinet were the leaders of the parties who made up Chamorro's electoral coalition, the National Opposition Union, many of whom had been actively engaged in opposition to the Sandinistas and were not prepared to abandon the conflict. She chose instead to call on technocrats who had spent the war years abroad and were concerned to restore the country.[29]

For other places in the cabinet, Chamorro turned to the opposition Sandinista National Liberation Front (FSLN), the largest single party represented in the National Assembly. To encourage a smooth and peaceful transition, she asked the Sandinista government's defense minister, Humberto Ortega, to stay on as her top military commander. Since she planned to decrease military spending and eliminate the draft, she needed the cooperation of the military leaders. She was also concerned to unify her country, and she felt this was "a golden opportunity to reject the long-held tradition...that called for the winners to banish the losers from the political scene and, if possible, send them into exile." Since the issues that divided her country had split her own family, she had an added incentive to heal the divisions. As she said: "I couldn't very well take a position that excluded [my children] from participating...."[30]

As several years had elapsed between her husband's term of office and her own rise to the top in 1991, Khaleda Zia included only a few who had served in his cabinet. Instead, she relied more on contacts of her own that she had made as leader of her party. Following her victory in 2001, Zia created a 27-member cabinet that included a number of new faces to accommodate the several interests in her party as well as the electoral coalition she had put together. Eight of these were newcomers to the cabinet.[31] While Zia did not include any women in her initial cabinet, following her second electoral victory, she did appoint an older sister to the ministry concerned with women and children.

Zia initially made few changes in her cabinet as she appeared to view a reshuffle "as an insult to her original judgment."[32] In her second term, she did reshuffle on more than one occasion, because some of the ministers were performing poorly[33] and others had engaged in corrupt practices.[34] In 2006, under pressure from her party, she reshuffled the cabinet three times in one month. Party leaders were concerned about their prospects in the upcoming parliamentary election, particularly considering the unrest over the power and water shortages that the country was experiencing.[35]

The daughters of politically prominent men as a rule did not have an independent power base and tended to rely on the followers of their fathers, but some found it difficult to work with the leaders of their parties. A widow had more than likely interacted with her late husband's colleagues, at least socially, but a daughter, who represented a different generation, was not likely to be seen as an equal. To counter this perception of her as well as to assert her independence, she might choose to deviate from her father's agenda.

Indira Gandhi was not comfortable working with her father's former colleagues, for they did not treat her as a serious politician and were quick to remind her that she owed her selection as prime minister to them. Her relations with the party leaders had been marred early on when as confidant and adviser to her father she attempted to control access to him. After she assumed office, she was forced to give in to the pressure of the party leaders and keep in place most of those who had served with her predecessor. To avoid a contest for the leadership of her party in the parliament in 1967, Gandhi agreed to include Desai in the cabinet as deputy prime minister and minister of finance. She preferred to have him in the government where he would not be in a position to cultivate opposition to her. She also believed that with Desai in the cabinet, she would be able to neutralize other competitors.

Following Gandhi's strong showing in the 1967 election, her party's impressive election victory in 1971, and her leadership during the 1971 Bangladesh war, support for her soared. She was in a position to remove those who disagreed with her, replacing them with loyal supporters.

Gandhi sought to deal with potential power rivals by shifting their portfolios. In reshuffling her cabinet, Gandhi gradually removed or demoted those who disagreed with her as well as those who were potential rivals for the leadership position. Following the 1969 split in the Congress Party, Gandhi removed Y.B.Chavan, who had been viewed as a possible successor to Nehru, from his powerful post as home minister and gave him the finance portfolio—an area in which he had little experience or expertise and was more likely to fail.

Though Benazir Bhutto had differences with the old guard in her party, she included in her first cabinet some who had served with her father, keeping on others who had held a cabinet post in the governments of her predecessors.[36] Bhutto, like Gandhi, filled out her cabinet with inexperienced men whose principal qualification was loyalty to her.[37] She included no women in the cabinet with the exception of her mother who was appointed senior minister without portfolio, thereby making provision for someone to take over the duties of the prime minister when Bhutto was away. Sheikh Hasina included in her cabinet some who had served with her father as well as representatives of different interests in the parliament. She also appointed two women to serve in her cabinet.

Unlike the other daughters, Gloria Arroyo and Megawati Sukarnoputri did not turn to their fathers' cabinet ministers as it had been many years since these men occupied the top political post. Instead, Arroyo looked to those who had supported her move against President Joseph Estrada. As education secretary, she appointed one of the senators, Raul Roco, who had voted to open the envelope containing evidence against Estrada, and as justice secretary, Hernando Perez, a prosecutor in the impeachment trial. To round out her cabinet with those who had experience, she included some who had served with her predecessors, Corazon Aquino and Fidel Ramos. She also appointed a number of technocrats as she was, according to one of her ministers, "willing to hire strangers based on track record and referrals from people she respects."[38] Vowing to increase political opportunities for women, she included seven women in her large cabinet.[39]

Megawati, who took office in the midst of the impression that she was "a bumbling housewife held hostage by the military, a scheming husband, and power-hungry politicians," made it clear that the cabinet was her creation and it worked for her, not the legislative body.[40] Although her first cabinet was seen as a highly professional one comprised of a market-friendly economic team and few politicians,[41] it faced calls for a reshuffle on the grounds of poor performance. For foreign minister she selected a career diplomat, but, despite her debt to the military, she chose a civilian with little experience in military matters for defense minister. To create a sense of continuity, she included seven men who had served with her predecessor, Abdurrahman Wahid.

Despite the considerable latitude she appeared to have in choosing her cabinet, Megawati failed to appoint a single woman among its 33 members. She had told an interviewer in 1998 that she was different from other Indonesian women, for in Eastern culture "it is still a tradition that the woman has the duty to stay in the background." In response to the interviewer's expression of surprise to her acknowledgment that she had no women advisers, Megawati said, "it's very hard and tough work. I am doing it, yes, but that is why I think I am rather unique."[42]

Selection by Temporary Leaders

Those who are appointed to the top position for a brief period may bring in a new team to govern since their very selection represents an attempt to break with the past to bolster a faltering government. Reneta Indzhova of Bulgaria ushered in a nonpartisan caretaker cabinet pejoratively referred to as a "government of experts." Claudette Werleigh replaced 13 of 17 cabinet members when she took over as prime minister of Haiti. In the cabinet Lydia Gueiler of Bolivia put together, only two ministers retained their posts. Madior Boye of Senegal, who was an advocate for women's rights, included 5 women in the 24-member cabinet assembled after she was appointed to a full term. She also selected several technocrats as well as some who were members of the previous government. Ertha Pascal-Trouillot who served as an interim president of Haiti appointed several friends and relatives to high-level positions.

Some leaders who are viewed as serving temporarily may feel constrained in selecting the members of a cabinet. When she first assumed office in 1969, Golda Meir did not see fit to make cabinet changes in the national unity government. In commenting on this decision, she remarked: "If I thought that there was need for such changes I would not have taken on this position."[43] Even after the election held later that same year in which the Labor Alignment lost seats, Meir chose to continue with a national unity government because of the growing tension with Israel's neighbors. Portfolios were assigned to the opposition parties, and, as part of an agreement to avoid a split in her own party, the factions of the Labor Alignment were given the opportunity to select their representatives in the government.

While Meir's predecessors as prime minister had assumed the portfolio for defense, Meir chose to appoint Moshe Dayan to fill that post despite her earlier differences with him. The imminent threat to Israel's security as well as Meir's lack of experience in the defense area made it important that she have someone with expertise in that slot. But she had a counterweight to Dayan in General David Elazar whom she appointed chief of staff in 1972. She had still another source of military advice when she invited former chief of staff Chaim Bar-Lev to join the cabinet. Within a few months, the national unity government broke down when the right-wing Gahal Party resigned from the cabinet following the government's acceptance of a United States-backed peace plan. The plan called for a cease-fire and negotiations for the withdrawal of Israeli troops from the occupied territories. Meir was able to form a new government, allowing the Knesset to serve the full term for which it was elected in 1969.

Portfolios Assumed by Leaders

In some countries, the constitution reserves specific portfolios for the political leader. The constitution in effect in Sri Lanka during the Bandaranaike years provided that the prime minister should head the defense and foreign affairs ministries. In other countries, the leader is authorized to assume responsibility for a ministry of her choice, giving her a greater measure of control over a specific policy area. Kumaratunga, in her first term as president, kept the finance ministry as well as the ministry of ethnic affairs and national integration. She chose to assume responsibility for the latter, more than likely, because of her concern to find a solution to the Sri Lankan civil war.[44] As far as the finance ministry was concerned, she told a reporter that she had taken on the work of this ministry because of the "corruption that has gone on at the presidential level and at the cabinet level." She went on to say that she had "to tend to these things myself because it's important to bring back the culture of honesty."[45]

Sheikh Hasina kept several of the more important ministries such as defense and planning for herself while Zia, at the beginning of her second term in 2001, took on responsibility for defense, power, and energy. Both were criticized for taking on too many roles, thereby placing undue burdens on themselves, and failing to meet their duties.

Other leaders who assumed responsibility for a ministry included Jenny Shipley and Helen Clark. Shipley continued to direct the Women's Affairs Ministry, a portfolio she held before becoming prime minister while Clark, as a close follower of the arts, took on the Ministry for Arts, Culture, and Heritage to convey their importance. She also assumed responsibility for the oversight of the ministries as she was concerned to run a more efficient and effective government. As the chair of the cabinet honors and appointments committee, Clark was in a position to bring more women into government. In an interview, she remarked that "people are well aware that if they serve up lists of men only, they will be told to go away and think again."[46]

Eugenia Charles assumed the portfolios of foreign affairs, finance, and development and during her second term that of defense. Her predecessor's alleged corrupt activities and his civil rights abuses had tarnished the image of Dominica, and Charles felt the need to shore up the country's reputation within the international community.[47]

Conclusions

Lydia Gueiler, who included two women in her cabinet, told an interviewer that she would have liked to have more, but she said that for "'political reasons' she had to appoint ministers acceptable to the more powerful factions in congress."[48] In putting together a cabinet, a political leader must include representatives of the various interests within her party or coalition as well as some with a record of service, especially if she has little experience herself. While these requirements serve to limit a leader's choices, they work against the inclusion of women who are relative newcomers to the political arena.

Since there have been so few women leaders, they have often identified with their male colleagues and have shown little interest in making changes, such as the appointment of more women, in a system that rewarded them. To demonstrate their loyalty, they acted as gatekeepers, making light of women's concerns, thereby reassuring the men who worked with them. By emphasizing that their success was the product of their personal attributes and that they were different from others of their gender, they were able to seal their co-optation by their male associates who saw them as "one of us." Margaret Thatcher spelled this out when she insisted that if she were able to reach the top, other women could also succeed without any special assistance. During the 1979 election campaign Thatcher remarked: "I didn't get here by being some strident female. I don't like strident females. I like people with ability. You get somewhere because of ability not sex."⁴⁹

Although women leaders may have gained more latitude in making changes in their cabinets after they have been in office for a number of years and, political considerations remain paramount. The impact of cabinet changes on coalition partners or on future electoral prospects will be viewed as more important than the goal of increasing the number of women in the cabinet.

Chapter Eleven

Political Decision Making and Management Styles

When asked whether being a woman had anything to do with her rising to the top, Tansu Ciller of Turkey replied that as a woman it was expected she would be a compromiser. She noted that some were "disillusioned in the sense that I would not give up on the issues that I thought that I should be leading in and this somehow did not fit with the image of... women."[1]

Ciller, an attractive woman, who used her feminine charms to break down the opposition, was a forceful leader.[2] Her abrupt manner made it difficult for her to get along with the bureaucracy as well as her colleagues.[3] According to a journalist, Ciller was adept at charming large crowds, but she came across as arrogant in more intimate settings.[4] She was not easy to work with, and during her early months in office she replaced almost 100 prime ministerial staff employees. Her tendency to make her own decisions while evading responsibility for her actions turned off some officials.[5]

More closely reflecting the leadership style expected of a woman was Hanna Suchocka, who was chosen to lead a multi-party Poland. Suchocka was viewed as having a low-key approach and was described by an aide as "very tough, but caring."[6] It was believed she would be able to forge a consensus and, in contrast to her predecessors, she quickly put together a governing coalition made up of several parties. In noting the importance of compromise in working out the differences that plagued her country, Suchocka indicated that she was able to deal with this situation because as a woman she had more patience. She remarked that "my closest staff frequently says, 'No! Enough! We just cannot go on like this' [whereas] I still feel that there is some work that can be done and that a compromise can still be found."[7]

Another leader who was described as having a calming effect on a volatile situation was Nino Burdzhanadze who took over as acting president following the removal of the longtime ruler of Georgia.[8] Burdzhanadze spoke on the differences between women and men when she told an interviewer that there were times when being "a woman manifests itself, especially in the different style of decision-making. With a woman's decision, it is easily visible that it was taken by someone who is more gentle, who tries to soften a situation rather than aggravate it."[9]

In discussing the advantages of the consensus approach, Maria Liberia-Peters said that as a woman she preferred the consensus type of leadership, noting that "you get the best results when you convince the other partner why we have to meet each other." In comparing this style with a hierarchical approach, she said that "if you can convince people why they have to go along with certain things, then their active participation can be longer lasting. She went on to say that you stimulate...them to be more creative, also, in adding their little grain...of sand to the finding of the solution."[10]

Corazon Aquino, who described herself as an effective mediator, pointed to a disadvantage of the consensus approach, especially for a woman, by observing that she was viewed as indecisive when she sought to reconcile the various interests in her government.[11] Aquino's eventual successor, Gloria Arroyo, also relied on a style of leadership that depended on consensus building. Pointing to the disadvantages to this approach, one commentator said Arroyo's style demonstrated "a capacity to bend this way and that as the wind turns" and by trying to please everyone, she was beginning to appear indecisive.[12]

Gro Brundtland, who enjoyed unusually high approval ratings throughout her tenure, combined feminine and masculine decision making styles. According to a Norwegian journalist, she could show emotion, yet she was not reluctant to use her power. Another journalist attributed her success to her abilities as well as the fact that she faced no strong opposition.[13] Arne Strand, who had served as Brundtland's state secretary, included in a list of her strong points her work ethic, intelligence, ability to get people to work together, and skills as an administrator. While she was not a particularly good speaker, she was a good listener. Her weaknesses included her temper, especially with reporters.[14]

The Cabinet's Role in Decision Making

During the early stages of the 1979 election campaign Thatcher in a speech in Cardiff, Wales, gave the voters a preview of her governing style. Describing herself as a reformer, she spoke of the accomplishments of her country but indicated that change was necessary if Britain were to reverse its downward spiral. She concluded this emotional address by saying "I am a conviction politician. The Old Testament prophets didn't say, 'Brothers, I want a consensus.' They said: 'This is my faith, this is what I passionately believe. If you believe it too, then come with me.' "[15]

Thatcher's conduct of cabinet meetings and her relationship with her ministers conformed to her view of herself as a conviction politician. It also reflected her training as a chemist in that a scientist begins with a hypothesis, examines relevant data, and then alters the hypothesis based on the findings. Typically she began these meetings by stating her own position, then permitting others to argue their views although she was not patient with those who spoke too long or rambled. She would interrupt those who put forward arguments with which she disagreed and sometimes berate those who opposed her. She was only willing to change her position if a convincing case could be made.[16] In commenting on her conduct of cabinet meetings, Thatcher, who was a forceful leader, said: "The idea that a prime minister is there just as a chairman to collect votes is absolute nonsense. You're there to give a lead. You may modify your approach as a result of discussion."[17] Her preference for the adversarial approach to decision making was undoubtedly reinforced by her training as a barrister.

William Whitelaw, who served as an invaluable conduit between Thatcher and her opponents in the party, easing the passage of her agenda, observed that she would listen and was easy to talk with individually. In a group situation, she appeared to know what she wanted and tended to talk quite a bit, emphasizing her viewpoint. In the shadow cabinet, if she disagreed with a view being expressed, she would "shoot it down pretty quickly." She was "tough in argument." Whitelaw also noted that she was not rigid, for she would change her mind in the face of effective argument.[18]

Thatcher, who was seen as having a hectoring style, was not considered a good listener. Whitelaw described incidents in the early days of her rule in which ministers were told to shut up in front of officials. Another colleague said that "...she talks too much. She comes into the conversation too early, gives her view—bang—and that pre-empts free discussion...there's no subject on which she has no views."[19] These were similar to the complaints made about her service in the cabinet as minister of education in the Heath government.

The fact that she worked with a cabinet that was not sympathetic to her views, as many to whom she had given posts were supporters of her predecessor, may also have influenced her approach to decision making. By setting the agenda and forcing others to examine a problem from her point of view and by dominating the meetings and intimidating the members of the cabinet, she may have felt she was in a better position to control the cabinet and to ensure approval of her agenda.

Golda Meir, who showed a commitment to building a consensus in multiparty Israel, went to cabinet meetings with a well-defined agenda. One of her aides described her conduct of cabinet sessions when he noted: "She listens to everyone, but she interrupts if they ramble. She has an open mind, but it's like arguing before a judge. When she makes a decision, it's made."[20] A government official noted that "she goes to all possible lengths to include the members of the Government in all the processes of consultation and decision."[21] Issues would be discussed until agreement was reached. Reliance on this rather cumbersome technique sometimes resulted in matters being left unattended, but it suited her style in relating to others. She had a long-term commitment to egalitarian values, and in her private life she had found it difficult to make use of servants, preferring the kibbutz-style of cooperative living. This is not to suggest that Meir used a consensus approach to avoid making decisions. On the contrary, she made decisions quickly and seemed comfortable in the world of action.

Despite the fact that her cabinet was a deeply divided one made up of people with little political experience and little in common other than opposition to Marcos, Corazon Aquino provided an opportunity for the various viewpoints to be expressed. When she reached a decision in cabinet meetings, which were opened with prayer, she would say, "This is what I feel," and the discussion would come to an end, but she could not be persuaded to make a quick decision.[22] When resolving differences, Aquino tended to favor the minister who was responsible for the particular matter being discussed. The meetings, at least in the early years, were rancorous and gave an appearance of indecisiveness. Following several reshuffles of her cabinet in response to military-led coup attempts, Aquino began to enforce a greater measure of discipline in the cabinet.[23]

Gloria Arroyo's cabinet meetings, which began at exactly 9 a.m., were disciplined affairs unlike the unstructured midnight sessions of her immediate predecessor, Joseph Estrada. Secretaries in her cabinet who made "sloppy presentations" were subjected to tongue-lashings as Arroyo had a vicious temper[24] that her father had told her was her "biggest obstacle to leadership."[25]

In meetings of her cabinet, Benazir Bhutto "was firm, business-like, quick to take a point and to keep the discussion on track."[26] In her second term of office, ministers in the Bhutto cabinet complained that she would not even listen to them when they talked of making overtures to the opposition.[27]

Indira Gandhi, who was cautious in making decisions and avoided making them quickly, used the cabinet meeting to listen to the views of the members, seldom speaking herself. The ministers would explain their proposals and await her reaction, but she was impatient with dissenting points of view. Decision making was primarily the province of the prime minister and her secretariat as she met each morning with some members of her staff to discuss important issues. She was able to maintain control of the cabinet since she determined the agenda as well as whether to postpone meetings or bypass the cabinet altogether.

In describing her approach to decision making, Gandhi said in a parliamentary speech in which she defended the Emergency: "Some members said that I proclaimed the emergency out of panic and fear. Panic and fear do not belong with my character. Whatever I do, I give serious thought, coolly and calmly. The decisions are cold headed."[28] Once she made up her mind, she acted quickly.

Other leaders paid scant attention to their cabinets. For example, Kim Campbell spent relatively little time with her ministers.[29] Of course, she was involved in a tight parliamentary election campaign after she won her party's leadership position, but she acknowledged in her autobiography that she could not ask for help and that she had "a habit of doing things herself."[30] Sheikh Hasina, who also had a tendency to act alone, often took decisions without consulting her cabinet. For example, no one knew of her decision to put those accused of killing her father on trial. On occasion, she actually defied her cabinet as in her choice of a new chief of the army before the 2001 election.[31] The members of Khaleda Zia's cabinet complained that they were ignored in so far as decision making was concerned, and Tansu Ciller made decisions alone or relied on a few favorite ministers.[32]

Alternatives to Formal Cabinet Decision Making

As cabinets have become larger and their fields of concern more technical, political leaders have come to rely more on small groups of ministers to solve problems. To maintain control over the policy agenda, a leader might use ad hoc meetings of cabinet ministers or private negotiations for making decisions. Thatcher wanted only disputed matters or sensitive issues to come to the cabinet. She disliked having arguments in cabinet that forced her to decide between ministers, and she expected the ministers to handle their own departments. Like her predecessors, Thatcher relied on meetings that included only a small number of ministers, scheduling comparatively few sessions with the full cabinet that usually had a short agenda and merely ratified decisions made elsewhere. In this way she was able to include some who disagreed with her in the cabinet and, at the same time, keep the doubters at bay.

Brundtland also relied on cabinet committees for resolving issues. To ensure her influence over matters of greatest personal concern, she chaired three of five small committees in the government she put together in 1986—security affairs, local government affairs and health policy, and polar affairs. Gloria Arroyo urged the members of her cabinet to work together to solve problems, bringing to her only a few important items.[33]

In an attempt to assert herself vis-a-vis the party bosses, Gandhi turned to advisers of her own choice, and this group was derisively referred to as her "kitchen cabinet." A number of cabinet ministers were included as well as some unofficial advisers, and the size and membership of the group varied over time.

In developing the cabinet agenda, Meir made use of a small circle of men whom she trusted and with whom she usually agreed. She met with these advisers on Saturday evenings at an informal gathering in her home, at which she often served light snacks. The issues to be discussed at the cabinet meeting the following morning were considered as well as matters related to the business of the party. Only the more significant questions as well as those issues in which agreement could not be reached within the committees were considered by the cabinet. Meir also delegated considerable authority to the cabinet ministers within their own sphere of activity, requesting to review only those matters that she believed most important.

These approaches to day-to-day decision making provided Meir with the time to concentrate her efforts on matters of foreign policy. Not only did she see international issues as relevant to the survival of the Jewish state, but she also saw herself as an expert on these matters, having served as foreign minister for a decade. She largely ignored her Foreign Minister Abba Eban, whom she felt was too dovish on foreign policy issues.

Another leader who looked to bodies other than the cabinet for advice was Helen Clark who relied on a policy advisory group. The group that was made up of individuals from the public and private sectors met before the regularly scheduled cabinet meetings. Clark held short sessions with her cabinet and much of the work was done in small groups of ministers and others with special expertise in the matter under consideration. Her predecessor, Jenny Shipley, created teams of ministers to resolve issues, limiting the cabinet to fortnightly meetings.

Personal Advisers and Outside Experts

Given the many considerations that a political leader must take into account in selecting the members of her cabinet, it is not surprising that leaders often seek advice from outside the cabinet. Initially Thatcher indicated that she would rely on her ministers and their departments, but she quickly turned to others for assistance. Because of her concern to make her influence felt in many areas of policy and to intervene in the work of the various departments, she got advice from sources independent of the departments. Having abolished the bureaucracy-based think tank staffed with civil servants, she created a policy unit in 1983 in the prime minister's office that was directly responsible to her. The policy unit, composed of individuals who specialized in specific policy areas, served as a check on the departments and offered alternative proposals for the prime minister's consideration.

Thatcher also made use of experts in specific fields, bringing in an adviser on economic matters and later one on foreign affairs. In time she relied more heavily on her personal advisers, and she sought the advice of free market and pro-business interests, using the staff of the Centre for Policy Studies that she cofounded in 1974. One former cabinet member criticized her use of these advisers when he wrote:

> ...within the Government the Prime Minister exercises direct control over more and more Departments.... She would like to run the major Departments herself and tries her best to do so...she cannot know enough to dictate the policy of each Department.... Her response has been to expand the Downing Street staff to include experts in every major area, thus establishing a government within a government.[34]

While Thatcher was thoughtful of her advisers and subordinates, she did not give praise readily. On position papers written by ministers and civil servants, she would write such comments as "this is incompetent." She scolded her cabinet colleagues in public, argued with ministers in front of their civil servants, and on occasion ignored ministers by turning to junior officials for their views.

Although Angela Merkel was referred to by some as "Germany's Maggie," the decision-making style of the two women was quite different. In contrast to the "iron lady," Merkel was far from firm when it came to holding her ground.[35] Her approach that was reflected in the two-month long negotiation with Gerhard Schroeder's Social Democratic Party (SPD) to determine who would rule Germany after the close of the 2005 election was one of patience and determination.

To a certain degree Merkel's style can be attributed to the fact that she was leading a grand coalition government that included the opposition SPD in a parliament in which the left slightly outnumbered the right. This has meant that she had to be somewhat more pragmatic in her legislative goals to maintain the shaky coalition.

Taking a more open and flexible approach to decision making than Thatcher, Merkel replaced the decades-long German practice of drafting legislation in round-table fashion as interest groups helped refine the ideas. Lobbyists were known to have drafted some of the legislation.[36] By reducing the direct influence of special interests, which often resulted in stalemate, it was hoped that much-needed economic reform might take place.

Chandrika Kumaratunga, who was slow to accept counsel from her colleagues, found that the members of her cabinet were inadequate when it came to providing good political advice, and she eventually turned to outsiders.[37] In contrast, Golda Meir did not depend on experts for advice but relied on the ministers instead. As one friend remarked: "She doesn't believe in building her own personal Cabinet."[38] In view of her lack of experience in the military arena as well as the importance of military related issues for Israel, she relied heavily on Moshe Dayan, her minister of defense, despite the long-running conflict between the two political veterans.

Indira Gandhi made use of experts and technocrats as she had great respect for their skills. She spoke of the role of the experts during a speech in the parliament when she said: "We, who are politicians, give guidance. We settle the objectives and the targets in the country. We must, however, rely on the advice of experts and specialists for carrying on these tasks."[39]

Gandhi, who had few advisers whom she felt she could trust, made frequent changes in her administration. She encouraged rivalries, thereby discouraging anyone from acquiring much power. Before the Emergency she looked to the "Kashmiri Mafia" that consisted of several young, left-leaning Kashmiri Brahmins. After the Emergency they were replaced by the "Punjabi Mafia," intimates of her younger son Sanjay.

Though Gandhi made heavy demands on her staff, she was considerate of the individual members. She had high standards of efficiency for those who worked for her, telling her aides, "Do away with the introductions, plunge into the subject."[40] Gandhi had a fairly informal relationship with those who worked for her, and when special service was performed, she would write notes of thanks. Although Gandhi could be irritable on occasion, she was not prone to lose her temper.

Edith Cresson relied on a special adviser who did not have an official position although he had an office next to the prime minister's and had ready access to her. When others began to doubt Cresson's ability to do the job, Abel Farnoux, an older man who had served in the French resistance, encouraged and reassured her. It was reported that he was influential in policy decision making.[41]

While most of the top-level political advisers were men, Helen Clark gave her chief of staff, Heather Simpson, a key role in decision making. Simpson's value to the prime minister was in "her sharpness at identifying unseen fishhooks and danger spots ahead."[42] Michelle Bachelet also named a woman to the post of chief of staff.

Given their inexperience and poorly developed power bases, the widows often relied on relatives and friends as well as close associates of their late husbands. For example, Sirimavo Bandaranaike, who spoke of her lack of political experience, placed great store in the advice of her nephew, Felix Bandaranaike, whom she also included in the cabinet as finance minister. During her first term, Felix proposed a reduction in the free ration of rice from two measures to one and one-half per person per week in view of the country's balance of payments problems. While this may have been an economically sound move, it was a politically unpopular one, and Felix was forced to resign. He continued to serve as an adviser to Bandaranaike and was soon brought back into the cabinet as minister without portfolio.

During her second term that began in 1970, Bandaranaike again looked to her nephew, particularly on domestic issues. Following the split with the Left at the end of 1975, Felix assumed the finance portfolio once again and the emphasis shifted toward the development of the private sector. Other relatives such as brothers and uncles served in a variety of governmental posts including that of president.

Isabel Peron relied on a small group of advisers, many of whom had been close to her late husband. She looked especially to Jose Lopez Rega, who was identified with the extreme right of the Peronist party. Lopez served as her minister of social welfare as well as her private secretary, a position he had held in General Peron's government. In his role as principal adviser to the president, he fashioned the cabinet to mirror his views. He was ousted in 1975 as a result of pressure from the labor unions and the military that took issue with the harsh measures used to deal with such serious problems as internal violence and inflation.

Violeta Chamorro relied primarily on her son-in-law, Antonio Lacayo, who some argued played the role of her prime minister, putting together support for the government's agenda.[43] Lacayo's role in decision making allowed Chamorro to become the peacemaker. Corazon Aquino's chief adviser was her executive secretary Joker Arroyo, who had been her late husband's lawyer. Arroyo, who saw Aquino as incapable of understanding complex issues, controlled access to the president and was described by some as the "little president."[44]

Since the era in which queens emerged as rulers, concern has been expressed that family members, particularly husbands, might have undue influence in decision making. Among the most influential spouses in the policy process was Benazir Bhutto's husband, Asif Zardari. He was viewed as having "a decisive say in most matters."[45] One disgruntled party member suggested that he was the de facto prime minister and that nothing moved without him.[46] For a time not only did Zardari have a seat in the Pakistani parliament, he also served as investments minister—a position created for him despite his reputation for taking money under the table in exchange for contract awards. His interference in government and economic policy was seen "as a major reason for the first Bhutto government's dismissal in 1990 by an angry army and bureaucracy."[47]

Although Denis Thatcher was seen as among the least intrusive of the husbands, he was a close confidant of his wife and had considerable influence in shaping her views. One of Margaret's biographers noted that she frequently announced in cabinet meetings that she had asked Denis's advice about this or that, and these were his feelings.[48] She had confidence in his judgment given his extensive experience as a businessman.

Children and other family members also played advisory roles. Perhaps the most involved was Sanjay, Indira Gandhi's younger son. She took him into her confidence at the time of the Emergency as she had turned over her advisers in rapid succession because they were too ambitious and were a threat to her political power.[49] Though Sanjay held no official position, he took part in the daily meeting of the Emergency Council. To get to Gandhi, other officials had to work through Sanjay or one of her other advisers. Sanjay was the architect of the forced sterilization program, from which Gandhi eventually sought to distance herself. He continued to advise his mother until his death in an airplane accident six months after the 1980 election that returned Gandhi to power. Gandhi then brought into the fold her older son Rajiv, who was an airplane pilot and until that time had shown little interest in politics. He gradually assumed more responsibility, and succeeded his mother as prime minister following her assassination in 1984.

Sirimavo Bandaranaike also expanded her small circle of advisers to include her daughter, Sunethra Rupasingle, who served as coordinating secretary to the prime minister with responsibility for pushing through key policy changes. Her younger daughter, Chandrika, was appointed as director of the Land Reform Commission, and her son, Anura, became chief of the SLFP's youth wing. He was also given the honorary post of adviser on youth affairs in the ministries of planning and education following his return from study in London.

Another son who played an important role as adviser to his mother was Khaleda Zia's older son, Tarique. After the 2001 election, which he masterminded, Tarique was appointed joint secretary general of his mother's party, and he played a role in selecting some government appointees. The opposition accused him of taking a cut of government contracts.

Siblings have also served as advisers. During her second term Zia brought her older sister, Khurshid Jahan Haq, into the cabinet that included only one other woman. Aquino's brother Jose "Peping" Cojuangco and her brother-in-law Paul Aquino were active in electoral politics and party affairs. Cojuangco proved especially embarrassing to his sister in light of questionable political and business deal-making.[50]

In other instances siblings have been adversaries. There was a bitter conflict for party leadership between Benazir Bhutto and her brother, Murtaza, who was believed to have been behind the hijacking of a Pakistan International Airways plane in the 1980s. Murtaza returned from exile in Damascus in 1993, and his mother suggested that he, not Benazir, was the true heir to his father's political legacy. In response, Bhutto removed her mother as head of the Pakistan People's Party so that she would not be in a position to appoint Murtaza as Benazir's successor.[51] Murtaza set up a faction of the PPP but was unable to elicit much support and was never a serious threat to his sister. In 1996, he was gunned down in front of his home in a confrontation with the police. Bhutto's husband was charged with a role in the planning of the assassination although he was never convicted.

Anura Bandaranaike, who it was expected would inherit the leadership of the SLFP when his mother left office, instead, found himself in competition with his sister, Chandrika Kumaratunga. When rebuffed by his mother, who played off her two younger children against each other, he left the party in 1993 and joined the opposition in the parliament. Following his mother's death in 2000, he was reunited with his sister. He once again joined the SLFP and became an adviser to Kumaratunga, but she refused to give him the prime ministership after her party regained control of parliament in April 2004—a position he wanted. Instead, he had to be satisfied with the minor cabinet portfolio of industry, tourism, and investment promotion. The assassination of the Sri Lankan foreign minister in 2005 enabled Anura to assume that important post.

Management Style

When commenting on decision making styles, Eugenia Charles of Dominica said that she saw no difference between women making decisions and men making decisions, but she felt that "women are inclined to...look after the details more than men. Men have the grand vision, and they pass it on to somebody else to put into practice. Women follow the details more, they want to know that it *is* being put into practice."[52] Asked about her success, Golda Meir told an interviewer that "I think that women, more than men, possess a capacity that helps in doing this job. It's that of going right to the essence of things, of taking the bull by the horns. Women are more practical, more realistic. They don't dissipate themselves in mystifications like men, who always beat around the bush trying to get to the heart of the matter."[53]

The management styles of the women leaders have varied from the largely hands off approach of the reluctant widows, Chamorro and Aquino, to the micro management style of the academics, Arroyo and Clark as well as Kumaratunga, who was, at least, in the early stages of her political career, a workaholic and one who relished the details of government. Still others like Meir selected a few issues on which they concentrated, leaving the remaining issues of governance to cabinet members and aides.

Chamorro in her autobiography described her role vis-a-vis her government when she wrote: "I see myself as the person responsible for setting the agenda...I provide the leadership and the inspiration. I sit in on all the big meetings, then turn to my advisers, get the consensus, and if it agrees with my own views and principles, I tell them to proceed."[54]

While Corazon Aquino was somewhat more involved in decision making than was Chamorro,[55] Aquino concentrated her efforts in a few areas, such as restoring democracy and developing support for a new constitution. Describing her approach to solving problems early in her presidency, she said on a television program: "I reason it out, 'Will it be solved if I stay awake at night?' I would be a wreck the following day if I don't sleep, and then I hope the next day would be better. So I sleep, and hope that the next day would be better than the previous day."[56]

Aquino viewed herself as the chairperson, laying out general policy goals and leaving the details to be filled in by the secretaries. She insisted that conflicts among the members of her government be settled by the feuding parties. When a secretary sought her help in getting the support of a colleague, she encouraged those who disagreed to work out any differences among themselves.[57]

Megawati also left the running of government to her ministers, resulting in each department's taking its own direction.[58] Decision making was often "arduous and too cautious," and she failed to communicate the reasons behind decisions when they were finally made.[59] Megawati had little appetite for long meetings and rarely immersed herself in briefing papers.[60] She left issues for her subordinates to handle, believing in delegating authority and receiving only the final results rather than getting involved in daily affairs. Megawati acknowledged that she often felt confused when her economic minister used "complicated economic theories" to explain policy options. She suggested that he follow the housewife approach, because "housewives usually know best how to stretch finances."[61]

In contrast, Gloria Arroyo, who described her management style as one of delegation, but "delegation without losing control,"[62] involved herself in all the details of an issue. When presented with new data or surprise briefings, she would use the phone to check the information herself.[63] Arroyo also followed up with her cabinet officers, chastising them when they failed to do their homework.[64] She created a "directives monitoring unit" to oversee the performance of her ministers.[65] Arroyo did her own homework thoroughly, working 16 hour days 6 days a week. One of her ministers described Arroyo as "impatient and anxious" to solve problems immediately. Another colleague described her as confrontational and said that this made her "unpopular" with her staff.[66]

Helen Clark known as the "Minister for Everything" closely supervised decision making, putting her stamp on the work of the several departments.[67] She kept close watch over the work of the ministries and was concerned to avoid surprises. She was quick to criticize her colleagues. The attention she focused on the activities of her ministers may in part reflect the fact that she did not select the members of her cabinet and in some cases did not believe that those who had been chosen by the party caucus were up to the job. Over time Clark came to rely more on her ministers, shifting some responsibility to those who served in the cabinet.

Michelle Bachelet was also "criticized for running too tight a ship, thus undermining her ministers' ability to produce results." One of her coalition partners suggested: "They're all inhibited. She needs to chart a clearer course and delegate more power."[68] Her response may be in part due to her inexperience and that of her ministers after only a few months in office.

Conclusions

Although the image of women as decision makers suggests that they will seek to build a consensus among different points of view, the roles women played in cabinet decision making have varied considerably. Some like Margaret Thatcher were forceful in presenting their positions at the outset of cabinet sessions, viewing their roles as more than counting votes. Others like Golda Meir listened to cabinet members and then presented recommendations.

Several women found their cabinets unwieldy and filled with troublemakers whom they sought to isolate by creating smaller cabinet committees or using "kitchen cabinets" outside the formal structure. Advisory groups, formed both inside and outside of government, and personal advisers also played a role.

Widows were likely to rely on relatives and their late husband's former associates for advice. Daughters, on the other hand, sought to distance themselves from their father's associates believing that they would always be viewed as the "little girl." Many of the married women leaders were accused of being unduly influenced by their husbands in making decisions. Several sons as well as daughters played important advisory roles.

The women who have broken the highest glass ceiling also varied in their management styles, ranging from the micro management approach of Helen Clark and Gloria Arroyo to the more detached style of Violeta Chamorro and Corazon Aquino. The management styles of the individual women were also found to have changed over time, perhaps as they became more confident and obtained a greater hold on power.

While some studies of legislatures have found that women are more likely to encourage compromise and cooperation and are more predisposed to encourage inclusiveness and the building of a consensus than are men who tend to rely on a hierarchical, authoritative approach to decision making, others have found few differences between the genders.[69] For those women who rose to the top, their style of decision making was likely to reflect the party and electoral systems found in their respective countries. That is, multiparty systems such as Norway that rely on a proportional distribution of the votes are more likely to promote consensus builders to positions of leadership, whereas two or three party systems such as that found in Britain with a winner-take-all electoral scheme are more likely to promote forceful leaders whether men or women.

Chapter Twelve

Political Leadership

Some of the leaders of her party considered Khaleda Zia's behavior at times to be despotic. It was reported that Gro Brundtland's "directness and aggressiveness offended many of her Labor colleagues...."[1] Tarja Halonen, a demanding boss, was viewed as feisty. Some described Golda Meir's style as autocratic, and an official in Chandrika Kumaratunga's government described her as a "combative personality."[2] Benazir Bhutto was viewed by many as "arrogant and headstrong" although she was not seen so in private where her manner, according to one writer, "only reflected impatience with and mistrust of the establishment."[3] Viewed as dictatorial, Gloria Arroyo's critics described her as headstrong and temperamental.[4] Jenny Shipley's opponents referred to her as an "armoured personnel carrier,"[5] and because of "her ability to push until she got what she wanted," she was described as the "perfumed bulldozer."[6] Helen Clark was viewed as bossy and opinionated. Edith Cresson who was a demanding boss, was seen as disputatious and petulant.[7] Her leadership was described as abrasive, and she was the subject of considerable criticism. It was said that she simply wore down her opponents rather than persuade them to a particular view.[8] Tansu Ciller was viewed as uncompromising, and one who had served on her staff said that she was "not an easy person to work with."[9] Eugenia Charles's detractors described her style as abrasive.[10] A reason frequently asserted as to why Margaret Thatcher's party summarily dismissed her as leader in 1990 was that her colleagues tired of her forceful style.

Most of the women who have risen to the top political position have at one time or another been described as autocratic. The tendency to label women leaders as overly aggressive may stem from the general perception that leaders and women do not share the same characteristics. While women are seen as nurturing, leaders are seen as competitive. If a woman behaves like a leader, she is viewed as too aggressive since such behavior in a woman is contrary to the expectations of one of her gender.

Gro Brundtland spoke to this issue when commenting on why her critics concluded that in her second term she was behaving less emotionally and confrontationally. She noted that since she had shown her effectiveness, the bias against her as a woman had faded. She said: "Because you're a woman they try to say she should be 'more feminine,' which means that she should have less deliberate and well thought through meanings and she shouldn't express them as well." Brundtland indicated that what they are really saying is that "a woman should not lead because she shouldn't be like a leader in what she says and does."[11]

As long as women remain few in number in the political arena, they may feel it necessary to behave like those in the dominant group. Maria de Lourdes Pintasilgo in commenting on the leadership style of women said: "[W]e [women] still don't have freedom of style. For that you need enough critical mass, enough women in power. Only then will the temptation to imitate male attitudes disappear."[12] To show that they belong they may feel it necessary to behave like those in the dominant group. In other words, they must behave like men and appear tough. Ertha Pascal-Trouillot, who served temporarily as president of Haiti, said that women must govern firmly.[13] Ruth Perry of Liberia said that the recipe for leadership is to be "firm, loving, kind and patient."[14] Helen Clark of New Zealand, in commenting on why women need to "toughen up," stressed that "if women are seen to be emotional they are almost written off as unfit to do the job."[15] Edith Cresson of France remarked to her aides, "What they [her colleagues] want is a male. Well I'll make like a male. They want me to shout. I'll shout."[16]

Party Leadership

A national leader reflects the aspirations of her constituents on whether to transform the country or maintain the status quo. She has a number of tools, such as political parties, other government bodies, and public opinion at her disposal, and she may use these to push her agenda and to meet challenges to her power. Corazon Aquino was not affiliated with any party, believing that she would be stronger if she remained above politics. She viewed political parties merely as devices for energizing the voters at the time of an election, and she failed to see the need to create a party to mobilize her base to secure passage and speedy implementation of her agenda.[17] As a result of her failure to institutionalize the support she had at the beginning of her term of office, it was difficult to secure the passage of any program, leading many to regard her as weak and indecisive.

In contrast, Golda Meir had a strong commitment to her party, making her a sound choice to lead the Israeli Labor Alignment during a period when the party was threatened by serious internal divisions, especially over the disposition of the territories captured during the 1967 war with Egypt. A split was a real possibility, but it would have been a disaster for the party's electoral prospects. When one faction moved to break away, Meir who had gone on record as saying, "I will not go down in history as the Prime Minister who watched this great party destroy itself at a time of national crisis,"[18] pressed the factions to avoid a split.

The Labor Alignment was threatened with another split over the disposition of the occupied territories during the months leading up to the 1973 election. Meir, who had secretly undergone cobalt treatment for a recurrence of cancer during the spring and who suffered from a number of other health problems, reluctantly agreed to head the list of party candidates in the general election. Downplaying the differences among the factions, in a radio interview she asserted that "we really don't have two sides to the debate, entrenched behind barricades. Nobody suggests there could be a resolution overnight on this issue."[19]

Paradoxically, it was the inability to find a resolution to the internal divisions within the party that accounted for Meir's considerable power. Her numerous threats to resign served to enhance her power. At the meeting in 1973 called for the purpose of announcing her proposed government, she surprised her party colleagues by offering her resignation. Her popularity had plummeted since the Yom Kippur war, and she did not have the strong support of some of the party leaders, but they remained concerned about a possible leadership struggle. The leaders of the different factions within her party begged her to withdraw her resignation, and she did. About a month later she announced her resignation again, saying that she had considered giving up her post before the election but that she agreed to remain in office out of a sense of duty to the party. This time she was not encouraged to reconsider.

Unlike Aquino, most of the widows who rose to the top belonged to their late husbands' political parties and, at least initially, took steps to strengthen these parties. For example, Khaleda Zia attempted to transform her husband's party, the Bangladesh Nationalist Party, into a "coherent political entity."[20] The party workers at all levels, primarily motivated by patronage and other rewards, were more concerned to please the chairperson than to build the party.[21] Zia may have contributed to the disorganized state of the party by failing to hold a single meeting of its National Executive Committee for a period of 13 years.[22] Although she had turned the top party position over to her son, Tarique, in 2002, it took four more years and an upcoming national election to schedule such a meeting.

Sirimavo Bandaranaike, who initially made appearances on behalf of her party but appeared to maintain an aura of semi-detachment from her position, set about to make changes following the Sri Lanka Freedom Party's defeat in 1965. She supervised the organization of local party associations throughout the country, becoming involved in the selection of candidates for parliamentary seats. She traveled extensively throughout the country, making speeches and working on behalf of SLFP candidates in by-elections. Her efforts were rewarded, for the SLFP once again captured control of the parliament in the election of May 1970, winning 91 of 151 seats.

Indira Gandhi experienced repeated challenges to her leadership and was not even consulted when the list of candidates for the Congress Party Working Committee, the policy-making body of the party, was being prepared. In the midst of rumors that plans were underway to remove her from office and that Desai was being used by the old guard Congress Party leadership to wrest power from her, Gandhi maneuvered a split in her party to reduce the power of those who sought to control her.

The break between Gandhi and the party bosses came in 1969 during the struggle over the selection of the Congress candidate for the presidency of India. At the meeting of the Congress Parliamentary Board in July to select the party's candidate for president, Gandhi proposed Jagjivan Ram, who served in the Gandhi cabinet. He was rejected as the board supported Sanjiva Reddy, a member of the Syndicate, who was speaker of the parliament. Bitterly opposed to Reddy and driven to tears in a public setting following the meeting, Gandhi viewed this move as a challenge to her leadership. The president would be in a position to remove her from office since he had the responsibility of selecting someone to form a government if a majority of parliament could not agree. After several months of maneuvering by both sides, Gandhi was expelled from the Congress. Most of the party members in the parliament remained loyal to her, allowing her to continue in office in a strengthened position. Gandhi was careful to select persons to serve on the party committees and boards who were loyal to her to prevent the development of competing power centers and to consolidate her position. She also traveled extensively throughout the country, meeting with party stalwarts.

Following her successful bid for reelection in 1971, Gandhi centralized party decision making. She did not hold a single intraparty election over the next 14 years. Chief ministers, state cabinets, and local party leaders were appointed by her or her appointees.[23]

Like Gandhi, Benazir Bhutto found it difficult to be accepted by her father's party colleagues not only because of her gender but also because of her age. She was only 35 when she became prime minister in 1988. The old guard of the Pakistan People's Party saw her as merely one who could be used to gain support for the party. Frustrated by their patronizing attitudes, she dismissed these men she called her "uncles" from party positions, replacing them with her own followers.

The PPP remained deeply divided throughout Bhutto's tenure. Opposition parties took advantage of these divisions and weaned away party members by offering them patronage and other benefits. Bhutto was ineffective in dealing with this situation as she often engaged in similar tactics vis-à-vis her opponents.[24]

Bhutto failed to strengthen the middle and local levels of the party that had been in disarray since her father's execution.[25] Instead, she blamed others for the weaknesses in her party, arguing that corruption charges brought against her government were responsible for her party's defeat in the 1997 election.

Although Sheikh Hasina, like Bhutto, was able to dominate her party by recruiting loyalists, she too presided over a highly divided political structure. As a result of her lack of interest in party affairs, according to one authority, the conflicts between party and government led to embarrassing policy decisions and antagonized a number of Western donors.[26]

Those leaders who neglected their parties often paid a price with comparatively short tenures in office. Canadian Prime Minister Kim Campbell failed to take the steps necessary to heal the wounds that plagued her party after the bitter fight for the leadership. Though she appointed to the cabinet the man who had challenged her, she had little contact with him.[27]

Tansu Ciller failed to shore up the traditional base of her party—its rural constituency. Instead, she brought businessmen and bureaucrats into the True Path Party, angering the old party leadership. By the time of the 1995 national election "she had eviscerated the party apparatus and replaced it with loyalists."[28] The fortunes of the True Path Party under Ciller's leadership deteriorated to such an extent that in the parliamentary election of 2002 the party failed to meet the 10 percent vote requirement for parliamentary membership.

Keeping a party coalition intact is not an easy task and can sometimes be made more difficult by attempting to be inclusionary. Violeta Chamorro lost support in the conservative coalition she rode to power because of her insistence on maintaining an association with the left-wing Sandinistas following her election in 1990. Bandaranaike's tilt toward the parties on the left in the early 1960s alienated many of her conservative coalition partners while Chandrika Kumaratunga, Bandaranaike's daughter, experienced a similar response when she sought alignment with the leftist People's Liberation Party (JVP)in her bid to hold on to power in 2001.

Legislative Leadership

In most parliamentary systems, the prime minister is expected to play a critical leadership role in the legislative body, but, among the several women leaders, the amount of involvement varied. Bandaranaike, who refused to contest a parliamentary seat, was appointed to the Senate to comply with the requirement that the prime minister be a member of parliament, and she remained content to play the role of the elder statesperson. Though she indicated that as soon as possible she would seek a seat in the House, the main body for debate, she remained in the Senate where she was treated with considerable deference, something she could not have expected in the House.

Bandaranaike's decision to stay in the Senate proved to be a costly one as it left the House virtually leaderless. Had she been actively involved in the lower chamber, working closely with supporters, the conflicts that came to threaten her government might not have reached such serious proportions. Her contributions to Senate debate were not particularly noteworthy as she was intolerant of the rough and tumble of the interaction on the floor. The ambivalence about her new position and her inability to become completely involved in the political fray affected her relationship with her colleagues as she found the important political arts of communication and persuasion difficult to master. Her conservative background and lifestyle did not make it easy for her to develop these skills.

Experience had its rewards, and as Bandaranaike's skills developed in office and her sense of confidence increased, she faced her responsibilities with greater commitment. She became more skilled in dealing with uncooperative party members within the parliament and more tolerant of political debate. One colleague said of her: "What she most admired and what she demanded from her colleagues was clear thinking and a practical approach to problems; quick, satisfactory solutions. Bandaranaike hated procrastination. And while lively argument stimulated her she disliked petty bickering or dissension for its own sake."[29]

Indira Gandhi, who had always been treated with some deference as the daughter of Nehru, also had little experience in parliamentary maneuver. Initially, Desai proved invaluable to her in dealing with hecklers during debate, but at times she became confused and on the verge of tears. According to one authority, Gandhi "had little intellectual curiosity towards the workings of parliament, or to the conventions and niceties of parliamentary activity."[30] She was increasingly absent from parliament after 1973 and even contemplated getting rid of it.

Khaleda Zia, who was viewed as arrogant, was not very effective in parliamentary debate and seldom attended the proceedings while she was prime minister.[31] She often came late to meetings, and her relationship with the media was poor.[32] Like Bandaranaike and Gandhi, Zia found the give-and-take of parliamentary debate unsettling.

Benazir Bhutto followed the pattern of previous Pakistani prime ministers in ruling by decree, often bypassing parliamentary procedures entirely.[33] During Bhutto's first term in office from 1988 to 1990 "not a single piece of legislation was placed before parliament by the treasury benches—a record that is unlikely to be surpassed easily."[34] Tansu Ciller of Turkey also made extensive use of the executive decree, relying on small groups of ministers in making decisions.[35]

Those who served in a legislature for a number of years before rising to the top appeared more comfortable with the legislative process. Gloria Arroyo's legislative leadership skills were developed during her time in the Philippine Senate when in a period of 6 years she filed more than 470 bills and resolutions, 55 of which were signed into law as socioeconomic measures.[36]

Margaret Thatcher, who had served 20 years in parliament before becoming prime minister in 1979, owed her elevation to party leader to the backbenchers in Parliament, making her sensitive to fostering their support. During her first term she met with the officers of the backbench party committees at least once a year and with the 1922 Executive more frequently. She regularly ate in the Members' dining room in the House of Commons, developing personal lines of communication with the members. She also liberally awarded titles to senior backbenchers and campaigned in by-elections for her party's candidates.

After the 1983 election, she did not maintain such close contact as there were more MPs with whom to deal. Also, her new parliamentary private secretary was not so sensitive to the thinking of the members as had been his predecessor. When compared to previous British prime ministers, Thatcher tended to participate in fewer parliamentary debates and made fewer speeches in the legislative body.

Over time some leaders veered toward the presidential style of leadership, paying less attention to the parliament. One journalist suggested that Helen Clark's focus "is squarely on her ability to go over Parliament, front for the Executive and work her way through and around the constitutional checks and balances, and persuade New Zealanders of the rightness and rectitude of her policies and unite them behind her."[37]

According to one authority, the principal reason why Violeta Chamorro had difficulty playing a strong legislative leadership role was due to the fact that the "president, her cabinet, and advisers had an agenda that differed radically from the plans of important parts of her legislative caucus."[38] This initially forced her to rely heavily on the opposition Sandinista National Liberation Front (FSLN) rather than on her own parliamentary coalition.

Popular Leadership

The ability to generate popular support can also be an important test of leadership. The women who have served as president in a largely ceremonial role have enjoyed the highest support levels as measured by public opinion polls. They serve as affect or symbolic leaders, while prime ministers, who often have to make difficult choices that can alienate segments of the population, are task leaders. As ceremonial presidents, Vigdis Finnbogadottir of Iceland and Mary Robinson of Ireland received approval ratings of more than 90 percent. Tarji Halonen, who was president in the Finnish dual system, achieved approval ratings of 95 percent, while Edith Cresson's approval ratings as prime minister in such a system suffered a severe drop during her short tenure.

Ceremonial presidents, whose powers are usually limited by the constitution and laws of their respective states, have little latitude in which to exercise their personal leadership. Despite the restrictions on their activities, some of the ceremonial leaders have had an impact in large part because of their popularity. But their success has also been a function of their willingness to work hard, particularly on issues that interested them.

During her seven-year tenure as president, Mary Robinson was said to have transformed the office. Whereas it had been the accepted practice for the Irish president to seek governmental approval before making statements, Robinson largely ignored this tradition, having made more than 700 speeches in 1991 alone.[39] Robinson used her largely powerless post to preach on social issues. She was particularly engaged in the plight of those suffering in the midst of the violence in Somalia and Rwanda—a concern that led her to accept the position of UN commissioner for human rights in 1997 despite the fact that she was virtually guaranteed a second term as president if she wanted it. By and large Robinson's immediate successor as Irish president, Mary McAleese, also took an inclusionary position but was not quite so strident in her interaction with others as was Robinson.

In assessing her role as president of Latvia, Vaira Vike-Freiberga declared that she did not involve herself in issues of finger pointing, arguing that it is not "a way of resolving problems. I have indeed tried to avoid situations in which the institution of the president is used as a club with which to beat an opponent over the head."[40] Nevertheless, during her first term in office she sent back seven laws for reconsideration by the parliament.

The only prime minister enjoying such high ratings was Gro Brundtland who scored more than 90 percent in her last years in office. Margaret Thatcher, on the other hand, demonstrated considerable political strength during her three terms in office, but she was never personally popular. Approval ratings for the Conservative Party consistently ran above those of Thatcher.

According to several opinion polls taken in 2007, Angela Merkel's approval ratings were in the 70s, the highest of any German Chancellor since the Second World War.[41] One poll even placed her chief Social Democratic rival, Kurt Beck, some 42 percentage points behind her.

Kim Campbell began her tenure as prime minister with the highest approval ratings of any Canadian political leader in several decades, only to see them decline so precipitously in five months that she lost her own seat in the parliamentary elections in 1993 and her party was reduced to two seats.

Charges of corruption and electoral fraud can wound the popularity of a political leader almost overnight as Gloria Arroyo discovered. Having been elected president of the Philippines just a year earlier, she saw her approval rating drop to 20 percent by July 2005.[42] Although she was successful in escaping impeachment, her position was seriously undermined, making it questionable whether she would be able to complete her term ending in 2010.

The support for several other women increased over time. Helen Clark as Labor Party leader before becoming prime minister was so unpopular that "her support ratings rivaled the polls' margin of error," but in time she became one of the most popular leaders in New Zealand history.[43] When asked to characterize her style of leadership, she described it as "direct, open, blunt, a lot of contact with media." She went on to say, "I think most journalists would admit that the reason I offer opinions on things is because they ring and ask, and I do have a fundamental belief that the buck stops at the top and that people are entitled to know what the Prime Minister thinks."[44] Clark's forceful leadership style as well as a growing economy accounts for her increased popularity. She was admired for her "decisiveness, down-to-earth style and personable manner."[45]

As the widows and daughters soon found out, trading on the name of a deceased husband or father has its limits. There comes a time when one's own record will determine her tenure in office as Megawati in losing the 2004 presidential election found out after only three years as leader of her country. Bandaranaike's ability to trade upon her martyred husband's name did not go much beyond her first term in office.

Shortly after she assumed office, satisfaction with Aquino's performance, according to nationwide polls, was 60 percent. Despite her extensive travels and frequent speech-making to reassure the people concerning the health of the country,[46] satisfaction with her performance fell to 48 percent in 1990.[47] Aquino initially failed to capitalize on "people power" that had played a role in her rise to the top. She waited four years before attempting to rally the population behind her policies. She then introduced *Kabesig* (Linking Arms Movement) to bring together nongovernmental and local leaders to complete a number of unresolved projects, but it was a matter of too little, too late.

Responding to Leadership Challenges

Concern has been expressed as to whether women are physically and psychologically prepared to be effective leaders in the rough arena of politics. Are they able to assert themselves when their tenure is challenged by legislative bodies or by their own political parties? When their authority is challenged, are they capable of engaging their opponents?

Few politicians can match the political maneuvering of Tansu Ciller in her attempts to gain and retain power. Professor Kemal

Kirisci, a political scientist at Bosporous University in Instanbul, was quoted as saying that "[s]he is probably the most Machiavellian politician Turkey has seen for a long time. For the sake of her goal she'll do anything."[48]

Not only were Ciller's political skills and machinations reflected in her rapid rise to the top, but she remained a powerful political broker in Turkish politics even after losing her post as prime minister. Although she had conducted a spirited campaign to regain power in 1996, her warnings of the dangers of a politicized Islam failed to win the day as the Welfare Party, which promised cheap food, clean government, and closer contacts with Islamic states, captured the most seats. Fearing the ascendance of an Islamic party, business and military groups urged Ciller and Mesut Yilmaz, the leader of the other center right party, the Motherland, to put aside their differences and form a government. They eventually reached an agreement that called for them to split the time left in the term, with Yilmaz serving as prime minister until 1997 when Ciller would take over and serve two years to be followed by a two-year term for Yilmaz. Ciller said in an interview that she was "prepared to do what I have to do" to keep the Welfare Party from assuming power. She described her decision to go along with the plan as a "sacrifice," comparing herself to the mother who gave up her infant rather than have it cut in half in the legend of King Solomon.[49]

Within weeks this forced marriage broke apart when, in a move inspired by the Welfare Party, motions were introduced in the parliament, calling for an investigation into corruption charges against Ciller. Yilmaz did nothing to check this action. Instead he permitted the members of his party to vote their consciences. In response, Ciller withdrew her party's support, referring to Yilmaz as a "cheap mudslinger" and a "backstabber."[50]

The Welfare Party was then given an opportunity to form a government, and it looked to the two center parties for a coalition partner. Ciller had a longheld and intense opposition to the Islamic Party whose leader, Necmettin Erbakan, had described her as "lower than an infidel" and insisted that "Turks do not want to be represented by women,"[51] but she agreed to bring the True Path Party into the coalition to the consternation of many of her former supporters. To compensate for her joining the coalition, she was given the post of deputy prime minister as well as foreign minister and the promise of a return to the office of prime minister after two years.

While Ciller stressed that her presence in the government would serve as a check on Erbakan, there was speculation at the time that her turn of mind was designed to protect her from the consequences of corruption charges.[52] Within months, she was cleared of some misdeeds in connection with the award of government contracts. Also, measures to have charges against her sent to the Supreme Court for investigation were defeated in the parliament.

When the Welfare-led government introduced an Islamic-inspired agenda shortly after taking office in 1996, it ran afoul of the Turkish military that warned the government to rescind the religious-based initiatives, but the party leaders rejected these demands. Pressure was put on members of the governing coalition to withdraw support, and many individual members of the True Path Party defected, leaving the government without a majority. Ciller refused to join her party colleagues. The leaders of the Welfare Party then pushed for a government headed by Ciller, but her candidacy was rejected. Her role in the formation of the Islamic-led government made her unacceptable to the military.

After Chandrika Kumaratunga sacked her trade minister in June 2001, the entire contingent of the Muslim Congress and 15 other members of her parliamentary coalition resigned, making her vulnerable to a vote of no confidence. To prevent such a vote, she suspended the parliament for a period of two months as she could not dissolve that body until a year after the last general election held in October 2000. In an attempt to retain a governing majority, she reached agreement with the left-wing People's Liberation Party, noting that "she would make a deal with any devil to end the crisis that was threatening her government."[53] In return for JVP support, Kumaratunga had to agree to reduce the size of her cabinet from 44 to 20 and make other concessions to the party that had opposed talks with the Tamil separatists. The agreement between the two was somewhat of a surprise as the JVP had sought to overthrow her mother in 1971 and was viewed as responsible for the assassination of Kumaratunga's husband several years later, but Kumaratunga concluded that the group had changed.

Experiencing more coalition defections in October, Kumaratunga chose to dissolve parliament. Since she did not achieve a majority in the ensuing parliamentary election, Kumaratunga agreed to accept the cabinet proposed by the opposition United National Party (UNP). Having failed to persuade the new prime minister, Ranil Wickremesinghe, to let her keep the cabinet posts of defense and finance, Kumaratunga committed herself to a government of cohabitation.

Kumaratunga attempted to reassert her power in November 2003 while the prime minister was in Washington. Concerned about parliamentary efforts to impeach the chief justice of the Supreme Court as well as herself, she suspended parliament for two weeks, established a state of emergency, and sacked the ministers of defense, interior, and information, assuming those positions herself. These actions were followed by a decision to dissolve the parliament, having reached the one year prohibition against calling a new election. This time the coalition she had put together was successful in the April 2004 election, enabling her to form a new government and thus end the difficult period of cohabitation.

Even more extreme steps were taken by Sirimavo Bandaranaike and Indira Gandhi as both women used emergency powers to hold on to their positions and extend their terms of office beyond constitutionally mandated periods. In 1960, Bandaranaike's party won a majority of the seats in the parliament, but as the problems facing the small nation mounted and the economy that was plagued by strikes deteriorated, the conflicts dividing the several factions within her party resurfaced. These differences had been set aside in the interest of success at the ballot box. With the defection of a number of SLFP members and the defeat of the party's candidates in by-elections, the government's majority was threatened. To deal with the growing crisis, in May 1963 Bandaranaike reshuffled her cabinet.

The following year Bandaranaike prorogued the parliament for a period of four months to stave off defeat. A state of emergency was declared and press censorship instituted. Although she attempted to reassure the populace that the constitution would not be suspended, the opposition UNP waged a campaign to sell itself as the true representative of democracy. Bandaranaike responded by saying that since she was a woman, her opponents believed that they could frighten her into calling an election, but she indicated that she would not be intimidated.[54]

Bandaranaike used the emergency period to mobilize her party and search for coalition partners, eventually turning to the Trotskyist Lanka Sama Samaja Party (LSSP)—a move that gave her more control over disruptive labor interests. As the price for cooperation, the LSSP received three cabinet posts, one of which was the important portfolio of finance.

Following Bandaranaike's return to power in 1970, support for her government began to erode as she was unable to turn the economy around. She applied emergency laws in response to a 1971 insurrection. A number of opposition MPs were arrested and imprisoned without a trial, opposition newspapers were nationalized, broadcasts were censored, and a series of laws were enacted without parliamentary debate.

To bolster her support, Bandaranaike sought to strengthen her position in the minority communities. Although Sinhalese was recognized as the official language in the new constitution, provision was made for the use of the Tamil language for administrative and judicial purposes. She also used patronage to develop a political base among the Tamils. Despite such efforts a new Tamil political party committed to a separate state was formed in May 1976, uniting the Sri Lanka and Indian Tamils in the United Liberation Front. Bandaranaike responded by again declaring a state of emergency. A prohibition was placed on the publication and distribution of "subversive" materials, but she also instituted some popular economic reforms such as price controls to make the restrictions more acceptable.

Faced with high unemployment, soaring inflation, student protests, several party defections, the breakup of the ruling coalition, and the threat of a no confidence vote, Bandaranaike in February 1977 again prorogued the parliament. Seeking to explain her action, she indicated that this step was taken to deprive "politicians who have no place in the country an opportunity of using the national state assembly as a forum to indulge in character assassination and mudslinging."[55] In time she instigated emergency rule and kept it in place until shortly before the 1977 election. Using her parliamentary majority to change the constitution, Bandaranaike was able to extend her term of office by two years, but she lost the 1977 election after a campaign in which the abuses of the emergency became the central issue.

Indira Gandhi, also, made use of extreme measures to stay in power. In response to economic and social unrest, the collapse of several state governments, and an Alhamra court decision declaring her election to parliament invalid, she took firm action by establishing a state of emergency in 1975 to deal with what she described as a threat to national security. In a broadcast to the nation, Gandhi said that the government had acted against a deep and widespread conspiracy that had "been brewing ever since I began introducing certain progressive measures of benefit to the common man and woman of India." Opposition politicians and dissidents within her own party were arrested. Press censorship was instituted and the right of habeas corpus was suspended. Many political organizations were banned and public meetings and strikes were declared illegal. Gandhi was later to acknowledge that her decision on the emergency was wrong although it enabled her to remain in power for two years beyond her term of office without facing the electorate.

The two women, who together ruled Bangladesh for more than 15 years, resorted to a number of extreme measures to hold on to power as well as to wrest power from one another. Disappointed that she had not won the 1990 election as was widely predicted, Sheikh Hasina took steps to impede the operation of government, including the use of *hartals* (general strikes) that brought work stoppages for more than 170 days during Khaleda Zia's first term in office. The Bangladesh Nationalist Party reciprocated with 85 days of total stoppage of public activities when Hasina came to power.[56]

Both women boycotted sessions of the parliament when the other was in power. Hasina's party did not attend most of the sessions during Zia's first term, and in March 1999 Hasina, who had become prime minister in 1996, complained that Zia had attended parliament only 24 days out of 224.[57] The Awami League paid little attention to the opposition when the BNP did attend. For example, only 13 minutes were given for the BNP to speak on the important issue of the Chittagong Peace Treaty, which the Hasina government had negotiated. Zia argued that the treaty was a sell-out to the insurgents in the Chittagong region and their Indian supporters. In Zia's second term in office, beginning in 2001, she failed for some time to appoint any AL members to the various parliamentary committees. Her excuse was that names were not provided.

Charges of corruption were filed with the courts by both parties against members of the opposition, including the two women leaders and some of their family members. After her defeat in 2001, Hasina filed thousands of cases against BNP leaders and workers, including 30 ministers. Zia issued a White Paper in January of the following year charging Hasina and a number of AL ministers with graft and irregularities.[58] Zia also prohibited a number of Awami League leaders from leaving the country and incarcerated some second rung leaders.

Several party leaders on both sides in Bangladesh were assassinated, and both Hasina and Zia asserted that various attempts were made on their lives. The two women have not hesitated to use incendiary language against one another as Zia was reputed to have suggested on at least four occasions that the AL would face the same fate as the League had in August 1975, referring to the killing of Hasina's father and other members of her family.

Conclusions

Despite reservations about women as leaders, considerable evidence suggests that they can be effective national leaders. According to a poll of 258 British political scholars, Margaret Thatcher came in fourth in a list of 20 British prime ministers in terms of degree of success. Another poll of experts placed Helen Clark fourth among New Zealand's prime ministers in the past 100 years; and Luisa Diogo of Mozambique was selected as one of only seven serving political leaders in *Time Magazine's* listing of the 100 most influential leaders—a listing that included such names as Vladimir Putin, George W. Bush, and Jaques Chirac.[59]

There have been failures as well. For example, on the whole, the widows got off to a slow start because of their lack of experience and inadequate education, forcing them to rely heavily on their husband's associates and family members. The daughters, although well-educated, turned in weak performances, especially those who were concerned with avenging the death of a father. They found it difficult to compromise on issues, particularly with leaders of the opposition whom they often regarded as complicit in their father's deaths.

The temporaries who had definite tasks to accomplish generally did so with dispatch. Their time in office was short, although the performances of Madior Boye and Luisa Diogo were viewed as so impressive that they were asked to stay on as prime ministers. The popularity of the ceremonial presidents allowed them to stretch their political influence, particularly in the case of Mary Robinson and Vigdis Finnbogadottir.

Epilogue

In the half century since Sirimavo Bandaranaike of Ceylon became the world's first woman prime minister, more than 60 women have assumed the position of prime minister or president. Although this represents slightly more than one woman per year, the trend has shown some acceleration. In the period, 1960–1975, only 5 women held the position of prime minister or president, while in the period, 1976–1991, 17 women rose to the top political position, and between 1992 and the end of 2007, the corresponding number totaled 42. By examining the experiences of the 64 women who have been able to break the highest political glass ceiling as of the end of 2007, an attempt has been made to shed light on why relatively few women have been able to reach the top as well as to identify trends that might suggest greater representation of women in the future.

Almost half of the women who reached the top were brought in as temporaries, ceremonial leaders, or were appointed to fill the less powerful position in political systems with both a president and a prime minister. In a number of African and Latin American states with strong presidents, the selection of a prime minister may have been influenced by presidents who felt that a woman without a strong power base would be easier to control. Also, troubled presidencies may have been motivated to select a woman, believing that as an outsider she might be viewed as more honest and more able to serve as a change agent. Several women prime ministers in the developing states were particularly attractive because they had degrees in economics and experience in international financial institutions. As former employees of these institutions, they were in a position to help obtain much needed developmental aid.

Selecting a woman for the job has sometimes been viewed as a last resort. For example, Peru's President Alejandro Toledo offered the position of prime minister to Beatriz Merino after being turned down by several male candidates who may have feared that such an appointment in an unpopular government would jeopardize their long-term political interests.

Until recently, prospects for a woman president in the United States as well as for a woman president in countries that have systems modeled after that in the United States have appeared remote. Before

2005, no woman had been elected president by popular vote unless she had the advantage of being part of a political legacy or was chosen to serve largely in a ceremonial role. With the election of Ellen Johnson Sirleaf as president of Liberia in 2005 and that of Michelle Bachelet in Chile a few months later, another barrier was overcome.

Among the most reliable indicators as to whether a woman will reach the top are her political connections, especially if she has been identified as a legacy. Most of the widows and daughters of former national leaders were recruited for the top position by their husband's or father's political party. In doing so, party leaders hoped to take advantage of the name of the husband or father and obtain a less-experienced candidate who might prove easier to manipulate. Daughters, particularly those whose fathers were martyrs as in the case of Sheik Hasina and Benazir Bhutto, took little persuading that they carry on their fathers' work. Once elected, they sometimes allowed their preoccupation with the legacy of their fathers to get in the way of sound policy choices.

As more qualified and experienced women professional politicians have entered the political arena, the percentage of political legacies has decreased. Whereas in the period from 1960 to 1975, three of the five women leaders were widows or daughters of prominent national political leaders, from 1976 to 1991 the number was 4 out of 17, while only 6 of the 42 women in the period from 1992 through 2007 had such a relationship. This is not to suggest that dynastic succession is likely to end. The latest pattern to emerge consists of a wife's succeeding her husband in the top position. In 2004, Marta Fox made comments to the effect that Mexico was now ready for a *presidente,* making it clear that she planned to be the one. Some suggested that her husband, Vincent, had allowed his wife to act as a virtual copresident, and his chief of staff resigned over the issue. The controversy that ensued led Marta Fox to relinquish her presidential ambitions.

In Argentina, which has already had a legacy couple with Juan and Isabel Peron, Néstor Kirchner agreed to have his wife Cristina seek the office of president in his stead in the October 2007 election—an election that she won. In part, the decision may have been influenced by economic problems looming on the horizon as well as a relatively poor showing for the Peronist party in recent local elections.

Néstor suggested that a government led by his wife "would be 'even better' than his and would 'deepen change.' "[1] Most commentators believed that either of the two would be able to win the election. Christina had been overwhelmingly reelected to the Argentinian Senate just two years earlier and also had considerably more national political experience than her husband. Whereas she had been serving in the Senate since 1995, he became president in 2003 directly from his position as a provincial governor. By rotating terms in office, the Kirchners would be in a position to establish a lengthy dynasty despite the two-term limit.

Another wife who sought to follow in the footsteps of her husband and become the first woman president of the United States was Hillary Clinton. Despite her ability to raise funds to finance her campaign, she failed to receive the nomination of her party. Although there was considerable disappointment among her supporters, Clinton claimed that the millions of votes she received in the presidential primaries represented some 18 million cracks for women in the highest glass ceiling.

Recently it has been sons, not daughters, who have been groomed for dynastic succession. Gloria Arroyo's two sons were elected to the Philippine House of Representatives in 2007. No longer did Arroyo seem as concerned about allegations of nepotism as she had at the beginning of her presidency in 2001 when she stopped her daughter, a graduate of Georgetown University, from assuming a foreign service post for which the daughter had qualified in competitive examinations.

Many thought that Indira Gandhi's charismatic granddaughter, Priyanka Gandhi Vadra, would inherit the Nehru mantle, but it was her grandson, Rahul Gandhi, who was elected to the Indian parliament in 2005 and two years later was made a secretary general of the Congress Party at the behest of his mother, Sonia Gandhi, the head of the party. Meanwhile, the sons of both Begum Zia and Sheikh Hasina in neighboring Bangladesh were being groomed for higher political office, but like their mothers they have been either arrested or accused of corruption. To carry on the Bhutto dynastic tradition, Benazir's son, Bilawel Bhutto Zardari, was designated chair of the Pakistan People's Party following the assassination of his mother in 2007, but because of his age and the concern that he first complete his university studies his father has assumed the functions of party leader.

Even though the percentage of women who reach the top primarily as a function of dynastic succession may be in decline, political connections can be useful for women leaders. The fathers and sometimes mothers of many of the women surveyed have held elected political positions, if not at the national level, at the provincial or local levels. Several held high military or civil service positions or had political interests that they instilled in their daughters at an early age. A few of the husbands also encouraged their wives in the pursuit of political office, perhaps in part reflecting their failure to achieve their own political ambitions as in the case of the husbands of Thatcher, Arroyo, and Megawati.

Whereas husbands and fathers played an important role in educating their wives and daughters in the ways of politics, a number of women leaders have also been helped along the way by political mentors. In some cases, this has led to accusations that the women political leaders reached the top only because of a relationship with a political mentor as in the case of Edith Cresson and Francois Mitterand of France.

As more women reach the top, there would appear to be greater opportunity for them to serve as political mentors. Yet a number of the women leaders were reluctant to do so. In the many years that Thatcher served as prime minister, she appointed only one woman to the cabinet and some women leaders, particularly those in Asia, failed to appoint any. Recently prime ministers have a better record on this score as Bachelet of Chile in 2007 had 48 percent of her cabinet positions filled by women, Germany's Merkel had 40 percent, while Sirleaf of Liberia had 30 percent women.[2]

A larger number of women national political leaders also provides the potential for more role models. The importance in paving the way for other leaders can be found in the comments of women political leaders themselves. For example, though she strongly disagreed with Margaret Thatcher on many issues, Edith Cresson said of the British prime minister that she "was very tough, very courageous, and she certainly had more difficulties, being a woman." Cresson remarked that as "a person, she stirs a certain admiration in me."[3] When asked which leaders outside the Philippines she admired, Arroyo said the strong women, and she specifically mentioned Thatcher and Meir as well as Queen Elizabeth I.[4] In her office, Hanna Suchocka kept a framed photograph of Margaret Thatcher.

A frequently asked question about women is whether they are qualified for higher political positions. Certainly in an earlier age women lacked the academic credentials for high political office at a time when few were able to obtain college degrees. In a number of universities they were not even admitted or were admitted only in small numbers. The situation has changed, as our findings indicate, the educational credentials of the women leaders are equal to or better than their male counterparts. Many of those who have reached the top have achieved advanced degrees in disciplines most relevant to political office such as law, economics, and politics. Moreover, their degrees have come from some of the world's most prestigious universities, such as Harvard and Oxford.

Despite the difficulties of balancing career and family responsibilities, many women have been able to build impressive political resumes. Some have had lengthy terms of office in national parliaments and have been able to serve in major cabinet positions such as foreign affairs, defense, and finance as opposed to those dealing with "women's issues."

Women who have served as vice president or deputy premier would seem to be the best positioned for rising to the top following the death or incapacity of the leader. Both Gloria Arroyo and Megawati served as vice president and in both cases they reached the top position as a result of widespread dissatisfaction with the sitting president, leading to his expulsion from office.

Women have slowly begun to make inroads as speakers of national parliaments—a position that enabled Lydia Gueiler of Bolivia, Anneli Jaatteenmaki of Finland, and Nino Burdzhanadze of Georgia to take the next step to the top. In 2007, the year in which Nancy Pelosi became the first woman speaker of the U.S. House of Representatives, more than 13 percent of the total global number of 262 posts of presiding officers of parliament or of one of its houses was held by a woman.[5]

Assuming the role of party leader can also be one of the most important avenues to the top position, particularly in a parliamentary system. Several of the women, including Thatcher, Shipley, Clark, and Merkel, directly challenged their party's leaders, often when no male was willing to take the risk. If the party is in power at the time, the challenger may be able to assume the top position immediately; otherwise she becomes leader of the opposition. In some countries, the functions of the party leader and the head of the government are divided between two persons who hold these positions.

The prominence of women politicians at all levels of government, sometimes aided by quotas as in the case of a number of political parties and legislatures throughout the world, does not automatically mean that women will be able to break the political glass ceiling. Even though states like Sweden and Denmark for many years have had parliaments and cabinets almost evenly divided between the genders, they have never had a woman at the top with the exception of a queen who performs ceremonial duties.

Recent trends suggest that it remains difficult for women to achieve the top political office and even those who do will often get such a position only as a temporary or ceremonial leader or as part of a legacy. The three who were successful in 2007 included Micheline Calmy-Rey for a one-year term as president in the Swiss plural executive system, a ceremonial presidency for Pratibha Patil of India, and a legacy presidency for Cristina Kirchner of Argentina.

The year was also one in which several former women prime ministers sought to make a comeback after losing the job. Only one of these, Yulia Tymoshenko, was successful as part of her effort to reestablish the Orange coalition in Ukraine. Assassination short circuited the effort of Benazir Bhutto for a third term as prime minister of Pakistan, while the efforts of Begum Zia and Sheikh Hasina to reestablish their positions as prime minister failed. The caretaker government in Bangladesh continued to suppress the activities of both on corruption charges and it is highly unlikely that either will be able to return to power.

Appendix: Background of Women Leaders

Name/position Dates in office/age	Education/ Occupation	Marital status/ Children	Previous Political Positions
Aquino, Corazon Philippines—President (1986–1992) / 53	college degree homemaker	widow 5 children	none
Arroyo, Gloria Philippines—President (2001–) / 53	PhD—economics college professor	married 3 children	vice president several minor ministries
Arteaga, Rosalia Ecuador—President (1997) / 40	law degree lawyer	married 3 children	vice president education minister
Bachelet, Michelle Chile—President (2006–) / 54	MD pediatrician	separated 3 children	defense minister health minister
Bandaranaike, Sirimavo Sri Lanka—PM (1960–1964; 1970–1977; 1994–2000) / 44	secondary education homemaker	widow 3 children	party leader
Barbara, Agatha Malta—President (1982–1987) / 59	secondary education politician	single	deputy PM several cabinet positions
Bhutto, Benazir Pakistan—PM (1988–1990; 1993–1996) / 35	graduate studies politician	married 3 children	party leader
Boye, Madior Senegal—PM (2001–2002) / 61	law degree jurist	married 2 children	justice minister
Brundtland, Gro Norway—PM (1981; 1986–1989; 1990–1996) / 41	MD and MPH physician	married 4 children	environmental minister parliament member

Continued

Appendix Continued

Name/position Dates in office/age	Education/ Occupation	Marital status/ Children	Previous Political Positions
Burdzhanadze, Nino Georgia—Interim President (2004–2005) / 39	doctorate and law degree college professor	married 2 children	parliamentary speaker environmental minister
Calmy-Rey, Micheline Switzerland—President (2007)	graduate degree politician	married 2 children	vice president foreign affairs minister
Camelia Romer, Susanne Netherlands Antilles—PM (1993; 1998–1999) / 35	law degree lawyer	married	deputy prime minister justice minister party leader
Campbell, Kim Canada—PM (1993) / 45	law degree and ABD lawyer	divorced no children	judicial minister defense minister
Chamorro, Violeta Nicaragua—President (1990–1996) / 60	some college newspaper publisher	widow 4 children	Sandinista junta; later in opposition
Charles, Mary Eugenia Dominica—PM (1980–1995) / 61	law degree lawyer	single no children	opposition leader parliament member
Ciller, Tansu Turkey—PM (1993–1996) / 47	PhD—economics college professor	married 2 children	economics minister
Clark, Helen New Zealand—PM (1999–) / 49	MA—political studies college instructor	married no children	deputy PM several minor ministries
Cresson, Edith France—PM (1991–1992) / 49	PhD—demography politician	married 2 children	agriculture and other minor ministries
Degutiene, Irena Lithuania—PM (1999) / 49	MD degree physician		social welfare minister
Das Neves, Maria Sao Tomé and Principe—PM (2002–2004) / 44	graduate degree World Bank UNICEF	married	economics and commerce minister

Continued

Appendix Continued

Name/position Dates in office/age	Education/ Occupation	Marital status/ Children	Previous Political Positions
Diogo, Luisa Mozambique—PM (2004–) / 46	MA—economics World Bank officer	separated 3 children	finance minister national budget director
Domitien, Elizabeth Central African Republic —PM (1975–1976) / 50s	secondary education businesswoman	married 1 child	party leader
Dreifuss, Ruth Switzerland—President (1999) / 58	college degree civil servant	single no children	federal council home minister Berne council
Finnbogadottir, Vigdis Iceland—President (1980–1996) / 50	college degree theater director	divorced 1 child	none
Gandhi, Indira India—PM (1966–1977; 1980–1984) / 48	some college politician	widow 2 children	party president information minister
Gueiler Tejada, Lydia Bolivia—President (1979–1980) / 56	secondary education accountant	divorced 1 child	parliamentary president party leader
Halonen, Tarja Finland—President (2000–) / 56	law degree lawyer	married 1 child	justice, foreign, and social ministries
Han, Myung-Sook South Korea—PM (2006–2007) / 62	doctorate in women studies politician	married 1 child	gender equality and environment minister
Hasina (Wajed), Sheikh Bangladesh—President (1996–2001) / 48	college graduate politician	married 2 children	opposition leader party leader
Indzhova, Reneta Bulgaria—PM (1994–1995) / 41	doctorate in economics college professor	divorced 1 child	executive director for privatization
Jaatteenmaki, Anneli Finland—PM (2003) / 48	law degree politician	married	parliamentary speaker justice minister
Jagan, Janet Guyana—PM and President (1997–1999) / 77	some college politician	widow 2 children	several cabinet posts

Continued

Appendix Continued

Name/position Dates in office/age	Education/ Occupation	Marital status/ Children	Previous Political Positions
Jongh-Elhage, Emily de Netherlands Antilles—PM (2006) / 59	college degree realtor teacher	Married	education and housing ministries
Kinigi, Sylvie Burundi—PM (1993–1994) / 40	graduate studies economics civil servant	widow 5 children	economic advisor
Kirchner, Cristina Argentina—President (2007–) / 54	law degree lawyer	married 2 children	senator
Kumaratunga, Chandrika Sri Lanka—President (1994–2005) / 49	graduate studies in econ. development politician	widow 2 children	provincial governor
Liberia-Peters, Maria Netherlands Antilles—PM (1984–1986; 1988–1993) / 43	graduate studies educational administration	married 2 children	parliament finance minister provincial council
Louisa-Godett, Mirna Netherlands Antilles—PM (2003–2004) / 49		married	none
McAleese, Mary Ireland—President (1997–) / 46	law degree law professor university admin.	married 3 children	none
Meir, Golda Israel—PM (1969–1974) / 70	secondary education politician	widow 2 children	foreign and labor minister ambassador to UN and USSR
Merino, Beatriz Peru—PM (2003) / 54	law degree lawyer	single no children	head national tax administrator parliament member
Merkel, Angela Germany—Chancellor (2005–) / 51	PhD-physics researcher	married no children	party leader family and environmental ministries

Continued

Appendix Continued

Name/position Dates in office/age	Education/ Occupation	Marital status/ Children	Previous Political Positions
Moscoso, Mireya Panama—President (1999–2004) / 52	some college businesswoman	widow 1 child	party leader
Pascal-Trouillot, Ertha Haiti—President (1990–1991) / 46	law degree lawyer	widow 1 child	supreme court justice
Patil, Pratibha India—President (2007–) / 72	law degree MA lawyer	married 2 children	state governor deputy chair of Rajya Sabha
Peron, Isabel Argentina—President (1974–1976) / 43	primary education entertainer	widow no children	vice president
Perry, Ruth Liberia—President (1996–1997) / 57	college degree politician bank executive	widow 7 children	senator
Pintasilgo, Maria de L. Portugal—PM (1979–1980) / 49	college degree in engineering researcher	single no children	ambassador to UNESCO social affairs minister
Planinc, Milka Yugoslavia—PM (1982–1986) / 57	college degree politician	married 2 children	communist party executive revolutionary
Prunskiene, Kazimiera Lithuania—PM (1990–1991) / 47	PhD in economics College professor	divorced 3 children	deputy prime minister
Robinson, Mary Ireland—President (1990–1997) / 46	law degree lawyer	married 3 children	Trinity College representative in senate
Shipley, Jenny New Zealand—PM (1997–1999) / 45	college degree teacher	married 2 children	cabinet member social affairs minister
Silveira, Maria do Carmo Sao Tomé and Principe—PM (2005–2006) / 44	college degree economist		central bank governor
Simpson-Miller, Portia Jamaica—PM (2006–2007) / 60	MA public admin. UN official	divorced 4 children	vice president-PNP party several minor ministries

Continued

Appendix Continued

Name/position Dates in office/age	Education/ Occupation	Marital status/ Children	Previous Political Positions
Sirleaf, Ellen Johnson Liberia—President (2006–) / 67	college degree social worker	married 1 child	finance minister
Suchocka, Hanna Poland—PM (1992–1993) / 46	doctorate in law lawyer	single no children	parliament member
Sukarnoputri, Megawati Indonesia—President (2001–2004) / 54	some college homemaker	married 3 children	vice president party leader
Thatcher, Margaret Great Britain—PM (1979–1990) / 54	law degree politician	married 2 children	opposition leader several minor ministries
Tuyaa, Nyam-Osoriyn Mongolia—PM (1999) / 41	graduate degree	married 3 children	foreign minister
Tymoshenko, Yulia Ukraine—PM (2005; 2007–) / 44	graduate degree economist businesswoman	married 1 child	deputy prime minister party leader
Uwilingiyimana, Agathe Rwanda—PM (1993–1994) / 40	Master's in chemistry secondary education teacher	married 5 children	education minister
Vike-Freiberga, Vaira Latvia—President (1999–2007) / 61	PhD—psychology college professor	married 2 children	none
Werleigh, Claudette Haiti—PM (1995–1996) / 49	college degree social service	married 2 children	foreign minister social affairs minister
Zia, Khaleda Bangladesh—President (1991–1996; 2001–2006) / 46	some college homemaker	widow 2 children	party leader opposition leader

Notes

One Introduction

1. "Women Greet World's First Woman Prime Minister," *Ceylon Daily News* (Colombo), Mar. 9, 1961, p. 3.
2. For a comparative study of the early women rulers, see Betty Millan, *Monstrous Regiment: Women Rulers in Men's Worlds* (Windsor Forest, Berks, UK: Kensal Press, 1982). For brief sketches focusing on the experiences of these women rulers, refer to Guida M. Jackson, *Women Who Ruled* (Santa Barbara, CA: ABC-CLIO, 1990) while for a more specialized study of women leaders, see Antonia Fraser, *The Warrior Queens* (NY: Alfred A. Knopf, 1989).
3. For a study of the life of Blanche of Castile, see Regine Pernoud, *Blanche of Castile* (London: Wm. Collins Sons & Co., 1975).
4. Among numerous biographies of Catherine de Medici are Jean Heritier, *Catherine de Medici* (NY: St. Martin's Press, 1963); R.J. Knecht, *Catherine de Medici* (NY: Longman, 1998); and Leonie Freida, *Catherine de Medici* (London: Weidenfeld & Nicholson, 2003).
5. Marina Warner, *The Dragon Empress: Life and Times of Tz'u-hsi* (NY: Macmillan, 1972).
6. Though Tz'u-hsi and the Empress Niuhuru served as co-regents, Tz'u-hsi proved to be the more effective leader. During the second regency, the once close relationship between the two women began to break down. Niuhuru died in 1881 under mysterious circumstances.
7. Among the biographies of Eleanor of Aquitaine are D.D.R. Owen, *Eleanor of Aquitaine* (Cambridge, MA: Blackwell, 1993); Alison Weir, *Eleanor of Aquitaine* (NY: Ballantine Books, 2000); and Bonnie Wheeler and John Parsons, *Eleanor of Aquitaine* (NY: Palgrave Macmillan, 2002).
8. C.P. Fitzgerald, *The Empress Wu* (London: Cresset Press, 1968).
9. Among the many biographies of Catherine the Great are Henri Troyat, *Catherine the Great,* trans. Joan Pinkham (NY: E.P. Dutton, 1980) and Isabel De Madariags, *Catherine the Great* (New Haven, CT: Yale University Press, 1990).
10. Among the numerous biographies of Elizabeth I are Anne Somerset, *Elizabeth I* (NY: St. Martin's Press, 1991) and David Loades, *Elizabeth I* (NY: Hambledon and London, 2003).
11. J.N. Hillgarth, *The Spanish Kingdoms* (Oxford, UK: Clarendon Press, 1978).

12. Quoted in Henri A. and Barbara van der Zee, *William and Mary* (NY: Alfred A. Knopf, 1973), p. 374.
13. Among the studies of the rule of Maria Theresa are C.A. Macartney, *Maria Theresa and the House of Austria* (London: English Universities Press, 1969); Karl A. Roider, Jr., *Maria Theresa* (Englewood Cliffs, NJ: Prentice-Hall, 1973); and Edward Crankshaw, *Maria Theresa* (NY: Atheneum, 1986).
14. For a comprehensive history of women, see Bonnie S. Anderson and Judith P. Zinsser, *A History of Their Own* (NY: Harper & Row, 1988).
15. Among more recent studies of the suffrage movements are Caroline Daley and Melanie Nolan (eds.), *Suffrage and beyond: International Feminist Perspectives* (NY: NYU Press, 1994); Eleanor Flexner and Ellen Fitzpatrick, *Century of Struggle* (Cambridge, MA: Harvard University Press, 1996); and Steven Hause, *Women's Suffrage and Social Politics in the French Third Republic* (Princeton, NJ: Princeton University Press, 1984).
16. For a more extensive discussion of the role of women in the development of the political party in Britain, see Janet Henderson Robb, *The Primrose League, 1883–1906* (NY: AMS Press, 1968).
17. Interparliamentary Union, *Women in National Parliaments*, www.ipu.org/parline/reports, Dec. 2007.
18. Women's Environment and Development Organization, *50/50: Getting the Balance Right in National Cabinets*, www.wedo.org.
19. Global Summit of Women, *Women Government Executives Worldwide*, www.globewomen.com/summit2004.
20. Among the numerous sources that include a discussion and evaluation of these explanations are Robert Darcy, Susan Welch, and Janet Clark, *Women, Elections, and Representation* (NY: Longman, 1987, 1994); Jenny Chapman, *Politics, Feminism and the Reformation of Gender* (NY: Routledge, 1993); Virginia Valian, *Why So Slow?* (Cambridge: MIT Press, 1998); and Jennifer L. Lawless and Richard L. Fox, *It Takes a Candidate: Why Women Don't Run for Office* (NY: Cambridge University Press, 2005). A study that measures the relative impact of various factors on female legislative representation is Pippa Norris, "Women's Legislative Participation in Western Europe," *West European Politics*, 8 (Oct. 1985), pp. 90–101.
21. Elizabeth Vallance and Elizabeth Davies, *Women of Europe* (NY: Cambridge University Press, 1986), p. 6.
22. Richard A. Seltzer, Jody Newman, and Melissa Vorhees Leighton, *Sex as a Political Variable* (Boulder, CO: Lynne Rienner, 1997) and Robert Darcy, Susan Welch, and Janet Clark,, *Women, Elections and Representation*.
23. The survey conducted by Mellman, Lazarus, and Lake for the National Women's Political Caucus in July 1994 found that more than 65 percent of the voters held to the view that women have greater difficulty than men getting elected.

24. Interparliamentary Union, "Women in National Parliaments," Dec. 2007.
25. Women's Environment and Development Organization, *50/50: Getting the Balance Right in National Cabinets.*
26. See Torild Skard and Elina Haavio-Mannila, "Women in Parliament," in *Unfinished Democracy,* ed. by Elina Haavio-Mannila. (NY: Pergamon Press, 1985), pp. 51–80; Anne Phillips, *Engendering Democracy* (Oxford, UK: Polity Press, 1991), p. 84; and Jill M. Bystydzienski, *Women in Electoral Politics* (Westport, CT: Praeger, 1995), pp. 16–51.
27. In a similar vein, a study of Brazil found that there was "a link between male emigration, the resulting female majority, and the election of a woman prefect." Eva A. Blay, "The Political Participation of Women in Brazil: Female Mayors," *Signs,* 5 (Autumn 1979), p. 49.
28. For a discussion of the effect of proportional representation on the numbers of women in public office, see Wilma Rule, "Why Don't Women Run: The Critical Contextual Factors in Women's Legislative Recruitment," *Western Political Quarterly,* 34 (Mar. 1981), pp. 60–77 and Pippa Norris, *Politics and Sexual Equality* (Boulder, CO: Lynn Rienner, 1987), p. 123–5.
29. A study that looks at the effect of the magnitude of a district on the proportion of women in a party's delegation is Richard E. Matland's, "How the Election System Structure Has Helped Women Close the Representation Gap," in *Women in Nordic Politics,* ed. by Lauri Karvonen and Per Selle (Brookfield, VT: Dartmouth, 1995).
30. See Darcy, Welch and Clark., *Women, Elections, and Representation,* pp. 114–6.
31. Jill Bystydzienski, "Influence of Women's Culture on Public Politics in Norway," in *Women Transforming Politics,* ed. by Jill Bystydzienski (Bloomington: Indiana University Press, 1992), pp. 11–14.
32. Richard E. Matland and Donley T. Studlar, "The Contagion of Women Candidates in Single-Member District and Proportional Representation Electoral Systems: Canada and Norway," *Journal of Politics,* 58 (Aug. 1996), pp. 707–33.
33. Quoted in Robert Fife, *Kim Campbell* (Toronto: Harper Collins, 1993), p. 120.
34. Ella Shcherbanenko, "Hello, Mrs. Prunskiene!" *Pravda* (Moscow), Sep. 26, 1992, p. 4.
35. Polly Toynbee, "World According to Gro," *Guardian* (Manchester, UK), Apr. 27, 1987, p. 10.
36. Jenny Shipley and Simon Robinson, "A Small But Cheeky Nation," *Time,* South Pacific (Dec. 15, 1997).

Two Political Legacies

1. See Anderson and Zinsser, *A History of Their Own,* Vol. II, pp. 212–213.

2. E.E. Werner, "Women in Congress: 1917–1964," *Western Political Quarterly*, 19 (Mar. 1966), p. 20.
3. Michael Gallagher, "166 Who Rule? The Dail Deputies of November 1982," *Economic and Social Review*, 15 (July 1984), p. 253.
4. Robert N. Kearney, "Women in Politics in Sri Lanka," *Asian Survey*, 21 (July 1981), p. 737.
5. "History's First Woman Prime Minister," *Ceylon Daily News* (Colombo), July 22, 1960, p. 6.
6. "Carrying on Husband's Work," *Ceylon Daily News* (Colombo), July 13, 1960, p. 5.
7. Manik de Silva, "A Birthday Bandwagon," *Far Eastern Economic Review*, 116 (Apr. 30, 1982), p. 34.
8. Steve Coll, "No 'Miracles' in Bangladesh for Leader Zia," *Washington Post*, Dec. 20, 1991, p. A40.
9. Quoted in S. Abdul Hakim, *Begum Khaleda of Bangladesh* (New Delhi: Vikas Publishing House, 1992), p. 11.
10. Larry Rohter, "A Guyana Favorite: U.S.-Born Grandmother," *New York Times*, Dec. 14, 1997, p. A1.
11. Ibid.
12. Joseph A. Page, *Peron* (NY: Random House, 1983), p. 471.
13. Guido di Tello, *Argentina under Peron, 1973–76* (London: Macmillan Press, 1983), p. 69.
14. Page, *Peron*, p. 391.
15. Patricia Burstein, "An Unlikely President Peron," *Newsday* (New York), July 5, 1974, p. 13.
16. See Robert Crossweller, *Peron and the Enigmas of Argentina* (NY: W.W. Norton & Co., 1989), p. 361 and Wayne S. Smith, "The Return of Peronism," in *Juan Peron and the Reshaping of Argentina*, ed. by Frederick C. Turner and Jose Enrique Miguens (Pittsburgh: University of Pittsburgh Press, 1983), p. 134.
17. "Interview with Guy Sacerdoti," *Far Eastern Economic Review*, 130 (Dec. 19, 1985), p. 41.
18. Lucy Komisar, *Corazon Aquino* (NY: George Braziller, 1987), p. 70.
19. Guy Sacerdoti, "The Aquino Clan Fight 'Guns, Goons and Gold,'" *Far Eastern Economic Review*, 130 (Dec. 19, 1985), p. 44.
20. Interview with William Stewart and Nelly Sindayen, *Time*, 129 (Jan. 5, 1987), p. 32.
21. Shirley Christian, *Nicaragua: Revolution in the Family* (NY: Random House, 1985), pp. 47–8.
22. Ibid.
23. Mark A. Uhlig, "Opposing Ortega," *New York Times Magazine*, Feb. 11, 1990, p. 62.
24. Tim Coome, "Ortega's Challenger Steps Forward," *Financial Times* (London), Nov. 13, 1989, p. 46.
25. Uhlig, "Opposing Ortega," p. 62.
26. Ibid., p. 72.

27. Richard Boudreaux, "The Great Conciliator," *Los Angeles Times Magazine*, Jan. 6, 1991, p. 13.
28. Stephen Kinzer, "Anti-Sandinistas Chosen Candidate," *Washington Post*, Sep. 4, 1990, p. 1.
29. Indira Gandhi. Letter of May 8, 1964, *Letters to an American Friend, 1950–1984*. Selected, with Commentary, from Correspondence with Dorothy Norman (NY: Harcourt Brace Jovanovich, 1985), p. 103.
30. Nayentra Sahgal, *Indira Gandhi's Emergence and Style* (New Delhi: Vikas Publishing House, 1978), p. 6.
31. Quoted in Nayana Currimbhoy, *Indira Gandhi* (NY: Franklin Watts, 1985), p. 59.
32. Rafiq Zakaria, *Women and Politics in Islam* (NY: New Horizons Press, 1989), p. 7. See also Polly Toynbee, "Bhutto Group," *Guardian* (Manchester, UK), June 20, 1983, p. 10.
33. Benazir Bhutto, *Daughter of Destiny* (NY: Simon & Schuster, 1989), p. 81.
34. Ibid., p. 124.
35. Ranesh Chandran, "The Persecution Continues," *India Today*, 9 (Feb. 15, 1984), p. 72.
36. Stephan Wagstyl, "Dynastic Triumph for Radical Kumaratunga," *Financial Times* (London), Aug. 18, 1994, p. 3.
37. Deidre Sheehan, "Ready to Rule," *Far Eastern Economic Review*, 163 (Nov. 9, 2000), p. 24.
38. John Aglionby, "Estrada to Stand Trial for Plunder," *Guardian*, www.guardianunlimited.co.uk/Archive, Jan. 21, 2001.
39. Rajiv Chandrasekaran, "Filipinos Get a Brainy Technocrat," *Washington Post*, Jan. 21, 2001, A32.
40. Keith B.Richburg, "Indonesian Says Slow Approach Avoids a Trap," *Washington Post*, Sep. 20, 1996, p. A25.
41. Keith B. Richburg, "Megawati Says She Has Mandate to Lead," *Washington Post*, July 9, 1999, p. A21.
42. "Ceylon's Lady Boss, Sirimavo," *Life*, 49 (Sep. 5, 1960), p. 47.
43. Komisar, *Corazon Aquino*, p. 81.
44. For further discussion of this reasoning, see Mary Fainsod Katzenstein, "Women and Politics in India," *Asian Survey*, 18 (May 1978), p. 481.
45. See Linda K. Richter, "Exploring Theories of Female Leadership in South and Southeast Asia," *Pacific Affairs*, 63 (Winter 1990–1991), p. 524 and Jahan Rounaq, "Women in South Asian Politics," *Third World Quarterly*, 9 (July 1987), p. 848.
46. For a similar interpretation of Bandaranaike's assumption of a political role after the assassination of her husband, see Krishna Prasanna Mukerji, *Madame Prime Minister Sirimavo Bandaranaike* (Colombo: M.D. Gunasenu & Co., 1960).
47. The unmarried sister of the founder of Pakistan unsuccessfully sought the presidency of her country in 1965. Fatima Jinnah, the sister of Muhammad Ali Jinnah, was chosen as its nominee by the Combined Opposition Party

when the candidate who had been selected to carry the party's banner died during the campaign. Though she had no political experience, she was called upon during an emergency to play an important role.
48. Claudia Dreifus, "Benazir Bhutto," *New York Times Magazine*, May 15, 1994, p. 38.

Three   Professional Politicians

1. Lea Ben Dor, "Why Choice Falls on Golda Meir," *Jerusalem Post Week-End Magazine*, Mar. 7, 1969, p. 5.
2. Mark Segal, "Labour Puts Up Golda Meir for Premier," *Jerusalem Post*, Mar. 9, 1969, p. 7.
3. James Feron, "Israel Has Found a Replacement for Golda Meir—It's Golda Meir," *New York Times Magazine*, Oct. 26, 1969, p. 52.
4. Ibid., p. 151.
5. Quoted in Penny Junor, *Margaret Thatcher* (London: Sidgwick & Jackson, 1984), p. 85.
6. Ibid., p. 119.
7. "Turkey's Thatcher," *Times* (London), June 15, 1993, p. 17.
8. Andrew Finkel, "Turkey Pins Hopes on Woman Leader for Change of Tack," *Times* (London), June 15, 1993, p. 13.
9. Dwight Bellanfante, "Portia Simpson Miller, A Woman of Courage, Still Seeking Full Acceptance," *Jamaica Observer*, Sep. 11, 2005, www.jamaicaobserver.com/news.
10. Robert Laiah, "Crusade for Change: Prime Minister Urges Christians to Help Unite Jamaica," *Jamaica Gleaner News*, www.jamaica-gleaner.com/gleaner/20060403.
11. Janis Valls-Russell, "France's New Face at the Top," *New Leader*, 74 (July 15–29, 1991), p. 13.
12. *Report of the 1998 Summit of the Council of Women World Leaders*, Cambridge, MA: Kennedy School of Government, 1998.
13. Gloria Steinem, "Gro Harlem," *Ms.* (Jan. 1988), p, 75.
14. Charles A. White, " 'Doing Politics' Differently," *Canada and the World*, 59 (Sep. 1993), p. 6.
15. E. Kaye Fulton, "The Rising Star," *Maclean's*, 106 (Jan. 31, 1993), p. 12.
16. Peter C. Newman, "Citizen Kim," *Vancouver* (May 1993), p. 90.
17. Ibid., p. 34.
18. William Drozdiak, "Europe's New Rage: Japan-Bashing," *Washington Post*, June 16, 1991, p. A19.
19. Steven Greenhouse, "French Leader Firm on Japanese," *New York Times*, May 20, 1991, p. D2.
20. Reported in "Cresson in the Soup," *Economist*, 320 (Aug. 3, 1991), p. 46.

21. Linnet Myers, "Poles' First Female Leader an Admired Loser," *Chicago Tribune,* Oct. 31, 1993, p. 4.
22. Linnet Myers, "New Polish Prime Minister Faces Gender Gap," *Chicago Tribune,* July 15, 1992, p. 2.
23. Stephen Engelberg, "Her Year of Living Dangerously," *New York Times Magazine,* Sep. 12, 1993, p. 55.
24. Myers, "Poles' First Female Leader an Admired Loser," p. 4.
25. Quoted in "Hanna Suchocka," *Current Biography Yearbook* (NY: H.W. Wilson, Co. 1994), p. 585.
26. Mary Milliken, "Peru's New Prime Minister Is Showing Her Independence," *Washington Post,* July 3, 2003, p. A24.
27. Andean Group Report, "Toledo Administration on the Rocks," *Asian Intelligence Limited,* Dec. 2, 2003.
28. Drew Benson, "Peruvian President Fires Premier, Then Shuffles Cabinet," *Washington Post,* Dec. 16, 2003, p. A24.
29. "A Highly Dubious Result," *Economist,* Nov. 22, 2004, www.economist.com/agenda/displaystory.cfm?story_id=E1_PQNTDGD.
30. Tom Warner, "Yushchenko Faces Early Test over Choice of Premier," *Financial Times* (London), Jan. 19, 2005, p. 6.
31. Stephen Paulika, "Strange Pair: The President Has an Ambitious Ally," *Newsweek,* Feb. 7, 2005, p. 28.
32. Jo Thomas, "Quietly, She Makes History as a Caribbean Leader," *New York Times,* Dec. 1, 1980, p. B16.
33. Some writers exclude women prime ministers from the Netherlands Antilles from their lists since it is not a totally independent state. In this study, the decision was made to include it since the Netherlands Antilles was given autonomy over its domestic affairs in 1954. Its former colonial ruler, the Netherlands, retains limited functions in the foreign and defense areas. On the other hand, Bermuda, which has had two women prime ministers—Pamela Gordon (1997–1998) and Jennifer M. Smith (1998–2003) has been excluded. Britain has played a slightly greater role in Bermuda's internal affairs than the Netherlands has in its territorial dependency.
34. "Sao Tomé: Former Premier Speaks Out against Her Dismissal, State Corruption," *BBC Monitoring Newsfile* (London: Sep. 17, 2004).
35. Gustavo Gonzalez, "Politics-Chile: Second Right-Winger Shakes up Presidential Race," IPS-Interpress Service, May 25, 2005.

Four   Temporaries, Tokens, and Ceremonial Leaders

1. Ray Bonner, "President Lydia Gueiler Tejada—Bolivia's Answer to Strongman Politics," *Ms.,* 8 (May 1980), p. 83.

2. Joseph B. Treaster, "Firm Leader for Haitians," *New York Times*, Mar. 15, 1990, p. A5.
3. Chris Simpson, "Senegal PM Sacked over Ferry Disaster," *BBC News*, Nov. 4, 2002, www.news.bbc.com.
4. "Africa's First Woman 'President,'" *West Africa* (2–8 Sep. 1996), p. 1395.
5. James Rupert, "Widow Leads Liberia With Power Only to Persuade," *Washington Post*, Jan. 26, 1997, p. A1.
6. "East and Central Africa; Burundi: New Prime Minister Outlines Domestic and Foreign Policy Priorities," BBC Summary of World Broadcasts, July 14, 1993.
7. Kevin Hill, "Sylvie Kinigi," in *Women in Law*, ed. by Rebecca Mae Saloker (Westport, CT: Greenwood Press, 1996), p. 120.
8. The constitution did not provide for a clear line of succession. When the constitution was codified in 1995, the provision calling for the vice president to succeed to the presidency was dropped. Fabio Castro, "New Struggle for Presidency in Ecuador," *Agence France Presse*, Feb. 10, 1997.
9. Diana Jean Schemo, "An Ecuadorean Resists Ouster, 3 Claim to Rule," *New York Times*, Sep. 8, 1997, p. A4.
10. Nora Boustany, "Diplomatic Dispatches: In Line of Great Georgian Women," *Washington Post*, July 1, 2005, A22.
11. "Luisa Diogo Sworn Into Office," Agencia de Informacao de Mocambique NEWS, allAfrica.com, Feb. 19, 2004.
12. *Radio Netherlands Wereldomroep*, www.rnw.nl, Aug. 19, 2003.
13. See Samuel Decalo, *Psychoses of Power* (Boulder, CO: Westview Press, 1989).
14. In Iceland, surnames consist of a combination of the first name of one's father, and, in the case of a daughter, the letters "dottir." However, one is referred to by her first name only, and a woman retains her name after marriage.
15. Denis Taylor, "Lady with a Love of Peace," *Times* (London), Feb. 17, 1982, p. I.
16. Ibid.
17. Barbara Gamarekian, "Iceland's President Disputes Some Myths," *New York Times*, Sep. 8, 1982, p. C16.
18. Bernhardt J. Hurwood, "Iceland's Optimist," *Christian Science Monitor* (Boston), Sep. 16, 1982, p. 15.
19. Robinson insisted that her departure was related to the party's support for the Anglo-Irish Agreement that had been negotiated without the participation of the Ulster Unionists. It gave the Republic of Ireland a role in the affairs of Northern Ireland.
20. Fergus Finley, *Mary Robinson* (Dublin: O'Brien Press, 1990), pp. 14–24.
21. Reprinted in ibid., p. 8.

Five   The Early Years

1. Interview with Winston Burdett, CBS, Feb. 18, 1966.
2. Indira Gandhi, *Speeches and Writings* (NY: Harper & Row, 1975), p. 14.
3. Quoted in Trevor Drieberg, *Indira Gandhi* (NY: Drake, 1973), p. 3.
4. Interview with Lord Chalfont, BBC television, Oct. 26, 1971.
5. Bhutto, *Daughter of Destiny,* p. 43.
6. Ibid.
7. Ahmed Fazl, "From Exile to Family Dynasty," *Times* (London), Mar. 26, 1998, p. 45.
8. Maureen Seneviratne, *Sirimavo Bandaranaike* (Colombo: Hansa, 1975), p. 111.
9. Quoted in Eliyahu Agress, *Golda Meir,* trans. By Israel I. Taslitt (NY: Sabra Books, 1969), p. 12.
10. Elizabeth Olson, "A First for Swiss: A Woman President," *New York Times,* Dec. 23, 1998.
11. Violeta Barrios de Chamorro, *Dreams of the Heart* (NY: Simon & Schuster, 1996), p. 34.
12. See Victoria Secunda, *Women and their Fathers* (NY: Delacorte Press, 1992).
13. See Speech at Mahila Vidyaapith, Allahabad, Mar. 31, 1928, reprinted in S. Gopal (ed.), *Selected Works of Jawaharlal Nehru,* Vol. 3 (New Delhi: Orient Longmans, 1972), pp. 361–2.
14. Ibid., Apr. 1, 1936, p. 251.
15. Sonia Gandhi (ed.), *Freedom's Daughter: Letters between Indira Gandhi and Jawaharlal Nehru, 1922–1939* (London: Hodder & Stoughton, 1989).
16. Ibid., May 6, 1935, p. 159.
17. Ibid., Dec. 22, 1938, p. 404.
18. Ian Jack, "The Destiny of Benazir Bhutto," *Vanity Fair,* 49 (May 1986), p. 73.
19. Bhutto, *Daughter of Destiny,* p. 47.
20. Ibid., pp. 69–70.
21. Oriana Fallaci, "Ali Bhutto," *Interview with History,* trans. John Shepley (NY: Liveright, 1976), p. 201.
22. Quoted in Junor, *Margaret Thatcher,* p. 67.
23. Tricia Murray, *Margaret Thatcher* (London: W. H. Allen, 1978), p. 19.
24. Ibid., p. 15.
25. Brian Edwards, *Helen: Portrait of a Prime Minister* (Auckland: Exisle, 2001), p. 78.
26. Quoted in Fife, *Kim Campbell,* p. 28.
27. Seneviratne, *Sirimavo Bandaranaike,* p. 165.
28. Celia W. Dugger, "The Blood All Over," *New York Times Magazine,* Oct. 8, 2000, p 76.

29. T. Sabaratnam, "Chandrika Takes Oath Today," *Daily News* (Colombo), Aug. 19, 1994, p. 1.
30. Agress, *Golda Meir*, p. 9.
31. Marie Syrkin, *Golda Meir Speaks Out* (London: Weidenfeld & Nicholson), p. 21.
32. Ibid., p. 15.
33. Seneviratne, *Sirimavo Bandaranaike*, p. 115.
34. Ibid.
35. Indira Gandhi, *My Truth* (NY: Grove Press, 1981), p. 12.
36. Jawaharlal Nehru, *An Autobiography* (Bombay: Allied, 1962), p. 240.
37. For a discussion of child rearing in India, see Sudhir Kakar, *The Inner World* (NY: Oxford University Press, rev. 2nd ed., 1981).
38. Seneviratne, *Sirimavo Bandaranaike*, p. 37.
39. Charles L. Sanders, "Dominica," *Ebony*, 36 (July 1981), p. 116.
40. Interview with William Stewart and Nelly Sindayen, *Time*, 129 (Jan. 5, 1987), p. 32.
41. Edwards, *Helen: Portrait of a Prime Minister*, p. 57.
42. Golda Meir, *My Life* (NY: G.P. Putnam's Sons, 1975), p. 15.
43. Laura A. Liswood, *Women World Leaders*, p. 59.
44. Chamorro, *Dreams of the Heart*, p. 26.
45. Nora Boustany, "Peru's Premier Puts her Perseverance to the Test," *Washington Post*, Dec. 12, 2003, p. A42.
46. "Nationwide International News: Hasina," United News of Bangladesh, Aug. 31, 2001, p. 1.
47. Fred Hauphfubrer, "On Top of the World," *People Weekly*, 27 (Apr. 20, 1987), p. 38.
48. Murray, *Margaret Thatcher*, p. 27.
49. See Benjamin Garber, "Mourning in Adolescence," *Adolescent Psychiatry*, 12 (1985), pp. 371–87.
50. E. Kaye Fulton and Mary Janigan, "The Real Kim Campbell," *Maclean's*, 106 (May 17, 1993), p. 19.
51. Liswood, *Women World Leaders*, p. 58.
52. Virginia Myers, *Head and Shoulders* (NY: Penguin, 1986), p. 151.
53. Blema S. Steinberg, "The Making of Female Presidents and Prime Ministers: The Impact of Birth Order, Sex of Siblings, and Father-Daughter Dynamics," *Political Psychology*, 22 (No. 1, 2001), p. 106.
54. Hauphfubrer, "On Top of the World," p. 38.
55. Nancy Gibbs, "Norway's Radical Daughter," *Time*, 148 (Sep. 25, 1989) p. 44.
56. Bhutto, *Daughter of Destiny*, p. 44.
57. Ibid., p. 42.
58. Maureen Orth, "Proud Mary," *Vanity Fair*, 55 (July 1992), p. 130.
59. Ibid.
60. Quoted in Charlotte Gray, "The New F-Word," *Saturday Night*, 104 (Apr. 1989), p. 19.

Six   Educational Experiences

1. Catherine Raissiguier, "France," in *International Handbook of Women's Education*, ed. by Gail P. Kelly (NY: Greenwood Press, 1989), p. 254.
2. Susan McCrae Vander Vost, "The Search for Women's Equality in Education and Employment," in *The Decade for Women*, ed. by Aisla Thomson (Toronto: Canadian Congress for Learning Opportunities for Women, 1986), p. 82.
3. Interview with Beverly McFarland, "Madame Prime Minister," *Tropic Miami Herald*, Feb. 26, 1984, p. 14.
4. "No One Faced Such Problems," *Ceylon Daily News* (Colombo), Mar. 16, 1965, p. 5 and "More Scare Stories Soon," *Ceylon Daily News*, Mar. 17, 1965, p. 5.
5. At the time her illness was described as pleurisy although she spent several months in a sanatorium that treated tuberculosis patients. A biographer, who debunked the notion that Gandhi suffered from pleurisy and, indeed, had tuberculosis, said that it was some years later when an effective treatment for tuberculosis was discovered that Gandhi's health made a remarkable improvement. Katherine Frank, *Indira* (NY: Houghton Mifflin, 2002), p. 240.
6. Bhutto, *Daughter of Destiny*, p. 43.
7. Ibid., p. 44.
8. Murray, *Margaret Thatcher*, p. 24.
9. George Gardiner, *Margaret Thatcher* (London: William Kimber, 1975), p. 25.
10. Hugo Young and Anne Sloman, *The Thatcher Phenomenon* (London: British Broadcasting Corporation 1986), p. 17.
11. Murray, *Margaret Thatcher*, p. 42.
12. Fulton and Janigan, "The Real Kim Campbell," p. 20.
13. Stephen Engelberg, "Her Year of Living Dangerously," *New York Times Magazine*, Sep. 12, 1993, p. 52.
14. Myers, *Head and Shoulders*, p. 158.
15. Jacqueline Redditt, "The Smiling Senhora's Path to the Top," *Daily Telegraph* (London), Aug. 30, 1979, p. 13.
16. Nadia Christensen, "Symbol of a Nation," *Scandinavian Review*, 69 (Mar. 1981), p. 11.
17. Michael Kilian, "Ireland's New Champion," *Chicago Tribune*, Dec. 16, 1990, Sec. 6, p. 1.
18. Redditt, "The Smiling Senhora's Path to the Top," p. 13.
19. Jack, "The Destiny of Benazir Bhutto," p. 73.
20. Simon Robinson, "Sticking to the Course," *Time*, South Pacific (Dec. 15, 1997).
21. Edwards, *Helen: Portrait of a Prime Minister*, p. 52.
22. Jean Blondel, *World Leaders* (Beverly Hills, CA: Sage Publications, 1980), pp. 121–23.

Seven Balancing Family and Political Career

1. Chris Morey, "PM Puts Husband Second," *Observer* (London), Feb. 8, 1981, p. 7.
2. Hauphfubrer, "On Top of the World," p. 38.
3. Galina Petriashvili, "I Am Open to Dialogue with the Women's Movement," www.we-myi.org/issue/32/nino.hml.
4. Melanie McFadyean and Margaret Renn, *Thatcher's Reign* (London: Chatto & Windus, 1984), p. 111.
5. Ibid.
6. Murray, *Margaret Thatcher*, p. 52.
7. Orth, "Proud Mary," p. 131.
8. Ibid., p. 130.
9. Arnold Michaelis, "An Interview with Indira Gandhi," *McCall's*, 93 (Apr. 1966), p. 188.
10. The Parsi religion is of ancient Persian extraction and follows the teaching of Zoroaster.
11. Indira Gandhi interviewed by Lord Chalfont, BBC Television, Oct. 26, 1971.
12. Drieberg, *Indira Gandhi*, p. 29.
13. Anand Mohan, *Indira Gandhi* (NY: Meredith Press, 1967), p. 202.
14. Betty Friedan, "How Mrs. Gandhi Shattered 'The Feminine Mystique,'" *Ladies Home Journal* (May 1966), p. 165.
15. Frank, *Indira*, p. 202.
16. Gandhi, *Letters to an American Friend, 1950–1984*, p. 28.
17. Friedan, "How Mrs. Gandhi Shattered 'The Feminine Mystique,'" p. 165.
18. Gandhi, *Letters to an American Friend, 1950–1984*, p. 78.
19. Rachel Kateenelsin-Rubashow (ed.), *The Plough Woman* (NY: Nicholas L. Brown, Inc., 1932), trans. Maurice Samuel, p. 207.
20. Nicholas Wapshott and George Brock, *Thatcher* (London: Macdonald & Co., 1983), p. 60.
21. Quoted in Zareer Masani, *Indira Gandhi* (NY: Thomas Y. Crowell Co., 1976), p. 91.
22. Ibid., p. 92.
23. Meir, *My Life*, p. 115.
24. Menachem Meir, *My Mother Golda Meir* (NY: Arbor House, 1983).
25. Kateenelsin-Rubashow (ed.), *The Plough Woman*, p. 207.
26. Bhutto, *Daughter of Destiny*, p. 353.
27. Craig Whitlock, "The Professor's Quantum Leap," *Washington Post*, June 8, 2007, p. A12.
28. McFarland, "Madame Prime Minister," p. 12.
29. Liswood, *Women World Leaders*, p. 70.
30. Maria Isabel Barreno, "The Woman Who Runs Portugal Is a Feminist," *Ms.* 8 (Dec. 1979) p. 126.

31. Julia Kagan, "My Side," *Working Woman*, 5 (Dec., 1980), p. 110.
32. "Switzerland Has a Woman President," *Christian Science Monitor* (Boston), July 22, 1999.
33. Miriam Dunn, "Agatha, the true socialist," *Malta Today*, Apr. 1, 2001, www.maltatoday.com.mt.
34. Ahmed Rashid, "Wheeler-Dealer," *Far Eastern Economic Review*, 157 (Apr. 28, 1994), p. 33.
35. "'I Never Asked for Power,'" *Guardian* (Manchester, UK), Aug. 15, 2002.
36. John McBeth and Michael Vatikiotis, "Lady in Waiting," *Far Eastern Economic Review*, 164 (May 17, 2001), p. 30.
37. Tim Dodd, "The Man Behind the Throne," *Australian Financial Review*, Feb. 5, 2003, p 43.
38. Ramon Tulfo, "That Interview with Max Soliveu," *Philippine Daily Inquirer*, Mar. 3, 2004, www.inq7.net.
39. Rina Jimenez-David, "'First Gentleman' Replies," *Philippine Daily Inquirer* (Manila), Feb. 10, 2001, www.inq7.net.
40. Carlito Pablo, "President Admits Building up Personal Political Group," *Philippine Daily Inquirer*, Apr. 23 2002, www.inq7.net.
41. "Why Mike Stays out of Rallies," *Manila Standard*, Mar. 22, 2004.
42. Quoted in Allan J. Mayer, *Madam Prime Minister* (NY: Newsweek Books, 1979), p. 129.
43. William Drozdiak, "France & the Female Prime Minister," *Washington Post*, May 18, 1991, p. G1.
44. Whitlock, "The Professor's Quantum Leap," p. A2.
45. Arshad Mahmud, "My Half-Educated Wife Is Not Fit to Govern, Says PM's Husband," *South China Morning Post* (Hong Kong), June 15, 1999.
46. Charles Trueheart, "In Canada, a Very Different Tory," *Washington Post*, Mar. 6, 1993, p. B5.
47. Taylor, "Lady with a Love of Peace," p. I.
48. Gamarekian, "Iceland's President Disputes Some Myths," p. C16.
49. See Marcia Manning Lee, "Why Few Women Hold Public Office: Democracy and Social Roles," *Political Science Quarterly*, 91 (Summer 1976), p. 306.

Eight   Early Political Experience

1. Margaret Thatcher, *Margaret Thatcher: The Path to Power* (NY: Harper Collins, 1995), p. 63.
2. Engelberg, "Her Year of Living Dangerously," p. 55.
3. Fiona Looney, "Queen Kingmaker," (Ireland), Apr. 2, 2006.
4. Steinem, "Gro Harlem," p. 75.
5. Liswood, *Women World Leaders*, p. 51.
6. Steinem, "Gro Harlem," p. 75.

7. Liswood, *Women World Leaders,* p. 52.
8. For her own account of this experience, see *La Mujer y la Revolucion* (La Paz, Bolivia, 1957).
9. Bonner, "President Lydia Gueiler Tejada," p. 84.
10. Quoted in Opfell, *Women Prime Ministers and Presidents,* p. 115.
11. "Minister Backs Press Admissions Bill," *Daily Telegraph* (London), Feb. 6, 1960, p. 13.
12. James Prior, *A Balance of Power* (London: Hamish Hamilton, 1986), p. 42.
13. Wapshott and Brock, *Thatcher,* p. 102.
14. Gro Harlem Brundtland, *Madam Prime Minister* (NY: Farrar, Straus and Giroux, 2002), pp. 114–115.
15. Steven Greenhouse, "'The Fighter' of France," *New York Times,* May 16, 1991, p. A3.
16. William Drozdiak, "New Premier Vows to Boost French Industry," *Washington Post,* May 17, 1991, p. A19.
17. Ben Dor, "Why Choice Falls on Golda Meir," p. 5.
18. It was at this time that the Prime Minister insisted that she Hebraize the name Meyerson, resulting in Meir.
19. Michael Brecher, *The Foreign Policy System of Israel* (New Haven, CT: Yale University Press, 1972), p. 304.
20. Ibid., p. 395.
21. Fife, *Kim Campbell,* p. 27.
22. Ibid., p. 162.
23. John Murray Brown, "Tansu Ciller and the Question of Turkish Identity," *World Policy Journal,* XI (Fall 1994), p. 60.
24. Philip Jackson, "A Brave Voice among the Blood and Bullets," *Times of London,* May 27, 1985, p. 9.
25. Graham Lovell Reuter, "Cory Aquino's Rise to Power," *Manila Times,* Feb. 27, 1986, p. 46.
26. Uhlig, "Opposing Ortega," p. 62.
27. Chamorro, *Dreams of the Heart.*
28. Seneviratne, *Sirimavo Bandaranaike,* p. 104.
29. Ibid., p. 102.
30. Chamorro, *Dreams of the Heart,* p. 197.
31. Masani, *Indira Gandhi,* p. 132.
32. Christine Avendano, "Arroyo Following in Father's Footsteps," *Filipino Reporter,* 28 (Nov. 2, 2000), p. 42.
33. Patrick Walters, "Megawati the Enigmatic Democrat," *Australian* (Canberra), Aug. 2, 1996, p. 13.
34. Ibid.
35. Drozdiak, "France & the Female Prime Minister," p. G1.
36. Ibid.
37. The rumors are explored at length in Ralph A. Martin, *Golda* (NY: Charles Scribner's Sons, 1988).
38. Michaelis, "An Interview with Indira Gandhi," p. 190.

39. Women's Environment and Development Organization, *50/50: Getting the Balance Right in National Cabinets.*
40. Blondel, *World Leaders,* p. 140.
41. Sally Halgesen, *The Female Advantage* (NY: Doubleday, 1990), p. 58.
42. Nora Boustany, "Finland's First Female President, Making the Best of It" *Washington Post,* Apr. 28, 2000, p. A26.
43. Myers, "Poles' First Female Leader an Admired Loser," p. 4.
44. Maria Buck, *Gloria Macapagal Arroyo* (Paranaque, The Philippines: Seagull, 2000), p. 132.
45. Halgesen, *The Female Advantage,* pp. 57–60.

Nine   Running for Office

1. Marcia Falkender, *Downing Street in Perspective* (London: Weidenfeld & Nicholson, 1983), p. 233.
2. The percentage was calculated from data available in Jacques-Rene Ralier and Ronald Ingelhart, *Euro-Barometer-3: European Men and Women* (Ann Arbor, MI: Inter-Union Consortium for Political and Social Research, May 1975), p. 42.
3. "It's Not Because She's a Woman," The Economist, 271 (Apr. 28, 1979), p. 23.
4. Jorgen Rasmussen, "The Electoral Costs of Being a Woman in the 1979 British General Election," *Comparative Politics,* 15 (July 1983), pp. 461–75.
5. Drozdiak, "France & the Female Prime Minister," p. G1.
6. Susan Riley, "Ms. Representing Feminism?" *This Magazine,* 26 (May 1993), p. 13.
7. Kevin Starr, "Priming the Minister," *Vogue* (Apr. 1989), p. 456.
8. Christopher Thomas, "Daughter of Turbulent Political Dynasty Takes Helm in Sri Lanka," *Times* (London), Aug. 19, 1994, p. 11.
9. Julian West, "Sri Lanka President Wounded in Blast," *Daily Telegraph* (London), Dec. 19, 1999.
10. Edwards, *Helen: Portrait of a Prime Minister,* pp. 241–2.
11. Uma Vasudev, *Indira Gandhi* (London: Vikas Publishing House, 1974), p. 406.
12. Keith B. Richburg, "Indonesia's Stealth Candidate," *Washington Post,* June 2, 1999, p. A15.
13. See Alan Watkins, "Maggie's Nerve Is the Target," *Observer* (London), Apr. 1, 1979, p. 11.
14. Ann Morrow, "Infectious Optimism at Campaign's End," *Daily Telegraph* (London), May 3, 1979, p. 1.
15. Finley, *Mary Robinson,* p. 38.
16. Gamarekian, "Iceland's President Dispels Some Myths," p. C16.
17. Nadia Christensen, "Symbol of a Nation," *Scandinavian Review,* 69 (Mar. 1981), p. 7.

18. Komisar, *Corazon Aquino*, p. 92.
19. Hakim, *Begum Khaleda Zia of Bangladesh*, p. 171.
20. Sirajuddin Ahmed, *Sheikh Hasina* (New Delhi: UBS Publishers' Distributors Ltd., 1998), p. 141.
21. "Sri Lanka Tilts to the Left," *Economist*, 332 (Aug. 20, 1994), p. 29.
22. Julian West, "Sri Lanka President Wounded in Blast."
23. Trish O'Kane, "The New Old Order," *NACLA Report on the Americas*, XXIV (June 1990), p. 29.
24. Andrew Phillips, "The Other New Woman PM," *Maclean's*, 100 (July 12, 1993), p. 26.
25. See Susan Delacourt, "Campbell Takes the Low Road," *Globe and Mail* (Toronto), Oct. 16, 1993, p. A-7.
26. Mari Tripp, "Letter from Finland," *Nation*, 270 (Apr. 10, 2000), p. 20.
27. Kate Connolly, "Merkel Shines in Schroeder Showdown,"
28. Carla Hall, "Iceland's First-Name President," *International Herald Tribune* (Paris), Sep. 13, 1982, p. 22.
29. Christensen, "Symbol of a Nation," p. 12.
30. "My Duty to Protect SLFP, Says Mrs. Bandaranaike," *Ceylon Daily News* (Colombo), Feb. 29, 1960, p. 5.
31. David English, "Maggie," *Daily Mail* (London), Apr. 17, 1979, p. 24.
32. David Butler and Dennis Kavanagh, *The British Election of 1979* (London: Macmillan, 1980), p. 251.
33. Liswood, *Women World Leaders*, p. 128.
34. Cathie Bell, "Women Leaders Square Off in N.Z.," *Vancouver Sun*, Nov. 26, 1999, p. A16.
35. Robinson, "Sticking to the Course," *Time*, South Pacific, Dec. 15, 1997.
36. Barbara Demick, "As Democracy Lurches Along, an Old Call Lures Polish Voters," *Philadelphia Inquirer*, Sep. 19, 1993, p. A2.
37. Mark Landler, "The Front-Runner in Germany Runs Scared," *New York Times*, Sep. 16, 2005, p. A3.
38. "Turkey Forges Customs Pact with Europe," *Washington Post*, Dec. 14, 1995, p. A35.
39. Peter C. Newman, "Kim Campbell's Descent into a Political Hell," *Maclean's*, 106 (Oct. 25, 1993), p. 38.
40. Quoted in Christopher Hitchens, "A Dynasty Divided," *Independent Magazine* (London), Feb. 17, 1990, p. 26.
41. Komisar, *Corazon Aquino*, p. 81.
42. Lane Hartill, "Liberia's 'Iron Lady' Goes for Gold," *Washington Post*, Oct. 5, 2005, p. A16.
43. Phillip Webster, "Protestors Provoke Attack on Labour," *Times* (London), June 9, 1983, p. 4.
44. Kelly Couturier, "Crackdown on Kurds Boosts Turkey's Ciller," *Washington Post*, Jan. 11, 1995, p. A12.
45. "Turkey Eyes Islam," *Economist*, 330 (Apr. 2, 1994), p. 46.
46. Simon Hoggart, "Honk and Click Every Time," *Guardian* (Manchester, UK), Apr. 20, 1979, p. 1.

47. Robin Lusting, "Mrs. Thatcher's Late Take-off," *Observer* (London), Apr. 15, 1979, p. 2.
48. "It's Not Because She's a Woman," *Economist*, p. 23.
49. See Richard L. Fox, *Gender Dynamics in Congressional Elections* (Thousand Oaks, CA: Sage Publications, 1997).
50. Clyde H. Farnsworth, "Campbell, Though Liked, May Not Win in Canada," *New York Times*, Oct. 15, 1993, p. A26.
51. Serge Kovaleski, "Moscoso Is First Woman Elevated to Panama's Presidency," *Washington Post*, May 3, 1999, p. A17.
52. For the results of a content analysis of the campaign speeches of the Bangladesh leaders, see Talukder Maniruzaman, "Bangladesh: The Fall of the Military Dictator," *Pacific Affairs*, 65 (Summer, 1992), pp. 203–24.
53. Komisar, *Corazon Aquino*, p. 90.
54. Boudreaux, "The Great Conciliator," p. 13.
55. Quoted in Vasudev, *Indira Gandhi*, p. 382.
56. Ahmed Rashid, "The Queen of Larkana," *Herald*, Oct. 1993, p. 40.
57. Maniruzaman, "Bangladesh: The Fall of a Military Dictator," p. 210.
58. Commissar, *Corazon Aquino*, p. 90.
59. A. Jeyaratnam Wilson, "Recent Political Developments in Ceylon," *The Round Table*, No. 241 (Jan. 1971), p. 139.
60. E. Kaye Fulton and Nancy Wood, "Playing Gender Politics," *Maclean's*, 106 (Oct. 4, 1993), p. 17.
61. For a systematic analysis of the themes addressed in the campaign speeches, see Shelley Pinto-Duschinsky, "Manifestoes, Speeches, and the Doctrine of the Mandate," in *Britain at the Polls, 1979*, ed. by Howard Rae Penniman (Washington, DC: American Enterprise Institute for Public Policy Research, 1981), pp. 307–30.
62. Gordon Greig, "Maggie Thatcher and Mary Wilson," *Daily Mail* (London), Apr. 27, 1979, p. 1.
63. Isabelo T. Crisostomo, *Cory: Profile of a President* (Boston: Branden, 1987), p. 140.
64. Commissar, *Corazon Aquino*, p. 83.
65. Ibid., p. 90.
66. Lewis M. Simons, *Worth Dying For* (NY: Wm. Morris & Co., 1987), p. 224.
67. See Michael Gallagher and Michael Marsh, "Republic of Ireland Presidential Election: 7 November 1990," *West European Politics*, 14 (Oct. 1991), pp. 169–73 and E. O'Reilly, *Candidate* (Dublin: Attic Press, 1991), pp. 150–1.
68. Joe Carroll, "Flynn Apologises for RTE Remark," *Irish Times* (Dublin), Nov. 5, 1990, p. 4.
69. Christine Newman, "'Full Steam Ahead' for Robinson Train on Pier," *Irish Times* (Dublin), Nov. 5, 1990, p. 4.
70. Stephanie Nolen, "Building bridges: a nationalist wins a four-woman presidential race," *Maclean's*, 110 (Nov. 10, 1997), p. 32.

71. Nicole and Hugh Pope, *Turkey Unveiled* (NY: Overlook Press, 1998), p. 314.
72. "Thatcher 'Glorifying in Slaughter,'" *Times* (London), June 2, 1983, p. 1.
73. Ibid.
74. "Mrs Gandhi Braves Shower of Stones," *Times of India* (New Delhi), Feb. 9, 1967, p. 1.
75. Kenneth J. Cooper, "Former Pakistani Leader Stresses Business Plan in Bid to Rule Again," *Washington Post*, Jan. 30, 1997, p. A15.
76. Stanley Kochanek, "Bangladesh in 1996," *Asian Survey*, XXXVII (Feb. 1997), p. 139.
77. Ibid.
78. M. Rashidzzaman, "Bangladesh in 2001," *Asian Survey*, XLII (Jan./Feb. 2002), p. 187.
79. Mari Tripp, "Letter from Finland," *Nation*, 270 (Apr. 10, 2000), p. 20.

Ten Forming Governments

1. Polly Toynbee, "World According to Gro," *Guardian* (Manchester, UK), Apr. 27, 1987, p. 10.
2. Ibid.
3. Barreno, "The Woman Who Runs Portugal Is a Feminist," p. 125.
4. Julia Kagan, "My Side," *Working Woman*, 15 (Dec. 1980), p. 110.
5. Kenneth Harris, "My Kind of Conservatism," *Observer* (London), Feb. 25, 1979, p. 33.
6. Ian Aitken, "Thatcher Bids Farewell to the Middle Way," *Guardian* (Manchester, UK), Apr. 17, 1979, p. 1.
7. Anthony King, "The Outsider as Political Leader," *British Journal of Political Science*, 32 (July 2002), p. 447.
8. Margaret Thatcher, *The Downing Street Years* (NY: Harper Collins, 1993), p. 418.
9. R.W. Apple, "Thatcher, Her Party in a Slump, She Shakes Up Cabinet," *New York Times*, Sep. 3, 1985, p. A3.
10. Quoted in Andrew Phillips, "The *other* new woman PM," *Maclean's*, 100 (July 12, 1993), p. 27.
11. Ibid.
12. John Doxey, "Turkey's Embattled Secularist: Tumult in the Republic," *New Leader*, 78 (Mar. 13, 1995), p. 6.
13. Opfell, *Women Prime Ministers and Presidents*, p. 107.
14. Mina Roces, *Women, Power, and Kinship Politics* (Westport, CT: Praeger, 1998), p. 86.
15. "Bachelet's Citizens' Democracy," *Economist*, Mar. 11, 2006.
16. A.E. Dick Howard, "Constitutional Reform," in *Transition to Democracy in Poland*, ed. by Richard F. Staar (NY: St. Martin's Press, 1993), p. 100.

17. "As You Were," *Economist*, 319 (May 25, 1991), p. 56.
18. "Edith the First," *Economist*, 319 (May 18, 1991), p. 52.
19. Alistair Cole, *Francois Mitterrand* (NY: Routledge, 1994), p. 91.
20. Liswood, *Women World Leaders*, p. 122.
21. Gamini Keerwella, "Sri Lanka in 1994," *Asian Survey*, 35 (Feb. 1995), p. 156.
22. Rajpal Abeynayake, "Sri Lankan MPs in 'Dogfight,'" *Straits Times* (Singapore), June 13, 2002.
23. "President Retains Defense, Takes Education and Constitutional Reforms." Online edition of *The Daily News* (Colombo), http://www.daily news.lk/2004/04/12/new11.html.
24. Quoted in Opfell, *Women Prime Ministers and Presidents*, p. 221.
25. Patrick Smellie, "A Controlling Vision," *Time International*, 155 (May 8. 2000), p. 16.
26. Jack Vowles, "New Zealand," *European Journal of Political Research*, 38 (Dec. 2000), p. 476.
27. Colin Espiner, "PM Quizzed on Peters' Role," *The Press* (Christchurch, NZ), Nov. 30, 2005.
28. Trish O'Kane, "The New Old Order," *NACLA Report on the Americas*, 24 (June 1990), p. 33.
29. David Close, *Nicaragua: The Chamorro Years* (Boulder, CO: Lynne Rienner, 1999). pp. 48, 69, and 73.
30. Chamorro, *Dreams of the Heart*, pp. 273–4.
31. Nazmul Ashraf, "A Motley Council of Ministers," *Daily Star* (Dhaka), Oct. 12, 2001, p. 1.
32. "Cabinet Changes," *Daily Star* (Dhaka), Jan. 3, 1998.
33. "Govt Now for 'Slim' Cabinet," *Daily Star* (Dhaka), Mar. 24, 2002.
34. Pan Xiaozhu, "Bangladeshi Cabinet Reshuffled Ahead of Opposition's Deadline," *Xinhua News Agency*, Mar. 26, 2004.
35. M. Abdulla "Futile Reshuffle of Cabinet," *Bangladesh OSC Report*, May 22, 2006.
36. Denholm Baretson, "Bhutto Cabinet Includes Associates of Zia and Her Father," *Washington Post*, Dec. 7, 1988, p. 37.
37. Lally Weymouth, "Pakistan's Imperiled Prime Minister," *Washington Post*, Oct. 8, 1989, p. C1.
38. Allen T. Cheng and Kevin Hamlin, "Thrilla in Manila," *Institutional Investor International Edition*, 27 (June 2002), p. 30.
39. Donna S. Cueto, "Macapagal: 'Woman power' very much alive in my gov't," *Inquirer News Service*, Mar. 9, 2001 (www.inq7.net).
40. John McBeth, "A Parade of Surprises," *Far Eastern Economic Review*, 164 (Aug. 23, 2001), p. 12.
41. Ibid.
42. Luisita Lopex Torregrosa, "Lives," *Vogue*, 188 (Apr. 1998), p. 250.
43. Segal, "Labour Puts Up Golda Meir For Premier," p. 7
44. Mervyn de Silva, "New Broom," *Far Eastern Economic Review*, 157 (Sep. 1, 1994), p. 16.

45. "Confidence in the Face of High Expectation," *International Herald Tribune* (Paris), Nov. 29, 1996.
46. Kathy Marke, "New Zealand PM Heads for Landslide Win," *Independent* (London), June 12, 2002, p. 14.
47. Lennon Honychurch, *The Dominica Story* (Roseau, Dominica: The Dominica Institute, 1984) p. 214.
48. Bonner "President Lydia Gueiler Tejada," p. 86.
49. *Daily Telegraph* (London), Apr. 27, 1979.

Eleven Political Decision Making and Management Styles

1. 1998 *Summit of the Council of Women World Leaders,* p. 4.
2. Nicole Pope and Hugh Pope, *Turkey Unveiled* (NY: Overlook Press, 1998), p. 305.
3. Ibid., p. 303.
4. Kelly Couturier, "Once Acclaimed Turk Fights for Her Political Life," *Washington Post,* June 7, 1996, p. A28.
5. Pope and Pope, *Turkey Unveiled,* p. 309.
6. Francine S. Kiefer, "Poland's Prime Minister Looks Ahead to Reform," *Christian Science Monitor,* May 7, 1993, p. 6.
7. Ibid., p. 8.
8. "Georgia's New Leaders," *CBC News,* Nov.24, 2003, www.cbc.ca/news/background/georgia/newleaders.
9. Petriashvili, "I am Open to Dialogue with the Women's Movement,".
10. Liswood, *Women World Leaders,* pp. 80–1.
11. "Cory Acts at Last," *Economist,* 301 (Nov. 29, 1986), p. 30.
12. Cited in Deidre Sheehan, "Time to Get Tough," *Far Eastern Economic Review,* 164 (June 7, 2001), pp. 21–2.
13. Bruce O. Soldheim, *On Top of the World* (Westport, CT: Greenwood Press, 2000), pp. 76–7.
14. Ibid.
15. Wapshott and Brock, *Thatcher,* p. 176.
16. See Graham P. Thomas, *Prime Minister and Cabinet Today* (Manchester, UK: Manchester University Press, 1998), pp. 36–40.
17. Leonard Downie, Jr., "Thatcher: No Doubt or Regrets," *Washington Post,* June 4, 1982, p. A1.
18. Murray, *Margaret Thatcher,* p. 141.
19. R.W. Apple, "Margaret Thatcher: A Choice Not an Echo," *New York Times Magazine,* Apr. 29, 1979, p. 56.
20. "Middle East: The War and the Woman," *Time,* 94 (Sep. 19, 1969), p. 32.
21. Agress, *Golda Meir,* p. 135.
22. Komisar, *Corazon Aquino,* p. 129.

23. David G. Timberman, *A Changeless Land* (NY: M.E. Sharpe, 1991), p. 193.
24. Deidre Sheehan, "Keeping Her Eye On the Ball," *Far Eastern Economic Review,* 164 (June 14, 2001), p. 20.
25. Maritas N. Sison, "Hope and Gloria," *Filipinas Magazine,* 9 (June 30, 2000), p. 56.
26. Iqbal Akhund, *Trial and Error* (NY: Oxford University Press, 2000), p. 52.
27. Ahmed Rashid, "Riches to Rubble," *Far Eastern Economic Review,* 158 (Jan. 12, 1995), p. 22.
28. William Borders, "Mrs. Gandhi Wins Parliament Vote," *New York Times,* July 23, 1975, p. 12.
29. Anthony Wilson-Smith and Mary Janigan, "A Struggle to Survive," *Maclean's,* 106 (Oct. 18, 1993), p. 20.
30. Kim Campbell, *Time and Chance* (Toronto: Doubleday, 1996), p. 252.
31. Manash Ghosh, "Shaping Bangladesh's Destiny," *Statesman Ltd.* (India), Feb. 22, 2001.
32. Ergun Ozbudun, "Turkey: How Far from Consolidation?" *Journal of Democracy,* 7, p. 136.
33. Belinda Olivares-Cunanan, "DNER Chief Has to Stand Up to the Politicos," *Philippine Daily Inquirer,* www.inq7.net, Feb. 14, 2001.
34. Francis Pym, *Politics of Consent* (London: H. Hamilton, 1984), p. 17.
35. "The Lady Is Not for Cloning," *Sunday Business* (London), Nov. 27, 2005, p. 1.
36. Bertrand Benoit, "Cold Shoulder: How Merkel's Coalition Is Spurning Lobbyists in Its Reform Push," *Financial Times* (London) Aug. 3, 2006, p. 11.
37. "Lonely at the Top," *Sunday Times* (London), July 12, 1998.
38. Feron, "Israel Has Found a Replacement for Golda Meir," p. 150.
39. N.B. Sen (ed.), *Wit and Wisdom of Indira Gandhi* (New Delhi: New Book Society of India, 1971), p. 200.
40. Masina, *Indira Gandhi,* p. 212.
41. "The Man at the Matignon," *Economist,* 322 (Jan. 4, 1992), p. 42.
42. Eugene Bingham, " Modest Room at the Top Is Where It All Happens," *New Zealand Herald,* www.nzherald.co.nz, Apr. 20, 2000.
43. Close, *Nicaragua: The Chamorro Years,* p. 73.
44. Roces, *Women, Power, and Kinship Politics,* p. 83.
45. Zaffar Abbas, "Who's Minding the Kitchen?" *Herald,* 25 (Oct. 1994), p. 34.
46. Ahmed Rashid, "Wheeler-Dealer: Opposition Baits Bhutto by Lashing out at her Husband," *Far Eastern Economic Review,* 157 (Apr. 28, 1994), p. 32.
47. Ibid.
48. Junor, *Margaret Thatcher,* p. 170.
49. Anser Kidwai, *Indira Gandhi: Charisma and Crisis* (New Delhi: Siddhi Books, 1996), p. 147.

50. Robert H.Reid and Eileen Guerrero, *Corazon Aquino and the Brushfire Revolution*, (Baton Rouge: Louisiana State University Press), pp. 178-9.
51. Veena Kukreja, *Contemporary Pakistan: Political Processes, Conflicts and Crises* (London: Sage Publications, 2003), p. 245.
52. Liswood, *Women World Leaders*, p. 82.
53. Fallaci, "Ali Bhutto," p. 119.
54. Chamorro, *Dreams of the Heart*, p. 312.
55. Elliott Abrams, "Who Won Nicaragua?" *Commentary*, 92 (July 1991), p. 26.
56. Reid and Guerrero, *Corazon Aquino and the Brushfire Revolution*, p. 175.
57. Ibid., p. 42.
58. John McBeth, "Indonesia: Nothing Changes," *Far Eastern Economic Review* (Nov. 1, 2001),
59. "Megawati Learns to Make Enemies," *Weekend Australian*, July 27, 2002.
60. Rajiv Chandrasekaran, "Indonesia's New Leader Shows Little Love of the Fray," *International Herald Tribune* (Paris), July 25, 2001, p. 5.
61. Harold Crouch, "Drifting Along: Megawati's Indonesia," *Australian Financial Review*, May 10, 2002, p. 4.
62. Antonio Lopez, "'My Example Is Integrity,'" *Asiaweek*, 27 (Feb. 2, 2001).
63. Tim McGirk, "Head Games," *Time*, www.time.com/asia/news, June 22, 2001.
64. Ibid.
65. Cheng and Hamlin, "Thrilla in Manila," p. 30.
66. Ibid.
67. Smellie, "A Controlling Vision," p. 16.
68. "Testing Times for Michele Bachelet," *Economist*, 379 (June 24, 2006), p. 46.
69. For a summary of studies that found differences between the genders in so far as styles of political decision making are concerned as well as those that found no differences, see Beth Reingold, "Conflict and Cooperation: Legislative Strategies and Concepts of Power among Female and Male State Legislators," *Journal of Politics*, 58 (May 1996), pp. 464-85.

Twelve   Political Leadership

1. R.W. Apple, Jr., "Labor Party Expected to Be Defeated in General Elections," *New York Times*, Sep. 14, 1981, p. A3.
2. John F. Burns, "Torn By War, Sri Lanka Faces Deepening Despair," *New York Times*, Jan. 19, 1997.
3. Akhund, *Trial and Error*, p. 318.

4. Cheng and Hamlin, "Thrilla in Manila," p. 30.
5. "Unlucky Jim," *Economist*, 344 (Nov. 8, 1997), p. 43.
6. Bell, "Women Leaders Square Off in N.Z.," p. A16.
7. "Cresson in the Soup," *Economist*, 320 (Aug. 3, 1991), p. 46.
8. "Au revoir, cher rival; bonjour, mon amie," *Economist*, 319 (May 18, 1991), p. 51.
9. Couturier, "Once-Acclaimed Turk Fights for Her Political Life," p. A28.
10. Honychurch, *The Dominica Story*, p. 220.
11. Francis X. Clines, "New Age of the Norse Goddess? Too Soon to Say," *New York Times*, Jan. 6, 1987, p. A4.
12. Barreno, "The Woman Who Runs Portugal Is a Feminist."
13. Elizabeth Barad, "Madame la Presidente," *MS*, 1 (July–Aug., 1990), p. 23.
14. Patrica A. Made, "Africa-OAU: What's She Doing Here?" *Inter Press Service*, June 8, 1997.
15. Myers, *Heads and Shoulders*, p. 166.
16. Ruth Marshall, "A French Sex(ist) Farce," *Newsweek* (July 22, 1991), p. 33.
17. Timberman, *A Changeless Land*, p. 239.
18. "She's Tough and Everyone Knows She's Tough," *Newsweek* (Sep. 29, 1969), p. 55.
19. *Jerusalem Post*, July 31, 1973.
20. Indranil Kumar Ghosh, "Khaleda Says Nation Needs Army," *India Abroad*, 21 (Mar. 8, 1991), p. 17.
21. Golam Hassian, "Bangladesh National Party: Military to Champion of Democracy," in *Political Parties in South Asia*, ed. by Subrata K.Mitra, Mike Enscat, and Clemen Speiss, (Westport, CO: Praeger, 2004), p. 212.
22. Rabib Hasnet Suman, "BNP Insiders Confused Over Party Positions," *Daily Star*, Aug.14, 2006, www.thedailystar.net.
23. Vijay Teshi and J.M.D. Little, *India: Macroeconomics, and Political Economy, 1964–1991* (Delhi: Oxford University Press, 1994), p. 70.
24. K. M. Arif, *Khaki Shadows:, Pakistan 1947–1997* (New York: Oxford University Press, 2001), p. 145.
25. Akhund, *Trial and Error,* p. 297.
26. Stanley A. Kochenek, "Governance, Patronage, Politics, and Democratic Transition in Bangladesh," *Asian Survey*, XL (May/June 2000), p. 537.
27. Wilson-Smith and Janigan, "A Struggle to Survive," p. 20.
28. Henry J. Barkey and Graham F. Fuller, *Turkey's Kurdish Question* (Lanham, MD: Rowman & Littlefield, 1998), p. 139.
29. Seneviratne, *Sirimavo Bandaranaike*, p. 182.
30. Vernon Hewitt, "The Prime Minister and Parliament," in *Nehru to the Nineties* (Vancouver: UBC Press, 1994), ed. by James Manor, pp. 54–5.
31. Sarojini Sharan, *Women Prime Ministers in South Asia* (New Delhi: Commonwealth, 1995), p. 34.

32. Kochanek, "Bangladesh in 1996," *Asian Survey,* XXXVII (Feb. 1997). p. 140.
33. Leo E. Rose and D. Hugh Evans, "Pakistan's Enduring Experiment," *Journal of Democracy,* 8 (Jan. 1997), p. 89.
34. Ayesha Jalal, *Authoritarianism and Democratic Politics in South Asia* (NY: Cambridge University Press, 1995), p. 111.
35. Ergun Ozbudun, *Contemporary Turkish Politics* (London: Lynne Rienner, 2000), p. 152.
36. Buck, *Gloria Macapagal Arroyo.*
37. Fran O. Sullivan, "The Presidential Predilections of Helen Clark" *New Zealand Herald,* www.nzherald.co.nz, May 7, 2005.
38. Close, *Nicaragua: The Chamorro Years,* p. 113.
39. John Horgan, *Mary Robinson* (Dublin: O'Brien Press, 1997), p. 171.
40. Ausma Cimdina, *In the Name of Freedom: President of Latvia Vaira Vike-Freiberga* (Latvia: Jumaava, 2003), trans. Karlis Streips, p. 202.
41. Nicholas Kulish, "Merkel Delivers What Germans Want: Status Quo," *New York Times,* Sep. 12, 2007, p. A4.
42. Alan Sipress, "Pressure Mounts on Philippine Leader," *Washington Post,* July 9, 2005, p. A8.
43. Smellie, "A Controlling Vision,", p. 16.
44. "New Zealand Prime Minister Helen Clark: In Search of a Nation's Soul," *Time International,* 156 (Aug. 14, 2000), p. 44.
45. Kathy Marks, "New Zealand PM Heads for Landslide Win," *Independent* (London), p. 14.
46. Jeanne-Marie Col, "Managing Softly: Corazon C. Aquino," in *Women as National Leaders* (Newberry Park, CA: Sage, 1993), ed. by Michael A. Genovese, p. 34.
47. Rigoberto Tiglao, "Poorer but Free," *Far Eastern Economic Review,* 153 (Sep. 5, 1991), p. 18.
48. Ustun Reinart, "Ambition for All Seasons: Tansu Ciller," *Middle East Review of International Relations,* 3 (Mar. 1999).
49. Celestine Bohlen, "Turkish Chief Ready for Deal to Bar Islamic Party," *New York Times,* Feb. 28, 1996, p. A 8.
50. Couturier, "Once-Acclaimed Turk Fights for Her Political Life." p. A28.
51. Roman Rollnick, "Islam Takes the Tiller in Turkey," *European* (London), 4–10 July 1996, p. 3.
52. Kelly Couturier, "Conservative Islamic Prime Minister Named in Turkey," *Washington Post,* June 29, 1996, p. A1.
53. Celia W. Dugger, "Sri Lankan President Makes Deal to Save Her Government," *New York Times,* Sep. 6, 2001, p. A9.
54. *Ceylon Daily News,* Apr. 1, 1964.
55. "Crises Rock Sri Lanka Regime," *Philadelphia Inquirer,* Mar. 13, 1977.
56. Steeradha Datta, "Bangladesh's Political Evolution: Growing Uncertainties," *Strategic Analysis,* 27 (Apr.–June 2003).

57. "Come to JS for Talks, Hasina Asks Khaleda," *Daily Star* (Dhaka), Mar. 5, 1999.
58. "Hasina, Most Ex-ministers Linked to 40 Cases of Graft," *Daily Star* (Dhaka), Jan. 24, 2002.
59. "Rating British Prime Ministers," www.mori.com/polls/2004/leeds; "Clark Ranks Fourth in Top of the Pops," *New Zealand Herald*, www.nzherald.com, June 6, 2004.

Epilogue

1. Larry Rohter, "Argentine Leader's Wife May Inherit His Troubles," *New York Times*, July 10, 2007, p. A9.
2. Women's Environment and Development Organization, *50/50: Getting the Balance Right in National Cabinets*.
3. *Current Biography Yearbook*, 1991, p. 167.
4. Sheehan, "Keeping Her Eye on the Ball," p. 18.
5. Interparliamentary Union, "Women Presiding Officers of Parliaments," *www.ipu.org/wmn-e/speakers.htm*.

Index

Adamkus, Valdas, 53, 70
Alvear, Soledad, 59, 60
Anne of Austria, 1
approval ratings, 43, 47, 50, 51, 160, 175, 215
Aquino, Benigno, 22
Aquino, Corazon
  breaking the glass ceiling, 22–24
  childhood, 83, 91, 109
  decision making, 192, 194, 200, 201–4
  early political experience, 35, 140–41
  forming governments, 178, 185
  political leadership, 208, 216
  running for office, 152, 159, 162, 164, 166
Aristide, Jean-Bertrand, 65–66
Arroyo, Gloria Macapagal
  breaking the glass ceiling, 33–34
  childhood, 82–83, 91
  decision making, 192, 194, 196, 202–4
  family and career, 122, 126, 225–27
  forming governments, 185
  political leadership, 155, 207, 213, 215
  running for office, 143–44, 147
Arroyo, Mike, 122, 155
Arteaga, Rosalia
  breaking the glass ceiling, 69
  education, 106
assassinations of
  fathers, 31–32, 169
  husbands, 15, 17–18, 22–24, 31, 142, 166, 169, 218
  women political leaders, 28, 68–69, 163–64, 225
Awami League, 18, 32, 81, 221

Bachelet, Michelle
  breaking the glass ceiling, 59–61, 224
  childhood, 84
  decision making, 179, 199, 204
  early political experience, 132–33
  education, 104
  family and career, 125–26
  forming governments, 226
Bandaranaike, Anura, 31, 202
Bandaranaike, Felix, 183, 199
Bandaranaike, Sirimavo
  breaking the glass ceiling, 15–17
  childhood, 82–83, 87, 89–90
  decision making, 199, 201
  early political experience, 28, 35, 140–41
  education, 99
  family and career, 31, 119
  forming governments, 180, 183, 187
  political leadership, 210, 212, 213, 216, 219–20
  running for office, 152–53, 156, 164, 168
Bandaranaike, S.W.R.D., 31, 82, 87
Bangladesh War, 86, 184
Barbara, Agatha, 120, 131
  breaking the glass ceiling, 76
  early political experience, 131
  education, 107
Bhutto, Benazir
  breaking the glass ceiling, 28–30

Bhutto, Benazir—*continued*
  career and family, 119, 120, 121, 126
  childhood, 80, 81, 86, 88, 91, 94
  decision making, 194–95, 200–1
  early political experience, 35–36, 142, 146, 147, 224
  education, 101, 108
  forming governments, 182, 185
  political leadership, 207, 211, 213
  running for office, 151, 154, 163–64, 166, 169
Bhutto, Murtaza, 201
Bhutto, Zulfikar Ali, 28–29, 81, 86, 146
Blanche of Castile, 2
Blondel, Jean, 109, 146, 147
Bokassa, Jean-Bedel, 72–73
Boye, Madior
  breaking the glass ceiling, 66–67, 78
  forming governments, 186
  political leadership, 222
Brundtland, Arne Olav, 111
Brundtland, Gro
  breaking the glass ceiling, 46–47
  childhood, 83, 92
  decision making, 192
  early political experience, 132, 136, 146
  education, 104, 107
  family and career, 111
  forming governments, 173
  gender differences, view of, 12
  political leadership, 207–8
  running for office, 158
Burdzhanadze, Nino
  breaking the highest glass ceiling, 69–70
  decision making, 191–92
  early political experience, 130, 227
  education, 106
  family and career, 111
Bush, George W., 55, 222

cabinet formation and activity
  decision making, 192–95, 198
  experience of leaders, 134–40
  reshuffling cabinets, 136, 179, 184, 186
  selection, 174–89
Calmy-Rey, Micheline
  breaking the glass ceiling, 55–56, 227–28
  education, 105
  forming governments, 181
Camelia-Romer, Susanne
  breaking the glass ceiling, 57–58
  education, 104
  running for office, 170
campaigning
  coping with the rigors of, 152–54
  meeting family responsibilities, 155–56
  physical limitations of women, 150–52
  running against a woman, 165–70
  showing competence and toughness, 156–61
Campbell, Kim
  breaking the glass ceiling, 47–49
  childhood experiences, 84, 87, 93, 95
  decision making, 12, 195
  early political experience, 129, 139
  education, 103, 104, 108
  family and career, 125
  forming governments, 177
  political leadership, 211, 215
  running for office, 150, 155, 156, 159, 161, 165
Cartwright, Sylvia, 73
Catherine de Medici, 2–3
Catherine the Great, 3
Chamorro, Violeta
  breaking the glass ceiling, 22, 24–26

childhood, 84, 88, 91
decision making, 200, 202, 203, 204
early political experience, 141–42
education, 99, 109
forming governments, 183
leadership, 212, 214
running for office, 152, 154, 159, 162, 167
Charles, Mary Eugenia
breaking the glass ceiling, 56–57
childhood, 83, 90
decision making, 202
early political experience, 133
education, 98, 104
family and career, 120
forming governments, 188
political leadership, 207
running for office, 151
Chittagong Treaty, 221
Christian Democratic Party, 44, 59, 177
Christian Social Union (CSU), 44
Ciller, Tansu
breaking the glass ceiling, 41–42
childhood, 84, 94
decision making, 191, 195
early political experience, 131, 139
education, 104–5
family and career, 123, 126
forming governments, 176, 177
political leadership, 207, 211, 213, 216, 217, 218
running for office, 155, 158, 160, 168
Clark, Helen
breaking the glass ceiling, 43–44
childhood, 87, 91, 94
decision making, 196, 197, 199, 202–4
early political experience, 137
education, 104, 105, 108, 109
family and career, 119, 120, 124, 129
forming governments, 181, 182, 188
political leadership, 207–8, 214, 216, 222
running for office, 151, 157, 170, 227
Clarkson, Adrienne, 73
Clinton, Hillary, 225
Congress Party, 17, 77, 142–43, 163, 185, 210, 225
Conservative Party, 39–41, 41–46, 123, 127, 135, 149–50, 174, 176, 215
corruption charges
Arroyo, Gloria, 122, 215
Arroyo, Mike, 122, 215
Bandaranaike, Sirimavo, 46, 168
Bhutto, Benazir, 30, 169
Ciller, Tansu, 123
Das Neves, Maria, 58–59
Hasina, Sheikh, 221, 228
Keimas, Taufiq, 121
Moscoso, Mireya, 30
Pascal-Trouillot, Ertha, 65
Peron, Isabel, 21
Tymoshenko, Yulia,130
Zardari, Asif Ali, 121
Zia, Khaleda, 32, 221, 228
Cresson, Edith
breaking the glass ceiling, 45, 49–50
childhood, 84
decision making, 8, 199
early political experience, 129, 136, 144
education, 104
family and career, 123, 155–56
forming governments, 179
political leadership, 207, 208, 214, 226
prime ministerial appointment, 150

Das Neves, Maria
breaking the glass ceiling, 58–59
early political experience, 132
Dayan, Moshe, 37–38, 138, 187, 198

decision making
  advisers and experts, 197–202
  cabinet's role, 192–95
  gender differences, 12, 191–92, 204–5
Degutiene, Irena
  breaking the glass ceiling, 70
  education, 106
De Menzes, Fradrique, 58, 59
Demirel, Suleyman, 41, 42
Desai, Morarji, 27–28, 184, 210, 213
Didda, Queen, 3
Diogo, Luisa
  breaking the glass ceiling, 70–71
  early political experience, 132
  education, 106
  family and career, 118–19, 123–24
  political leadership, 222
Domitien, Elizabeth
  breaking the glass ceiling, 72–73
Dreifuss, Ruth
  breaking the glass ceiling, 55–56
  childhood, 84
  early political experience, 130
  education, 105
  family and career, 120

Eleanor of Aquitaine, 3
Elizabeth I, 4, 5, 226
Elizabeth II, 73
emergency rule, 28, 143, 168–69, 195, 198, 200, 220
Ershad, H.M., 18, 32, 141, 169
Estrada, Joseph, 33, 34, 144, 185, 194
European Parliament, 9, 53, 55

Falkland Islands, 159, 168
family and career
  ambivalence about marriage, 117–23
  divorce and widowhood, 125–26
  husbands as helpmates, 111–14

husbands as political liabilities, 120–24
father/daughter relationships, 85–88
Finnbogadottir, Vigdis
  breaking the glass ceiling, 73–74
  education, 106
  family and career, 125
  political leadership, 214, 222
  running for office, 153, 156

Gandhi, Feroze, 115–17
Gandhi, Indira
  breaking the glass ceiling, 26–28
  childhood, 79–81, 85–86, 89–90, 94
  decision making, 195–96, 198–99, 200–1
  early political experience, 142–43, 145
  education, 100–1, 108
  family and career, 115–17, 118
  forming governments, 184, 185
  political leadership, 36, 210–11, 213, 219, 220
  running for office, 152, 154, 162–63, 169
Gandhi, Rahul, 225
Gandhi, Rajiv, 116, 201
Gandhi, Sanjay, 28, 116, 198, 200
Gorbachev, Mikhail, 52–53
Gueiler, Lydia
  breaking the glass ceiling, 64–65
  early political experience, 134, 227
  education, 106
  family and career, 125
  forming governments, 186, 188

Halonen, Tarja
  breaking the glass ceiling, 54
  early political experience, 138, 146
  education, 104
  family and career, 113
  political leadership, 207, 214
  running for office, 151, 156

Han, Myung-sook
  breaking the glass ceiling, 70–71
Hasina, Sheikh
  breaking the glass ceiling, 32–33
  childhood, 81, 88, 92
  early political experience, 142, 147
  education, 101, 108
  family and career, 124
  forming governments, 185, 187
  political dynasties, 224–25, 228
  political leadership, 211, 221
  running for office, 18–19, 154, 163, 169, 170
Heath, Edward, 39–41, 135, 175, 193

Indzhova, Reneta
  breaking the glass ceiling, 66
  education, 106
  forming governments, 186
Isabella, Queen, 4–5
Islam, 30, 42, 101, 158, 166, 217

Jaatteenmaki, Anneli
  breaking the glass ceiling, 54–55
  early political experience, 132, 227
  education, 104
Jagan, Cheddi, 19
Jagan, Janet
  breaking the glass ceiling, 19–20
  early political experience, 142
  education, 99
Jongh-Elhage, Emily de
  breaking the glass ceiling, 57–58
Joseph, Keith, 33, 39, 175, 194

Kamaraj, Kumaraswamy, 27, 28, 143
Kinigi, Sylvie, 132
  breaking the glass ceiling, 68
  early political experience, 132
Kirchner, Cristina
  breaking the glass ceiling, 224–25
Kohl, Helmut, 44, 137

Kumaratunga, Chandrika
  breaking the glass ceiling, 31–32
  childhood, 82, 87–89
  decision making, 198, 202, 207, 212, 218
  early political experience, 142
  education, 101, 108
  forming governments, 17, 179–80, 187
  running for office, 151, 154, 163, 170

Labor Alignment, 37, 39, 166, 186, 187, 209
Landsbergis, Vytautas, 52
legacies, 15, 17, 19, 21, 23, 25, 27, 29, 31, 33, 35
  electoral advantages, 162–65
  lack of political experience, 140–44
Liberia-Peters, Maria
  breaking the glass ceiling, 57
  childhood, 91
  early political experience, 133
  education, 105, 109
  political leadership, 192
  running for office, 157
Louisa-Godett, Mirna
  breaking the glass ceiling, 71

Macapagal, Diosdado, 33, 82, 83
management style, 202–4
Marcos, Ferdinand, 22, 23, 24, 83, 162, 164, 166, 178, 194
Maria Theresa, 5
Mary I, 4
Mary II, 5
Mary Tudor, 4
McAleese, Mary
  breaking the glass ceiling, 76
  education, 106
  political leadership, 215
  running for office, 167
Megawati
  breaking the glass ceiling, 33–34

Megawati—*continued*
  childhood, 82, 93
  decision making, 203
  early political experience, 144, 225–27
  education, 101
  family and career, 121–22, 126
  forming governments, 182, 185–86
  political leadership, 216
  running for office, 152
Meir, Golda
  breaking the glass ceiling, 37–39
  childhood, 83–84, 88, 91, 94
  decision making, 194, 196, 198, 202, 204
  early political experience, 128, 137–38, 144–45, 147
  education, 97, 102, 108
  family and career, 113–14, 115, 117–18
  forming governments, 186–87
  political leadership, 207, 209
  political mentors, 144–46
  running for office, 150–51, 158, 165–66
Merino, Beatriz
  breaking the glass ceiling, 51–52, 223
  childhood, 91
  early political experience, 131
  education, 104
  family and career, 120
Merkel, Angela
  breaking the glass ceiling, 44
  decision making, 198
  early political experience, 137
  education, 104–5
  family and career, 120, 123
  forming governments, 177
  leadership, 215, 226–27
  running for office, 151, 156, 158
Meyerson, Morris, 114
Mitterrand, Francois, 49, 50, 129, 136, 144, 150, 179
Moscoso, Mireya
  breaking the glass ceiling, 20–22
  childhood, 88
  early political experience, 141
  education, 99
  running for office, 162
Mulroney, Brian, 47, 48, 139

Nehru, Jawaharlal, 26–27, 80, 85–86, 89, 90, 100, 116, 145, 152, 162–63, 185, 213, 225
Netherlands Antilles, 56, 57, 58, 72, 105, 133, 139

Ortega, Humberto, 183

Pakistan People's Party (PNP), 29–30, 81, 201, 211, 225
parental political activities, 79–84
Pascal-Trouillot, Ertha
  breaking the glass ceiling, 65, 66
  childhood, 88
  decision making, 208
  education, 106
  family and career, 124
  forming governments, 186
Patil, Pratiba
  breaking the glass ceiling, 77, 228
  education, 106
paucity of women, 9, 12, 170
Peron, Eva, 21
Peron, Isabel
  breaking the glass ceiling, 20–21
  childhood, 88
  decision making, 199–200
  early political experience, 140, 142
Peron, Juan, 20, 199
Perry, Ruth
  breaking the glass ceiling, 67
  decision making, 208
  education, 106
Peters, Winston, 57, 139, 181, 182
Pintasilgo, Maria de Lourdes
  breaking the glass ceiling, 63–64
  decision making, 208
  early political experience, 131
  education, 105, 107

forming governments, 173–74
on marriage, 120
Planinc, Milka
  breaking the glass ceiling, 55
  early political experience, 134
  education, 105
  forming governments, 180
  political leadership
    leadership challenges, 216–21
    legislative leadership, 212–14
    party leadership, 208–12
    popular leadership, 214–16
    women seen as autocratic and aggressive, 207–8
Prunskiene, Kazimiera
  breaking the glass ceiling, 52–53
  early years, 88
  women as decision makers, 12, 45

Queens who ruled, 1–5

Rahman, Mujibur, 17, 18, 32, 81, 162
Robinson, Mary
  breaking the glass ceiling, 74–75
  childhood, 93–95
  early political experience, 131
  education, 106, 108
  family and career, 112–13
  political leadership, 214, 215
  running for office, 153, 155, 165, 167
Rupasingle, Sunethra, 201

Sandinistas, 24, 25, 142, 167, 183, 214
Sapir, Pinhas, 37, 166
Sauve, Jeanne, 73
Scandinavian women leaders, 10
Schroeder, Gerhard, 44, 156, 198
Shastri, Lal Bahadur, 27, 28, 142, 143
Shipley, Jenny
  breaking the glass ceiling, 42–43
  childhood, 88, 94
  decision making, 12, 197

early political experience, 130, 137
education, 105, 109
family and career, 113
forming governments, 181, 188
political leadership, 207
running for office, 157, 170
Silveira, Maria do Carmo
  breaking the glass ceiling, 58–59
Simla Agreement, 86
Simpson-Miller, Portia
  breaking the glass ceiling, 44–45
Sirleaf, Ellen Johnson
  breaking the glass ceiling, 59–60
  early political experience, 132–33
  education, 104–5
  family and career, 125
  toughness, 159
Sri Lanka Freedom Party (SLFP), 15–17, 31, 82, 153, 164, 183, 201, 202, 210, 219
Suchocka, Hanna
  breaking the glass ceiling, 50–51
  childhood, 93–94
  decision making, 191
  early political experience, 130, 146
  education, 104
  forming governments, 45, 179, 181
  running for office, 157, 158
Sukarno, 33, 82, 93, 121, 144
Sukarnoputri, Megawati, see Megawati

Tamil, 31, 164, 218, 220
Tejada, Lydia Gueiler, see Gueiler, Lydia
Thatcher, Denis, 112–13, 123, 168, 200
Thatcher, Margaret
  breaking the glass ceiling, 39–41
  childhood, 83, 86, 87, 92, 94
  decision making, 192–94, 195–96, 197, 200
  early political experience, 127–28, 134–36, 139, 146

Thatcher, Margaret—*continued*
  education, 102–4, 108–9
  family and career, 111–13, 115, 117, 123
  forming governments, 173–76, 188
  political leadership, 207, 213–15, 222, 226–27
  running for office, 149, 151–53, 155, 157, 159, 160–61, 165, 168
Tito, Josip Broz, 55, 134
Tizard, Catherine, 73
Toledo, Alejandro, 51–52
Trouillot, Ernst, 124
True Path Party, 41, 42, 131, 160, 177, 211, 217, 218
Tuyaa, Nyam-Osoriyn
  breaking the glass ceiling, 71
  early political experience, 138
  education, 106
Tymoshenko, Yulia
  breaking the glass ceiling, 53–54
  early political experience, 130
  education, 104–5
  running for office, 151, 228
Tz'u-hsi, 2

United National Party (UNP), 16–17, 31, 170, 180, 218–19
Uwilingiyimana, Agathe
  breaking the glass ceiling, 68–69
  education, 106

Vike-Freiberga, Vaira
  breaking the glass ceiling, 76–78
  education, 107
  political leadership, 215

Wade, Abdoulaye, 67
Wahid, Abdurrahman, 34–35, 122, 186
Wajed, Mia, 124
Wajed, Sheikh Hasina, see Hasina, Sheikh
Walesa, Lech, 50–51, 179

Weah, George, 60
Werleigh, Claudette
  breaking the glass ceiling, 65–66
  childhood, 83
  education, 106
  forming governments, 186
Wickremesinghe, Ranil, 180, 218
women's issues
  abortion, 50, 75, 132, 137, 139, 155
  appointment of women, 173–74, 177, 179, 182, 184–85
  child rearing, 157
  gay and lesbian rights, 52, 75, 151
  women's rights, 71, 73, 75, 186
  women's suffrage, 5–6, 122
women political leaders
  competence of, 156–59
  number and importance, 7, 12
  reasons for paucity, 7–10
  as role models, 8, 13, 36, 89, 92, 95, 226
  special case of Scandinavia, 10–12
  toughness of, 159–63
Wu Chao, 3

Yanukovich, Victor, 54
Yilmaz, Mesut, 168, 217
Yom Kippur War, 39, 166, 209
Yushchenko, Victor, 53–54

Zardari, Asif Ali, 119, 121, 200, 225
Zia, Khaleda
  breaking the glass ceiling, 17–19
  decision making, 195, 201
  dynastic politics, 225
  early political experience, 141
  education, 99
  family and career, 119
  forming governments, 183–84, 187
  political leadership, 207, 209, 213, 221
  running for office, 32–33, 152, 154, 169, 228
Zia, Tarique, 201
Zia ul-Haq, 29, 163

HQ 1236 .J46 2008
Jensen, Jane S.
Women political leaders

MAY 2 7 2009